Medical Law in Israel

Medical Law in Israel

Fifth Edition

Mohammed S. Wattad

This book was originally published as a monograph in the International Encyclopaedia of Laws/Medical Law.

Founding Editor: Roger Blanpain
General Editor: Frank Hendrickx
Volume Editor: Herman Nys; Associate Editor: Tom Goffin

Wolters Kluwer

Published by:
Kluwer Law International B.V.
PO Box 316
2400 AH Alphen aan den Rijn
The Netherlands
E-mail: lrs-sales@wolterskluwer.com
Website: www.wolterskluwer.com/en/solutions/kluwerlawinternational

Sold and distributed by:
Wolters Kluwer Legal & Regulatory U.S.
920 Links Avenue
Landisville, PA 17538
United States of America
E-mail: customer.service@wolterskluwer.com

ISBN 978-94-035-0939-6

e-Book: ISBN 978-94-035-0949-5
web-PDF: ISBN 978-94-035-0959-4

This title is available on www.kluwerlawonline.com

Printed in the Netherlands.

The Author

Prof. Mohammed S. Wattad is a full professor and president of Ramat Gan Academic College.

For sixteen years, he was a member of the founding senior academic staff of the school of law at Zefat Academic College; there, he served as dean of law school from 2018 to 2024 and as deputy vice president for academic affairs from 2022 to 2023.

Prof. Wattad is also a Senior Researcher at the Institute for National Security Studies at Tel-Aviv University, a Senior Research Fellow at the Institute for Israeli Thought, a Research Fellow at the International Institute for Counter-Terrorism at Reichman University, and a Research Fellow at the Minerva Center for the Rule of Law under Extreme Conditions at Haifa University. Between 2018 and 2021, he served as a Research Fellow at the International Center for Health, Law, and Ethics at Haifa University.

In addition, he serves as an Adjunct Professor at several law schools in Israel and abroad. From 2014 to 2016, he served as a visiting associate professor at the University of California at Irvine, both at the Department of Political Science and the School of Law.

Between 2003 and 2004, he served as a legal clerk at the Supreme Court of Israel under the supervision of Justice Dalia Dorner.

Prof. Wattad is a legal scholar specializing in international and comparative criminal law, comparative constitutional law, international law, the laws of war, torture, and terrorism, conflict resolution, professional ethics, medical law, and the interaction between law and political science. Additionally, Prof. Wattad has expertise in the history of Israel and issues of self-image and identity in multicultural societies.

Prof. Wattad is a Haifa University School of Law graduate from Israel, having studied as an exchange student at Oxford University. Additionally, he accomplished higher academic education in Law at the Hebrew University of Jerusalem Columbia University, New York, in the USA, the Munk Center of Global Affairs & Public Policy and the Toronto University in Canada, the Max Planck Institute in Germany, and the International Institute of Higher Studies in Criminal Sciences in Italy. Wattad graduated with distinction from all academic institutions he attended and was on the Dean's List. During his studies, Prof. Wattad has received several prizes of excellence and other prestigious fellowships, including Fulbright, Halbert, Minerva, and Humboldt.

He is the 2020 winner of the prestigious *Zeltner* Young Scholar Award by the Faulty of Law at Tel-Aviv University; the 2015 winner of the prestigious Young Scholar Award on Israel Studies (the law field) by the Association for Israel Studies; and the 2007 and the 2008 winner of the Best Legal Oralist Award of the International Institute of Higher Studies in Criminal Sciences. In 2014 and 2018, he was granted the 'Excellent Lecturer Award' by Zefat Academic College.

Prof. Wattad serves on editorial boards at several prestigious academic journals. Between 2010 and 2015, he was the Editor-in-Chief of *the International Journal of Medicine and Law*. He is also a member of several professional associations and, among other things, a member of the board of governance at the Association for Public Law in Israel and the Association for Israel Studies.

Besides, Prof. Wattad serves in many important public and professional positions, leading, among others, as a member of the Public Committee for Recommending Nominees for the Position of the *Knesset*'s Legal Advisor, member of the Bar Examination Committee, co-chair (together with Deputy Chief Justice (ret.) Prof. Elyakim Rubinstein) of *Kav-Mashve* – Developing Employment Leadership in Israeli Arab Society, member of the Board of Governance at the Israeli Institute for Press and Media Board of Governance, and member of the Presidential Board of Israel Press Council.

Prof. Wattad is highly involved in professional ethics; among other things, he serves as Vice President of the Bar Disciplinary Tribunal of the Northern District in Israel, Head of the Ethics Forum in Rotary Israel, and a member of the Ethics Tribunal of Israel Press Council.

In addition, between 2006 and 2016, Prof. Wattad engaged in diplomatic work related to Israel's public affairs. In this capacity, he collaborated with Israel's Foreign Ministry, including several of its embassies and consulates abroad, leading among them in the USA, Canada, and Germany.

Besides, Prof. Wattad has been devoted to volunteering activities in the community and society. He led, among others, through the Rotary organization, where he was elected District Governor for Rotary Israel for 2025–2026. Prof. Wattad is the recipient of the prestigious Paul Harris Award by the Rotary Foundation of Rotary International in appreciation of tangible and significant assistance to further better understanding and friendly relations among people worldwide.

He is married to Lana, a physician who specializes in Internal Medicine and Immunology at Rambam Medical Centre in Israel and is the father of Lady Lorraine and Emily. They live in Haifa City in the northern part of Israel.

Table of Contents

Table of Contents

List of Abbreviations

AIDS	Acquired Immune Deficiency Syndrome
DNA	Deoxyribonucleic Acid
GSS	General Security Service
HMO	Health Maintenance Organization
IMA	Israel Medical Association
IUD	Intrauterine Device

List of Abbreviations

Acknowledgement

My research assistant, Noor Abed Elrhman, deserves special thanks for her valuable work and assistance. I am grateful and indebted to her.

Acknowledgement

General Introduction

Chapter 1. General Background

§1. Geography and Climate

1. Israel is a small country with an area of 20,770 km^2 and a total population of approximately 9,900,000 inhabitants, of which 73.2% are Jews, 21.1% are Arabs, and 5.7% are non-Arab Christians and others who do not follow any religion. Israel lies at the eastern end of the Mediterranean Sea. Lebanon borders it in the north, Egypt in the south, Syria in the northeast, and Jordan in the east. Jerusalem is Israel's capital and largest city, with Tel Aviv and Haifa following. The country's climate is the Mediterranean, namely, subtropical. Its main characteristics are two contradictory seasons: hot, dry summer and cold, wet winter.

§2. Culture

2. Every year, Israel publishes approximately 7,300 books, of which 89% are in Hebrew, and 1,000 newspapers, of which eighteen are dailies. Eighteen active theatres perform before audiences of more than 2.5 million people. Israel's seventeen orchestras play before more than a million people every year. The country's numerous dance groups are patronized by over one-third of a million spectators annually.

§3. Political and Judicial Systems

I. The President of the State

3. The head of Israel's state is its President. He is elected for seven years by the Knesset, Israel's Parliament. He signs every new law apart from the one defining his powers. The President acts to achieve the formation of every new government and accepts the resignation of a government. He accredits the diplomatic representatives of the state, receives the credentials of diplomatic representatives of other states, and signs conventions with foreign countries. In addition, the President has the power to pardon offenders and to reduce penalties.

II. The Knesset, Israel's Parliament

4. The Knesset is the Parliament of the state. It consists of 120 members. The Knesset is elected by general, national, direct, equal, secret, and proportional elections. The Knesset's term of office is four years.

III. The Government

5. The government is the executive authority of the state. It comprises the Prime Minister and the ministers. The Prime Minister serves by being elected by the President – after being recommended before the president by all elected parties in the Knesset. The Prime Minister appoints the ministers; their appointment requires the approval of the Knesset. The Prime Minister determines the ministers' roles and conducts the government's functioning. For example, the Prime Minister or the minister charged with implementing the law is empowered to determine regulations for its implementation.

IV. The Judiciary

6. The President of the state appoints judges upon their election by a judges' election committee. Judicial judges are not subject to any authority but that of the law. A judge's tenure ends upon retirement on a pension (70 years old) or resignation. The Supreme Court hears appeals against judgments or other decisions of the district courts. The Supreme Court also sits as the High Court of Justice; as such, it hears matters in which it may deem it necessary to grant relief in the name of justice and which are not within the jurisdiction of any other judicial tribunal. Thus, the judicial system comprises the Supreme Court, district courts, magistrate courts, religious courts, and different courts and judicial tribunals.

V. The State Comptroller

7. The Knesset elects the state comptroller. This person oversees state inspection and inspects the economy, assets, finance, obligations, and administration of the state, government ministries, and local authorities. Thus, the state comptroller is independent of the government and responsible before the Knesset in exercising their functions.

§4. Population and Vital Statistics

8. Life expectancy in Israel is 81 years for males and 84 years for females. The birth rate is 21.5 births/1,000 population per year. More than a million cases are heard in courts every year. The legal establishment employs approximately 661 judges, and police and prison authorities use more than 36,000 police and prison officers and more than 50,000 volunteers. In Israel, there are more than 70,000 lawyers; most of them engage in private practice.

Chapter 2. General Description of the Healthcare System

§1. General Survey

9. Israel's health services have an elaborate infrastructure managed in accordance with parallel branches of activity in different spheres, as follows:

- Hospitalization services provide beds and treatment in medical centres, psychiatric institutions, and hospitals for long-term illnesses.
- The clinical services supply casual treatment within the hospital precincts and outside through the agency of the sick funds.
- The preventive, environmental treatment services limit the incidence of ecological infection, local epidemics, and the spread of disease.
- The community services provide psychiatry treatment for senior citizens, one-day care, and home care.
- The complimentary services render first aid, the evacuation of casualties, and other kindred activities.

All these facilities are available to Israel's population through the agencies of private, governmental, and public actors, such as the Ministry of Health, sick funds, public institutions, and local authorities.

§2. Regularization of the Healthcare System

10. The Ministry of Health is responsible for the regular supply of medical services to Israel's population and is charged with the overall planning, inspection, and coordination of the entire health establishment.

In ensuring the health of the country's inhabitants, the ministry concentrates on the following objectives: programming, licensing, directing, and supervising the state's health services; initiating and updating health legislation; ensuring hospitalization at general, psychiatric, rehabilitative and nursing institutions; safeguarding preventive and curative medical services; awarding licences to members of the various branches of the medical or paramedical profession; inspection, regularization, and conformation in the spheres of pharmacy, registration of medical preparations and determination of their contents as well as those of cosmetics and poisonous substances; control over the manufacture, preparation and marketing of foodstuffs for local and overseas consumption; vigilance with respect to environmental health hazards by prevention and by the enforcement of laws to purify the atmosphere, water and solid garbage; the preparation of a master plan for medical development which will encourage research and divert considerable resources to medical progress; as well as the training of nursing and paramedical personnel for medical institutions.

The hospitalization setup consists of around 15,000 beds. However, the ratio of available beds to population is on the decline. Alongside the data for 2023, and in order to address the acute needs of the healthcare system, according to the Ministry of Health's multi-year plan for allocating hospital beds, additional beds are expected to be added in the coming years. Between 2023 and 2028, the Ministry of Health plans to allocate an additional 1,790 beds to hospitals, resulting in a total of approximately 17,500 general beds in Israel, an increase of 11%. The Ministry of Health and the sick funds manage approximately twenty hospitals, while another ten are private institutions.

The services include treating chronic and geriatric patients, providing hospitalization for acute, rehabilitative, or nursing cases and ambulatory aid, home attendance, and visits for observation. In addition, mental health services coordinate mental health hospitals, civic centres, and stations with the object of promising overall benefits, consisting of prevention, treatment, and rehabilitation, by safeguarding continuity and regular treatment and providing for mental health services on a regional basis. On their release from the hospital, mental health patients are offered rehabilitation programmes which include jobs and accommodation.

The public health service is dedicated to the prevention of epidemics and the promotion of public health. It provides nutrition services, environmental health, epidemiology and laboratories, mother and child care, dental health, and hygiene. In addition, the nutrition service exerts its control over food, ensuring its standard of wholesomeness, quality, ingredients, packing, and classification. This service works on the three levels of legislation, inspection, and enforcement.

The Department for Environmental Health is responsible for maintaining a high standard of drinkable water, bathing pools, food marketing, sanitary conditions in public places, and the processing of garbage. In this connection, mention should be made of the sanitation law which makes it a crime to dump any sort of rubbish in or pollute places and ordaining that every local authority must define sites where waste may be deposited for disposal.

The Department of Epidemiology checks the spread of infectious diseases and epidemics. Its public health laboratories provide for microbiological and chemical analysis of water and food samples. The Department for Mother and Child Care lays down the procedure and supervises its implementation to treat women capable of childbirth, pregnant women, babies, and school children in more than a thousand family care stations. The Dental Health Department devotes its activities to the formulation of preventive measures to preserve dental health. The Department of Hygiene Education prepares explanatory material and training syllabuses on public health for the population in general and teachers of hygiene in particular, emphasizing the prevention of smoking, sensible nutrition, dental health, measures against accidents at home, and general hygiene. The Medical Institute for Road Safety aspires to reduce the number of traffic accidents caused by the ill health of drivers. The institute examines the health and tests candidates' aptitudes for licences to drive public transportation and drivers and applicants for permits if their health is defective.

The Nutrition Department collects and classifies data on the country's nutritional condition and disseminates guidance and advice among the general public.

The Institute for Preparing Formulae and the Inspection of Medical Substances safeguards the quality of medicines and inspects and examines the manufacture of medical products.

§3. Regularization of the Healthcare System During a Pandemic

11. Healthcare Regulations regarding the Coronavirus.

Due to the vast spread of the coronavirus pandemic, the government had to conduct and regulate laws, orders, and emergency regulations to limit the spread of the novel coronavirus.

Isolation

The purpose of the isolation period is to stop the infection and prevent the spread of the coronavirus disease in Israel. The isolation includes entering a place of isolation and avoiding contact with those around, including those staying in the house. The isolation is by order of the Director General of the Ministry of Health.

Active patients with a positive COVID test result are required to isolate until approved by attending physicians or nurses or registered nurses to be defined as 'recovering,' according to the Ministry of Health directives.

Moreover, anyone who suffers from a temperature of 38 degrees or more is required to isolate themselves, and it is highly recommended that they do a COVID test. In addition, those who experience one or more of the other COVID symptoms, such as cough, difficulty breathing, or other respiratory symptoms, or a change in the sense of smell or taste, are recommended to be examined for COVID or consult a caregiver before being exposed to other people.

However, as a rule, holders of a valid Israeli immunization certificate or recovery certificate are not required to go into isolation, even if they have suspected corona symptoms (fever over 38 degrees, cough, difficulty breathing or other respiratory symptoms, or loss of sense of taste or smell).

On 15 May 2023, the mandatory isolation order for those confirmed with COVID-19 was lifted.

Namely, since the lifting of the mandatory isolation order, the Ministry of Health has instructed that there is no longer a mandatory quarantine for those who have been confirmed with a COVID-19 test, whether conducted institutionally or at home, and there is no obligation to isolate.

However, it is important to remember that COVID-19 is still a contagious disease that primarily threatens those in high-risk groups. Therefore, according to the guidelines from the Ministry of Health, every COVID-19 patient should act responsibly towards the community based on the recommendations for those confirmed with COVID-19. The Ministry of Health recommends that those who test positive test for COVID-19 stay at home for five days from the date of the positive test or until the symptoms of the disease subside, such as a fever above 38 degrees, cough, and difficulty in breathing or other respiratory symptoms. Additionally, the Ministry of Health recommends that if it is necessary to leave the house, it is advisable to wear a mask for the entire duration outside the home.

Indeed, these are only recommendations from the Ministry of Health and not mandatory guidelines.

Enforcement

Violating the provisions of the Public Health Order (New Corona Virus) (Home Isolation and Various Provisions) (Temporary Order) is liable to imprisonment for six months or a fine in accordance with the Penal Law, 1977.

A police officer may order the dispersal of a crowd gathering or gathering made in violation of the Public Health Order. If a person refuses to comply with a police officer on such distribution, a police officer may use reasonable force to disperse the crowd. Anyone who rejects the instructions of a police officer is liable to imprisonment for six months or a fine per the Penal Code.

According to the Penal Code, any person staying in a place other than their residence without wearing a mask, contrary to the provisions of the Public Health Order, is liable to imprisonment for six months or a fine.

Emergency Regulations (Enforcement of the Public Health Order) (The New Corona Virus) (Home Isolation and Various Provisions) (Temporary Order), 2020, were repealed and replaced by the Law to Amend and Implement the Emergency Regulations (New Coronavirus Enforcement), 2020, which regulated all enforcement matters, with penalties determined for each offence. The Law came into effect on 17 June 2020, until 10 August 2020, and included a provision allowing the Knesset, upon request of the government and in accordance with the recommendation of the Knesset's Constitution, Law, and Justice Committee, to extend the extension period for the entire law or part of it for an additional period not exceeding twenty-one days or to shorten the extension period.

Assistance from the General Security Service and Location Data

The purpose of the Authorization of the General Security Service (GSS) to Assist in the National Endeavour Law is to enable the GSS to be authorized to assist the Ministry of Health in conducting an epidemiological investigation to reduce the spread of the new coronavirus, to protect the safety and health of the public, as part of the efforts of the State of Israel in dealing with the rapid spread of the virus. Furthermore, the face of urgency resulting from the rise in morbidity rates that poses a severe and immediate danger to the citizens and inhabitants of Israel requires the use of exceptional measures, all for a limited period at the same time, promoting and assimilating the use of civilian technology among the public to locate those who have been in close contact with active patients.

The law enables the GSS to track anyone who is registered with the Ministry of Health as in need of isolation from the moment of registration onward, anyone who was a COVID patient fourteen days back, and anyone who was near the cell phone of that patient fourteen days back – whether in the train, on the street, or at work, namely everywhere. The tracking method works by using the location data of the cell phone.

Other information that may be possible to monitor is the history of calls and text messages without the content, credit history, street cameras, and cameras in public spaces (e.g., hospitals) that can be managed, among other things, using artificial intelligence systems. Regulations authorizing the GSS were set to expire on 20 January 2021. The rules regarding the location history of patients allow a qualified officer to permit the receipt of a person's location data who is liable for isolation from a database of a *Bezeq* licence holder, without a court order to supervise the observance of the isolation order; obtaining location data under this subsection shall be done on a sample basis only and in a non-continuous manner. The information obtained under this section shall not be used for purposes other than what it is intended for. However, these regulations expired on 22 April 2021.

The Supreme Court sitting as the High Court of Justice adjudicated a petition submitted regarding the authorization granted to the GSS to assist in conducting epidemiological investigations, pursuant to the Authorization Law of the GSS to assist in the national effort to reduce the spread of the new coronavirus and promote the use of civilian technology to trace those who have been in close contact with patients (Emergency Regulation), 2020. The petitioners were four civil organizations working to defend human rights. In their petition, they requested the Court to rule on the annulment of the GSS Authorization Law, or alternatively, the annulment of the government's declaration regarding the GSS' authorization under this law.

The GSS' authorization method evolved through various forms until the enactment of the principal law discussed in the petition. Initially, the GSS was authorized to act through emergency regulations under section 39 of the Basic Law: Government. Subsequently, after the convening of the 23rd Knesset and the establishment of the Foreign Affairs and Security Committee, the government decided to use section 7(b)(6) of the GSS Law, 2002, which, allows it to authorize the GSS to operate in areas not within its core areas of operation, provided it is for 'vital national security interests of the state' and with the approval of the Foreign Affairs Committee.

The authorization decision was deliberated in the *Ben Meir* case. The Supreme Court's judgment determined that 'section 7(b)(6) of the General Security Service Law should be interpreted as allowing the government to authorize the GSS even in areas not directly related to security in the narrow sense, but the test to be adopted regarding the expression national security in this context is a severe and immediate danger to the citizens and residents of the country or its law enforcement agencies'.

Following the ruling in the *Ben Meir* case, the possibility of initiating legislation for GSS authorization to assist the Ministry of Health in conducting epidemiological investigations was deliberated, and simultaneously, the validity of the authorization decision was extended from time to time until the completion of the examination of the mentioned possibility. However, due to a significant decrease in the infection rate at the beginning of June 2020, it was decided in an inter-governmental discussion not to advance the bill at that stage. Therefore, on 10 June 2020, the authorization decision expired. However, towards the end of June 2020, there was a significant increase in the virus infection rate, prompting the government to reutilize GSS tools and return and promote the bill. Accordingly, on 24 June 2020, a government bill was placed on the Knesset table. Initially, an intern law was passed, allowing the government to rely on the GSS for three weeks until the completion of the full legislative process. During this period, the Foreign Affairs and Security Committee held three meetings, mostly public, to discuss the bill and the subject of the petition, and one of them also heard the positions of public representatives and academia.

The GSS Authorization Law was approved in the Knesset in the second and third readings on 20 July 2020, with the majority of forty-eight supporters versus twenty-three opponents. It was published in the *Official Gazette* on 21 July 2020 and came into effect on the same day.

The petitioners' main claim is that the use of the GSS for contact tracing severely and disproportionately violates the right to privacy and freedom. The essence of privacy infringement lies in the government's ability to forcibly collect location data that may reveal personal information. Especially given that the de-anonymization of data can now be relatively easily done technologically. According to the petitioners, the GSS Authorization Law does not pass the tests of limitation clauses, as its infringement on the right to privacy and freedom is very severe. Conversely, the benefit derived from it is limited.

Regarding the petition, the Supreme Court's decision was made by a majority opinion, as mentioned in the judgment of Chief Justice of the Supreme Court Esther Hayut, who proposed to partially accept the petition in the sense that as long as the government chooses to continue relying on the GSS after 14 March 2021, it must formulate criteria for exercising its discretion in accordance with paragraph 48 of the judgment. In any case, from that date onwards, the government's authority to authorize the GSS will be limited only to those cases where the confirmed patient does not cooperate in the epidemiological investigation or has not reported any contacts.

§4. The Financing of Healthcare

12. The 1994 government law partly covers health insurance in Israel for National Health Insurance, which is based on justice, equality, and mutual aid. In addition, the law entitles every person residing in Israel to health services.

The state is responsible for funding the whole package of health services using resources detailed in the law. The sick fund is responsible for supplying all its health services to every one of its registered members in accordance with the law. Health services from the contents of the whole package are supplied as ordered by the physicians, are of reasonable quality, will reach the patient within a reasonable period, and are obtainable within good distance from the home of the insured patient – all from resources made available to the sick fund, as laid down by the law. Health services are provided while human dignity remains sacrosanct, confidentiality is preserved, and secrecy is maintained.

Every resident in Israel who has reached the age of 18 must register with the sick fund of their choice and have any minor who is a child inscribed. The sick fund of any person's choice must accept their registration without any reservations, conditions, or payment. No employer may condition an employee's job on the latter's belonging to any specific sick fund, nor shall the employer oblige their employee to register with any fund of the country's various sick funds.

13. The whole package of health services is divided into the following spheres:

(a) Personal preventive medicine and health education.
(b) Medical diagnosis.

(c) Ambulatory treatment, including mental care at a clinic or home.
(d) Hospitalization – general, psychiatric, psychogeriatric, and chronic nursing.
(e) Rehabilitation – medical, psychological, physiotherapy, linguistic, occupational therapy, and social, health-restoring work.
(f) The supply of medicines.
(g) Medical equipment and supportive instruments.
(h) Children's preventive dental care.
(i) Medical first aid and transport to and from hospitals and clinics.
(j) Medical services in factories, offices, and other places of work.
(k) Medical and mental treatment for the rehabilitation of drug and alcohol addicts.

14. The law obliged the sick fund not to distinguish supplying all the people for whom it is responsible with such medical services as they require, whether directly or through its auxiliary services. Lack of payment or arrears in charge of health insurance dues can be no excuse for the sick fund not to honour its commitment to supply any of the services in the whole package. The sick fund, or the party that provides treatment for a person who has contracted an illness or suffered an injury as a result of a third party's misconduct, has the right to claim from that third party, from the insurance agent, or some other person, given the liability of any of them, by law or insurance contract, all costs incurred by the health services that have restored the health of or repaired the injury to, the first party. A sick fund member has the right to choose their treatment supplier, for themselves or any registered offspring, from among the fund's medical staff or any medical personnel affiliated with the fund.

15. The law has set up a Council for National Health Insurance, consisting of forty-six members, over whom the Minister of Health presides. Its functions are as follows:

(a) To advise the Minister of Health concerning matters appertaining to the law as listed below:
   (1) Health insurance dues.
   (2) Changes in the health service package, usually owing to new techniques and their costs.
   (3) The promotion of uniformity in the quality of the medical services and their accessibility as required by the regulations of the law.
   (4) The evaluation of requirements for the allocation of funds for expanding the health services.
   (5) Payments by insured persons for health services rendered.
   (6) Ethical issues in the health sphere at the government level.
   (7) A list of priorities in the health sphere for the expending of resources on various requirements.
   (8) The supply of health services on a regional or interregional basis.
   (9) Any other matter to be determined by the Minister of Health, or a third of the members of the Health Council shall seek to discuss it.

(b) To keep the implementation of the law under constant observation and to establish an institution under the minister's appointees to organize research, carry out surveys, and submit recommendations to the Council.
(c) To circularize up-to-date and regular information among sick fund members about their legal rights, the types of services at their disposal, where these services are obtainable, and who the purveyors of the services are in every kind of sick fund.

In 2023, The Financing of Healthcare was updated based on the contents of the basic services basket and as detailed in the second amendment to the law and requests from health funds according to section 8(a1) of the law approved by the Knesset Finance Committee according to section 8(a2) of the law. This is in accordance with the following sections:

(1) According to section 8(h) of the National Health Insurance Law, due to the rise in the health cost index starting from 1 April 2023, the payments have changed, and the measurement also applies to reimbursements, funding, or financial participation of the health fund.
(2) A directive on National Health Insurance (Medications in the Health Services Basket) (Emergency Regulations), 2023, froze insured individuals' out-of-pocket payments as part of the health fund billing plan for the months of July through December 2023, so they will not be affected by the increase in the price list.
(3) After expanding the Health Services Basket for 2023, as of 1 July 2023, glasses for children up to the age of 7 were included in the basket.
(4) Starting 1 July 2023, seniors aged 72 and above were entitled to preventive dental care and dentures. Additionally, new services such as root canal treatment, installation of up to four implants, and other services that were not previously available were added.
(5) In addition, according to the directive on National Health Insurance (Amendment – Second Amendment to the Law) (No. 2), 2022, self-participation for hospitalization day was reduced according to the health cost index for 2022 starting from 30 June 2022.

§5. THE ADMINISTRATION OF HEALTHCARE

16. In 2005, the Minister of Health had enacted the Regulations on National Health Insurance (Arrangements for Choosing Between Services Suppliers), whereby every Health Maintenance Organization (HMO) must detail, in its published selection arrangement, the services it offers to its insured persons. The selection arrangement has been formulated in accordance with the categories of services listed in the regulations. In addition, each HMO must submit its selection arrangement to the Minister of Health, thus bringing it to attention and placing it before the insured person in the various clinics of each HMO. Furthermore, a copy of the selection arrangement shall be provided to the insured person, upon their request, free of charge, and it shall also be published on the website of the HMO. According to the 2024 amendment to the Regulations on National Health Insurance (Arrangements for Choosing Between Services Suppliers), the HMO must inform the insured of their right to perform the procedure with any service provider included in the fund's choice arrangement. They must also provide the insured with a list of all service providers in the choice arrangement, based on their residence, including the provider's name and contact details. The information shall be sufficiently provided to the insured to ensure freedom of choice and compliance with the provisions of the law and regulations. The insured shall be informed clearly and prominently in writing, including digitally, allowing them to print and revisit the list. Service providers shall inform the insured in writing when the insured approaches them for service or when the fund issues a committee. This shall be confirmed in advance by the fund's administrator. Moreover, in 2007, further regulations were enacted (Regulations on National Health Insurance (Medical Service for Insured Persons of HMO for Small Communities)).

17. The Minister of Health further enacted the Regulations for National Health Insurance (Notification on Closure of a Clinic or Terminating Medical Service Contact) 2005, which established a set of procedures to guarantee the lawful closure of a medical clinic or termination of medical service contact.

18. By this authority, the Minister of Health amended the National Health Insurance Ordinance (Funding the Health Council) in 2015, thus holding that the monthly fund to be transferred to the Health Council by the National Insurance Institute is ILS 958,334.

Chapter 3. Medical Law

§1. Definition and Function of Medical Law

19. Forensic medicine is a medical science sphere distinct from medical law. The discipline of forensic medicine is a speciality of medicine and a sub-speciality of pathology. Modern forensic sciences began in the middle of the nineteenth century due to biological, physical, and medical discoveries and technological developments. Forensic medicine deals with the problems related to unnatural deaths and various types of trauma to the living.

20. As an independent body in the legal galaxy, medical law is still in its early years and started its juvenile growth in the 1950s and 1960s of the twentieth century. More recently, its development has been boosted by expanding social trends and ideologies contemporaneously with tremendous scientific and technological breakthroughs. As a result, medical treatment has ceased to be a matter entirely controlled by physicians alone; a considerable portion of it is subject to the directions and decisions of the patient. This development first crystallized in law-court decisions and has gradually earned the recognition of the legislators. As a result, legal decisions concerned with medical treatment have begun to be determined by such ethical factors. They are given expression in such socio-legal factors as 'respect for the individual,' 'respect for autonomy,' 'respect for dignity,' 'informed consent,' 'confidentiality,' and 'truth-telling'.

21. The 1980s and 1990s of the twentieth century witnessed a tremendous expansion of medical law, qualitatively and quantitatively. This expansion found expression not only in law-court decisions of broad proportions, particularly in damage claims but also in legislation, which is making rapid strides towards providing for most, if not all, of the health contingencies, as well as in the publication of professional and scientific literature enriched by an abundance of research work that appears in print in book form or as articles in professional journals.

22. Medical law today is only a section of a far wider legal field known as Health Law. While medical law, in its legal aspect, covers the whole gamut of relationships between physician and patient, such as the physician's responsibility for and duties to their patient and the patient's rights, health law deals with these, among many other subjects in a less specific form. It makes direct or indirect provisions for all the normative aspects relating to for all the normative aspects relating to mankind's health. Consequently, health law deals with subjects concerning the beginning of life, such as abortions, artificial reproduction, and genetic engineering; with the cessation of life, such as euthanasia; and with such effects on life as transplantations and experimentation on humans. With health laws' increasing consideration for and preservation of the individual patient's rights, it has focused on the interests of society in general and of third parties in particular.

23. The legal sources of medical law may be found primarily in statutes enacted by the Knesset, in subsidiary regulations, and in decisions of the law courts.

National legislation also incorporates international charters like the Helsinki–Tokyo Declaration, adopted and legalized in Israel. The primary sources of medical law are civil law, particularly the law of torts, contracts, and criminal law. The law of torts applies to the wrongs of negligence and of assault. Most legal actions that arise from the physician's professional conduct concerning the patient are brought in the tort of negligence. Although, as we shall later show, the legal source of this wrong lies in the Torts Ordinance, Articles 23–35 of the same Ordinance refers to the wrong of assault, which is committed by intentionally bringing about harmful contact with the body of another without the person's consent. The Law of Contracts has limited application in regulating the relationship between doctor and patient. Most governmental or public authorities employ most Israeli doctors, and national or public legal arrangements govern most medical treatments. In general, it is only in the context of private practice that the Law of Contracts operates.

24. Several crimes in criminal law are solely related to physicians. For example, the revised version of the Physicians' Ordinance fixes a prison sentence and a fine for a physician who uses fraud to obtain a licence or illegally employs assistants.

The Penal Code decrees a prison sentence and a fine for a physician who performs an illegal abortion or one who is so negligent in treating a patient whose life is endangered or is guilty of assault in treating a patient without the latter's consent. In addition, the Law of Patients' Rights imposes fines on physicians who contravene specific directives detailed in the law.

The Law on Treatment of the Mentally Ill decrees a prison sentence for a physician who signs a certificate stating that a person is mentally ill knowing that the person is of sound mind. Furthermore, anyone who does not render emergency aid to a person who needs it may be fined in accordance with the 'Neither shalt thou stand against the blood of thy neighbour' Law.

Part I. The Medical Profession

Chapter 1. Access to the Medical Profession

§1. MEDICAL EDUCATION

25. As will be seen hereinafter, the revised version of the Physicians' Ordinance decrees that an applicant for a physician's licence may obtain one on condition that they have completed their education in medicine that may be acquired in Israel or abroad. In Israel, medicine may be studied in that section of a university called as a section of a university called medical faculty or medical school. The first of Israel's medical schools was founded in 1949 at the Hebrew University in Jerusalem. Today, medicine is taught at five Israeli higher-education institutions: the Hebrew University of Jerusalem, Tel Aviv University, Ben Gurion University in Beersheba, the Technion in Haifa (Technological Institute), and Bar-Ilan University through its branch in Sefad. In general, the courses at Israel's medical schools are six years and are followed by a one-year internship. The Physicians' Ordinance stipulates that anyone who wishes to proceed to an internship must first pass examinations. The Director General of the Ministry of Health is equipped with the power to withhold a licence from an intern if the Director of the hospital where the intern has spent his or her internship cannot report favourably on his or her work. The 1988 Physicians' Regulations (Examination of Candidates for Internship) specified that the subjects for examination would be internal, surgical, children's, gynaecological medicine, and psychiatry. A person who has been awarded the recognized diploma of a medical school and has passed the interns' examination is regarded as a physician's licence, if he or she complies with the various other conditions detailed in the law.

§2. MEDICAL SPECIALISTS

I. General Authorization

26. After consultation with the Israel Medical Association (IMA), the revised version of the Physicians' Ordinance is empowered by the Minister of Health, after consultation with the IMA, to determine specialist titles in the different branches of medicine and conditions for their award to applicants after succeeding in examinations as determined by the minister. In accordance with the Ordinance mentioned above, the minister laid down Regulations for Physicians (Authorization of Specialist Titles and Examinations) in 1973. The regulations ordain that only such specialist titles named in the appendix to the regulations may be awarded to physicians.

The Physicians Ordinance of 1976 was amended in 2005, thus providing that, on certain occasions, a special medical commission shall be established to determine the mental capability or the physical state of the person who seeks to apply for a licence for performing medicine as a physician or for an already-licensed physician. Any information to be gathered in accordance with these procedures enjoys the duty of secrecy.

II. Application for Specialization

27. A candidate for specialization must address the application for enrolment as a specialist student to the Scientific Council of the Physicians' Association, attaching proof of completion of a medical doctorate course at a medical school, together with notifications from the departmental head and the chairman of the specialization committee at a hospital, stating their willingness to accept the candidate as a specialization student. He who has accomplished one-third of his residency before 21 May 2014 may complete his specialization in accordance with the original residency plan that initially applied to him.

28. The duration of medical residency ranges from 4 to 7 years, depending on the chosen speciality. Residents are employed by medical institutions accredited by both the scientific council and the Ministry of Health for residency training. Throughout the residency period, institutions are bound by obligations defined by the scientific council, outlined in Ministry of Health regulations, and stipulated in employment agreements. Residents work under the guidance and supervision of specialized physicians in their chosen field. It's important to note that residents are licensed physicians and are held to the same legal responsibilities and authority as any other doctor. At the conclusion of their residency, residents must successfully pass examinations administered by the scientific council.

III. Specialization

29. Specialization will take the form of full-time employment at a recognized establishment, inclusive of several duty shifts as allocated by the scientific council for the branch of medicine chosen by the applicant, who will be guided by and under the observation of a specialist in the branch of medicine of the student's choice. The period of specialization shall be as ordained in the appendix to the regulations mentioned above, in addition to a term of specialization in basic science. The latter is categorized in paragraph 1 of the regulations as one of the following: immunology, anatomy, pathological anatomy, anthropology, epidemiology, medical ethics, biology, biochemistry, biophysics, genetics, chemistry, physical chemistry, microbiology, computer science, sociology, statistics, physics physiology, psychology, pharmacology, the history of medicine, and nutrition.

IV. Examinations

30. The oral and written examinations take place in two stages: intermediate and final. The intermediate, relating mainly to theoretical knowledge, may be taken by the candidate after completing half the period of specialization. The student must pass the intermediate examination before sitting for finals, especially with concrete cases in the candidate's particular branch of medicine. Examinations occur at least once a year, and failed candidates may sit for either examination again. Everything connected with the examinations is confidential. Anyone whose functions link with them will divulge nothing unless the law obliges or permits the person to do so. After the aspirant for the specialist title has completed his examinations and studentship, the Council will present the Director General with a survey of all its probes, including examination results, together with its reasoned recommendation.

31. More precisely, in Israel, medical specialization exams are conducted in two stages: Stage A and Stage B.

32. During medical residency in Stage A, candidates undergo a comprehensive exam consisting of written and oral components. This stage is intended to evaluate the candidates' clinical and theoretical knowledge. During the specialization, a wide range of topics in medicine, including internal medicine, surgery, neurology, nephrology, emergency medicine, psychiatry, and more, must be reinforced.

33. Stage B is also a comprehensive exam that focuses on specific topics related to the candidate's specialized field. The exam includes a written component and a clinical examination in the context of real patients or in focused patient case scenarios. Its aim is to assess the candidate's ability to become a proficient specialist in their chosen field.

34. Successful completion of both stages is required to recognize medical specialization in Israel.

V. Approval of Title

35. A physician who seeks confirmation of his or her title will address the application to the Director through the agency of the Scientific Council of the Israel Physicians' Association. The physician will attach the following six documents to his application:

(1) A diploma attesting to the successful completion of his or her studies at a university or medical faculty recognized by the Director.
(2) A licence or temporary permit to practise medicine in Israel.
(3) A document certifying completion of specialization or exemption from specialization.

(4) A specialization record issued by the Scientific Council to a specialization student, containing details of his or her specialization and including the endorsement of all the stages of his or her specialization.
(5) Confirmation of success in specialist examinations at each stage or proof of exemption from examination.
(6) A recommendation from the head of the department of the main subject or of the advanced subject in which he or she specialized, whichever is relevant, in proof of the candidate's unreserved suitability for the specialist title.

VI. Cancellation and Suspension of Title

36. The Director General is empowered to cancel or suspend the award of a title in the following two contingencies:

(1) He or she has discovered that the approval was obtained by false evidence.
(2) The possessor of the title has demonstrated gross negligence or incompetence in performing his or her specialist duties.

Pending a decision, the specialist must be allowed to air his or her objections before a special committee consisting of the Director's representative, the Chairman of the Scientific Council, and the Dean of a Medical School. It is forbidden for a person to use the title of specialist, or any other title which is misleading, if he or she has not been awarded such a title or if it has been cancelled.

It should be noted that Suspension is an urgent and immediate process aimed at protecting the public from potential future harm that may arise if that doctor continues to work for another day. This is until the matter is clarified in an orderly manner within a legal or disciplinary process if initiated as such. In this sense, the suspension is similar to an arrest aimed at keeping dangerous offenders off the streets until the legal process against them is concluded the suspension is similar to an arrest aimed at keeping dangerous offenders off the streets until the legal process against them is concluded and they are incarcerated (if convicted).

VII. Specialist Titles

37. To date, the following are Israel's fields of specialization:

Internal medicine, cardiology, haematology, clinical immunology and allergies, pneumonia, gastroenteritis, endocrinology, nephrology, paediatrics, neurology, psychiatry, general surgery, child surgery, neurosurgery, breast surgery, orthopaedic surgery, plastic surgery, urologic surgery, skin and sex diseases, nose, ear, and throat diseases; optic diseases, anaesthesiology, childbirth and gynaecology, diagnostic radiology, oncology, family medicine, public health (academic and certified), physical health and convalescence, clinical laboratory subjects (microbiology or clinical biochemistry), pathological anatomy, nuclear medicine, geriatrics, forensic medicine, child and adolescent psychiatry, medical administration, neonatology, medical genetics, rheumatology, arm surgery, blood vessel surgery, infectious diseases, occupational medicine, general intensive care, child neurology, child cardiology, children's lung diseases, children's clinical and allergic immunology, children's haemato-oncology, children's gastroenterology, children's nephrology, children's endocrinology, children's intensive care, clinical pharmacology, and emergency medicine.

Chapter 2. Practice of Medicine

§1. Legal Conditions for the Practice of Medicine

I. General Rule

38. The Supreme Court of Israel ruled (H.C. 1/49):

> the natural right to play the trade or profession of his own choice, as long as his occupation is not illegal. No person may practice any trade or profession for which the legislature has created restrictions or conditions with which he must comply before he begins to engage in the occupation of his choice, having satisfied the requirements of the law. For example, a person may not practice as a lawyer until he has acquired a licence to do so, in accordance with the Lawyers' Ordinance. Moreover, he cannot acquire his licence unless he has been qualified by taking a course in legal studies:
>
>> He who would practice … medicine must first obtain the required licence … If he practices any of these professions without such a licence, he will face dire consequences.

II. Legal Monopoly of Physicians

39. The practice of medicine is confined only to licensed personnel. The 1976 revised version of the Physicians' Ordinance defines the profession as examining sick or injured persons, diagnosing their disabilities, curing them, prescribing for them, examining women's preparations for conception and childbirth, and other services regularly rendered by physicians, including acupuncture. The Ordinance decrees that a licensed physician shall not engage in any other work whose nature may confront him or her with a conflict of interest. In addition, the law ordains that a physician should not advertise any misleading activity that may undermine the dignity of the profession.

40. In Israel, the legal monopoly of physicians is governed by the Physicians Ordinance, which aims to uphold the quality of medical care and ensure public safety. This legislation delineates the criteria and prerequisites for licensing physicians and accrediting medical institutions. It restricts medical practice exclusively to licensed physicians authorized by local authorities.

41. The law also specifies physicians' professional duties and obligations, empowering the Ministry of Health to revoke the licence of any physician who fails to meet these standards. These measures ensure that medical treatments are administered solely by competent and licensed professionals, thereby safeguarding public health and safety.

III. Legal Conditions for the Practice of Medicine

A. Licence

42. The Ordinance's purpose is twofold: It regularizes procedure for the award of physicians' licences and prevents the infiltration of undesirables into the profession. A licensed physician authorized to practice medicine in Israel is a person in possession of a licence as specified by the Physicians' Ordinance.

A licence to practise medicine may be awarded only to an Israeli citizen or to the holder of a certificate of permanent residence in Israel. The Director General is empowered to issue a 'limited permit' for the practice of medicine to a person who does not possess a certificate of permanent residence in Israel if he or she has been invited to a hospital with the Director General's consent, for work during a specified period; or if he or she has applied for, and obtained, the Director General's consent to a period of extra training in medicine or medical specialization to attain the status of a specialist. The Director General is empowered to condition the award of a limited permit on a period of internship, success in examinations, or both. He may also limit the permit concerning time, place, or a branch of medicine. Three conditions determine the award of a licence. The applicant must be an honest person; his or her medical education must be sound, and he or she must have passed all examinations. Persons of proper medical education include, among others, students from abroad who hold diplomas recognized by the Director General. As defined by the Ordinance, a diploma consists of any degree, certificate, proof of status, certification, or written communication issued by a university or other institution, by the governing body of a country, or by its official representatives.

B. Application for Licence

43. An application for a licence to practise medicine shall be addressed to the Director General of the Ministry of Health through the agency of the District Health Officer. Attachments to the application must comprise a completed questionnaire for professional workers in health services; a certified copy or photocopy of a diploma in evidence of the medical education of the applicant; and a certificate in proof of his or her Israeli nationality or residential status in compliance with the law for entrance to Israel. The Inspector General will award an applicant, who fulfils all the conditions detailed in the Ordinance, a licence. The Ministry of Health's Director General is also empowered to issue a temporary permit for the practice of medicine during a period not exceeding twelve months.

C. Advisory Board for Medical Licences

44. As stated, the Director General of the Ministry of Health is empowered to issue licences for medical practice or temporary permits for the same purpose. The law provides the 'advisory board' to enable the Director to perform the duties. This body, appointed by the Minister of Health, consists of three members: a physician employed by the Ministry of Health and two other physicians of the minister's choice from a list compiled by the IMA and containing the name of at least one physician who is a member of the teaching staff of a medical school with the status of a senior lecturer or professor. The board is empowered to interview an applicant for a licence or permit and question him or her about medical qualifications and experience. The Director General is expected to consider the advisory board's recommendations before finally deciding to approve or turn down any application for a medical licence. However, the Director General may refuse to accept the board's recommendations if he finds them mistaken or resulting from the irregular procedure.

D. Appeal

45. Following Amendment No. 12 to the Physicians Ordinance, section 38A was added, defining therein the Appeals Committee appointed by the Minister. This committee will review all appeals regarding decisions on licence applications. Thus, an applicant for a medical licence is entitled, within thirty days from receipt of the administrative decision on their application, to submit a written appeal to the Appeals Committee appointed by the Minister according to the provisions of subsection (C).

E. Obtaining a Licence by Fraud

46. A person who obtains, or attempts to obtain, a licence, or permit to practise medicine or to achieve the status of a certified specialist, by evidence or statement that is false or misleading, whether orally or in writing, whether he or she has exhibited such fictitious proof, or caused it to be exhibited, will be subject to a three-year prison sentence. Any accessory will be liable for the same punishment.

IV. The Practice of Medicine Without a Licence

47. The Physicians' Ordinance states that a person who is not a licensed physician may not practice medicine or masquerade, on a temporary or permanent basis, as one who is engaged in healing or is prepared to heal. Any infringement of this rule carries a penalty of a year's imprisonment or a fine. In addition, a person who is not a licensed physician cannot be compensated by the law court for services or be awarded any emolument for such work done, or such services rendered, as should have been provided by a licensed physician; nor may he or she be reimbursed for medicine prescribed or dispensed.

The Ordinance disqualifies any person other than a licensed physician from dubbing him- or herself a 'physician,' a 'medical worker,' a 'surgeon,' or the holder of any similar title in words or initials which create the impression that he or she is medically competent. A licensed physician may call himself or herself a 'doctor'. Still, the Ordinance rules out the use of any title or similar attribute that might imply the achievement of status or professional skills, different from those that he or she possesses recognized by the Director. A person who contravenes this order uses the title of 'specialist' in a specific branch of the profession, assumes any other title that may mislead, and for which he or she is not licensed, is liable to a three-month term of imprisonment. It should be noted that a licensed physician has no authority to engage in dentistry except in the ordinary course of his medical treatment.

48. The Physicians' Ordinance lists the following five exemptions from the rule that persons may not practice medicine without a physician's licence:

(1) A licensed dentist.
(2) A licensed chemist.
(3) A certified midwife.
(4) A nurse or other person who tends sick people.
(5) Any person who offers advice or chance assistance with no monetary or other personal gain or acts under direct control.

None of these persons has the right to present him- or herself as a licensed physician. Still, all are permitted to exercise their skills in a confined medical sphere, as detailed in the definition of that particular 'medical practice' that is covered by the expertise of the practitioners or laymen in the above list. The Director is also empowered to make exceptions to the rule laid down in the Ordinance, as follows:

(a) Personnel employed as male or female nurses and assistants whom the Director has appointed and certified to diagnose or heal in such situations as he has specified or permitted.
(b) Personnel designated by the Director as approved medical students.
(c) Specialists invited from abroad to perform specific operations or to participate in specified medical consultations.

However, it should be noted that the current situation in Israel is set to change regarding the practice of medicine following the introduction of a new profession into the law known as the Physician Assistant. In 2023, Amendment No. 8 to Israel's Health Profession Order Law introduced the Physician Assistant as a new healthcare profession; the work of a Physician Assistant (PA) in Israel involves assisting physicians by performing medical procedures within their speciality under supervision. They undergo rigorous academic and practical training, obtaining the Ministry of Health certification. Personal authorization, renewable every two years, ensures compliance with safety and quality standards for medical procedures. This new profession aims to enhance medical service delivery and improve healthcare across Israel.

In addition, Amendment No. 16 to the Physicians Ordinance regulated all aspects of personal authorization for Physician Assistants. It should be noted that section 3 stipulates that individuals who are not physicians are not authorized to practice medicine or represent themselves, explicitly or implicitly, as practicing medicine.

Subsection (b) specifies a list of professions exempt from the provisions of Subsection (a). As part of the amendment, the profession of Physician Assistant was added, thus exempting it from the provisions of subsection (a).

V. Performing Exceptional Actions

49. In 2008, the Physicians' Regulations (Qualifications for Performing Exceptional Actions) were amended, thus permitting the performance of exceptional actions by authorized nurses, on the condition that these nurses have studied these actions in a nursing school where he or she completed his or her studies. 'Exceptional Actions' include medical actions that can be performed by people other than physicians, for example, arterial lines. In 2017, the aforementioned regulations were amended, thus enlarging the scope of actions that amount to 'exceptional actions.'

50. The Physicians' Ordinance (Amendment No. 15), 2023, dated 29 March 2023, amended section 59(b1) of the ordinance and expanded the list of authorized personnel to administer treatments at the patient's home, including assistants authorized by the appointed administrator. Until this amendment, the delegation of special procedures for execution at the patient's home was only permitted to qualified nurses.

51. However, following the amendment to the Physicians Regulations (Qualifications for Performing Exceptional Procedures), the eighth addition was introduced, allowing phlebotomists to draw blood at the patient's home from the age of 7 and above.

52. Regulation 8 was amended in this amendment, which pertains to granting permissions to nurses to perform special procedures in the hospital. Subsection (g) of subsection (3) was amended to specify that in any other medical institution, the granting authority shall be the medical director of that medical institution.

53. In the amendment, section 10A was added, concerning 'personal authorization for an assistant to perform a special procedure in the hospital.' Subsection (a) stipulates that a medical director who has received permission to exercise the authority to perform special procedures is entitled to grant personal authorization to the appointed assistant from the eighth addition to perform the specified special procedure in the eighth addition, In the hospital, if the assistant meets the conditions mentioned Regulation 10(b), and additional conditions determined in the eighth addition.

54. Subsection (b) specifies from whom the authorization to perform a special procedure in the hospital shall be granted.

55. Subsection (c) specifies that a personal authorization is valid for one year and may be extended for additional periods not exceeding one year each, based on the opinion of the person directly responsible for the assistant.

56. In the amendment, the eighth addition was added, which includes the list of assistants and a detailed description of the permitted special procedures, according to the physician's instructions:

1. Phlebotomists

Venous blood collection from age 7 and above provided that the assistant has performed the specified procedure satisfactorily at the medical institution for at least 3 months prior to performing the special procedure in the hospital, and has written approval from the medical director of the institution, along with an additional condition of CPR renewal once every two years.

§2. Illegal Practice of Medicine

I. Legal Definition of the Offence

57. The revised version of the Physicians' Ordinance decrees that any person who practices medicine or masquerades as a medical practitioner without being a licensed physician shall be fined and sentenced to a year's imprisonment.

II. Medical Activities

A. General Remarks

58. Paragraph 2 of the Patient's Rights Law defines 'medical treatment' as including medical diagnosis, preventive medical treatment, and psychological and nursing treatment. The legislator has adopted a broad enough definition to provide directives that advantage the most significant possible number of sick people.

59. Paragraph 1 of the revised version of the Physicians' Ordinance defines the 'practice of medicine' as inclusive of the examination of the sick and injured, diagnoses, cures, prescribing medicines, an inspection of women linked with conception and childbirth, and any other services customarily rendered by a physician, including acupuncture.

B. Specific Medical Activities

1. Preventive Medicine

60. The Patient's Rights Law determines that the physician who engages in preventive medicine is bound by duties and liabilities to his or her patients, whether they are ill or healthy. It is clearly stated that a physician is entitled to practise preventive medicine, among other types of medicine. However, the Physicians' Ordinance's revised version does not explicitly include preventive medicine in its definition of the 'practice of medicine'. Whereas paragraph 1 of this Ordinance may be interpreted as having such preventive medicine as may be considered part and parcel of the business or services customarily rendered by a physician. Furthermore, the 1973 Physicians' Regulations (Approval of Specialist's Title and Examinations), laid down by virtue of the Ordinance, deal, among other matters, with medical specialization in the field of public health, which, of course, includes the practice of preventive medicine. Hence, preventive medicine belongs to the legal monopoly of physicians insofar as activities mentioned in Article 3 of the Ordinance are practised.

61. Regarding preventive medicine, it should be noted that on 3 April 2024, a bill on preventive medicine was placed on the Knesset's table.

62. One of the conclusions from the intern report of the Parliamentary Examination Team of the functioning of the Rehabilitation Department, Families and Commemoration Department in the Ministry of Defence, dated 24 February 2010, established during the Eighteenth Knesset by the Foreign Affairs and Defence Committee, is the necessity to establish a preventive medical system within the various relevant security bodies. Its purpose is to preserve the health, fitness, and readiness of its personal and to minimize instances of injury and illness during and following service.

63. Given that a significant portion of the entitlement claims are due the occupational diseases, it is proposed that the aforementioned security bodies be mandated to implement a preventive medical system as stated. The head of the relevant security body will determine the directives for carrying out this task. Additionally, the head of the relevant security body will annually report to the Foreign Affairs and Defence Committee on the previous year regarding the number of occupational diseases and injuries among the personnel of the security body, categorized by professions and roles, and the actions taken by the security body to reduce and prevent occupational diseases and injuries among its personnel.

64. Furthermore, it is proposed that a security body failing to submit such a report will face penalties, and the allocated funds will be directed towards the rehabilitation of disabled individuals who served in that security body.

2. Self-Care

65. Self-help, or self-care, is not considered an illegal practice of medicine because the Ordinance envisages only the situation in which medical activities are practised vis-à-vis another person.

66. A particular directive in the same spirit may be found in the Penal Code. It deals with the crime of illegal abortion.

Paragraph 320 of the Code decrees that a woman who has undergone an abortion will not be criminally responsible for what has happened to her.

3. Venepuncture: Taking of Blood

67. The blood analysis is an examination in the sense of Article 3 of the Physicians' Ordinance. The taking of blood also falls under the legal monopoly of physicians. However, paragraph 59 of the Ordinance empowers the Director General of the Ministry of Health to decree that nurses may be given authority to treat patients in certain situations. The Director laid down regulations for physicians in 2001 (Competencies for the Performance of Extraordinary Tasks). Paragraph 2(1) of these regulations authorizes nurses who have been trained and certified for the task to carry out venepuncture for analysis.

68. In addition, following the amendment to the Physicians Regulations (Qualification for Performing Exceptional Procedures), section 10A allows medical directors to grant personal authorization to Phlebotomists listed in the eighth addition to perform venous blood draws from patients aged 7 and above at hospitals. This authorization requires prior satisfactory performance of the procedure at a medical institution for at least three months, written approval from the medical director, and renewal of CPR certification once every two years.

4. Radiography

69. Radiography is a purely technical procedure that, as such, does not belong to the practice of medicine. As long as the maker of the radiogram does not use it to establish a diagnosis or treatment, he or she cannot be condemned for the illegal practice of medicine. The 1968 Order Controlling Appliances and Services (Radiology Appliances for Medical Treatment) regularizes the conditions under which a licence may be obtained for the possession of radiology appliances but does not stipulate that the applicant must be a physician. Similarly, the applicant for a permit to activate a radiology appliance or a radioactive complex in accordance with the 1980 Pharmacists' Regulations (Radioactive Components and Commodities) is not required to be a physician. However, the 1973 Physicians' Regulations (Approval of Specialist Title and Examinations), formulated in consequence of the Ordinance, deal, among other matters, with medical specialization in the field of diagnostic radiology, which is a branch of medicine in which only certified specialists in diagnostic radiology hold a monopoly.

70. The Pharmacists' Regulations (Radioactive Components and Commodities) was amended in 2005, thus prohibiting a person's employment in, *inter alia,* a radioactive facility unless all instructions in accordance with the law are met. The regulations provide a detailed apparatus of instructions and supervision on such employment.

5. The Use of Blood Pressure and Other Simple Appliances for Measurement

71. If simple appliances are used for blood pressure measurement or measurement of heartbeat and pulsation, it cannot be considered a practice of medicine in the context of self-examination and self-care. However, if such appliances are used to examine the state of health of another person, it can be considered an act of medicine reserved for physicians. In Israel, the day-to-day chores of a nurse include using these appliances, which can therefore be regarded as contained in the work of nursing as authorized by paragraph 3 of the revised Physicians' Ordinance. Paragraph 2(6) of the 1977 Physicians' Regulations (Competencies for the Performance of Extraordinary Tasks) authorizes nurses who have been trained and certified for the work to measure venous blood pressure for analysis after a licensed physician has attached the apparatus.

6. Eye Examination and the Measuring of Eye Deviations

72. The regular eye examination is part of a physician's practice. The 1973 Physicians' Regulations (Approval of Specialist Title and Examinations), formalized by virtue of the Ordinance, deal, among other matters, with medical specialization in the sphere of ophthalmic diseases, which is a legal monopoly of certified eye specialists. Eye tests by nurses in the ordinary course of their nursing activities are legitimate. In addition, optometrists and ortho-opticians are empowered to engage in certain types of eye measurements, subject to the conditions detailed in the Law on Optometry, as described in a later chapter of this work.

7. Psychoanalysis and Psychotherapy

73. On the question of whether psychoanalysis and psychotherapy are parts of medicine, opinions widely diverge. Therefore, the discussions concentrate on the following matters:

- Can psychoanalysis and psychotherapy be considered a treatment in the sense of Article 1 of the Physicians' Ordinance?
- Is the use of verbal and non-verbal forms of communication a treatment?
- Are psychoanalysis and psychotherapy directed towards a pathological state?

Paragraph 1 is not a sufficiently direct, lucid answer to these questions. It can be assumed that mental therapy recommended by a physician to his patient is included in the general definition of 'medical practice'. However, this positive assumption will not solve whether members of other professions are prohibited from exploiting such therapy. The solution is that mental therapy may be used by professionals who are not physicians whenever the authority to do so has been vested with them by the legislator. Whatever has been stated above or will be recorded later is also applicable to group therapy.

74. As for the physicians, the revised version of the Physicians' Ordinance empowers them to 'treat patients' and, in the absence of particulars, it may be assumed that the term includes any mental treatment, except such as is specifically entrusted to a specialist in a definite branch of mental therapy. The 1973 Physicians' Regulations (Approval of Title and Examinations) – formulated by virtue of the Ordinance – deal, among other matters, with medical specialization in the sphere of psychiatry, in general, and child and adolescent psychiatry, in particular – which are the exclusive preserves of specialists who have been licensed to engage in them.

75. The 1991 Law for the Treatment of the Mentally Ill allots certain types of treatment to psychiatrists who are recognized specialists in psychiatry or child and adolescent psychiatry. The 1992 Regulations for the Treatment of the Mentally Ill empower a social worker to conduct psychological diagnoses.

76. The 1977 Psychologists' Law empowers psychologists to diagnose and assess conditions and problems of mental, intellectual, or behavioural nature in humans and engage in treatment, rehabilitation, and guidance, as well as advise in matters appertaining to their occupations mentioned above.

8. Acupuncture

77. In the revised version of the Physicians' Ordinance, the legislator has included acupuncture treatment among the activities defined as 'medical practice'.

However, it appears that laypeople who practice acupuncture are not prohibited from doing so.

Instructions regarding acupuncture are found in a specific section, section 59A of the Physicians' Ordinance. This section stipulates that the administrator is authorized to permit non-licensed physicians who satisfy the conditions set by the Minister in the regulations to practice acupuncture under the supervision of a licensed physician. Such regulations will be enacted following consultation with the Scientific Council and approval by the Health Committee of the Knesset.

9. Written and Oral Advice and Recommendations

78. Written and oral advice and recommendations may be regarded as medical acts if they constitute an essential part of the treatment.

10. Prescriptions

79. Physicians' prescriptions may be a virtual source of damage in different ways. Individual doses may be too large; intervals between doses may be too long or too short; safety precautions for dangerous drugs may be inadequate; mistakes in the wording may lead to disastrous results. In addition, medicines with varying after-effects or concentrations are marketed under patent names that sound the same or have similar spelling. This fact makes the deciphering of the physician's prescription difficult, especially because physicians often do not excel in the legibility of their handwriting. When the injury or death results from a physician's wrong prescription, the physician will be declared guilty, even if the pharmacist who supplied the medicine is proved liable for negligence. However, the physician bears no blame for the carelessness of a pharmacist who has prepared the medicine from a faultless prescription. However, he or she may be liable if his or her prescription or designation of a drug is illegible.

11. Inoculation

a. Compulsory Inoculation

80. The 1940 Public Health Ordinance decreed that the Director of Public Health Services or a government physician is empowered to impose the obligation of vaccination on people who live in areas where infectious disease is liable to assume or has already considered the proportions of an epidemic. This is essential for the confinement of the disease. The Ordinance mentioned above defines an infectious disease as one of those listed in the second appendix of the Ordinance. The new coronavirus 2019 infection nCoV-2019 Coronavirus Novel was added. The Ministry of Health's Director of Health Services is authorized to publish a proclamation in *Reshumoth*, the official government bulletin, that any other disease may be classified as infectious in accordance with the Ordinance. He or she is also required to pinpoint the area in which the directives of the Ordinance must be implemented and the period during which the proclaimed directives will be valid. Any person who wilfully refuses inoculation or vaccination against chickenpox, cholera, or any other plague may be charged with the commission of a crime, fined, and sent to prison. Suppose it appears that the danger of a virulent disease in the form of a local or infectious epidemic is looming over areas of Israel or that a part of Israel has already been affected by such a disease as plague, cholera, yellow fever, smallpox, typhus, or any other disease is classified by the Minister of Health in *Reshumoth* as dangerous and infectious. In that case, he or she is authorized to issue a public proclamation in *Reshumoth* to the effect that the health of the nation is seriously jeopardized by the threat or incidence of the epidemic in Israel or neighbouring countries. As a result of this proclamation, the Director of Health Services is empowered to prevent or contain the spread of the epidemic by ordering that the population, new immigrants, or any individuals suspected of recent contact with the disease be inoculated with a protective vaccine or other preventive substances. The Ordinance mentioned above is the most stringent in ordering immunization against smallpox. When called upon to do so by the Director of Health Services, the commissioner of a district may request the residents of the district to be vaccinated immediately if they have not been successfully vaccinated during the previous three years. A traveller, who arrives in Israel by land, sea, or air, if so, required by the quarantine authorities, must produce his international vaccination certificate unless he or she can satisfy that he or she has become immune to the disease by having successfully recovered from it. The international vaccination certificate must conform to the one approved by the WHO:

(a) Valid for three years beginning eight days after the date of vaccination.
(b) Complete in every detail, without deletions or corrections.
(c) Approved and stamped by the health authorities in the country of issue.

Any traveller who does not possess the certificate must be vaccinated free of charge by the quarantine officials. If the person refuses vaccination, the authorities may detain him or her under observation for up to fourteen days from when he or she left the country from which he or she has come to Israel. A traveller who arrives from a country where cholera is rife is obliged to produce an international vaccination certificate against the disease for their inspection when requested by quarantine officials. A traveller who does not possess the certificate may be held under guard for up to five days from the date on which he or she left the infected area.

81. The 1989 Law on the Insurance of Immunization Victims deals with types of immunization that are not part of the physician's treatment. These consist of triple inoculation of Diphtheria, Tetanus, and Pertussis or each of its components against croup, tetanus, or whooping cough, infantile paralysis inoculation; combined inoculation of Neonatal Morality Rate, or each of its components, against measles, mumps, and German measles; immunization against meningitis caused by haemophilia's influenza; immunization against hepatitis B, as well as a vaccine against the new SARS-associated Coronavirus (severe acute respiratory syndrome coronavirus–2; SARS–CoV–2). For any person who is inoculated and any person who comes into contact, the law decrees that the state must provide insurance policies against such injury as disablement or death resulting from the injection. The insurer is the Internal State Insurance Fund. The insured establishments are:

(a) The state of Israel.
(b) The Sick Fund.
(c) A municipality or local council.
(d) The physician who inoculates.

The beneficiary is the person inoculated by an insured party and any other person who meets the one who undergoes inoculation. As for the immunizations, which are insured, the insurance policy covers all the types of vaccination listed above except those for meningitis or hepatitis B. Concerning the insurance coverage; it is effective in the event of death and physical, mental, or intellectual deficiency, which may result from vaccination after the policy has become valid. The cost of the insurance, exacted by the Ministry of Finance, fluctuates in accordance with the cost-of-living index. The person undergoing vaccination, or the person's guardian, will make a one-time payment of this sum for all the immunizations received. The insurance fee during the policy's validity period shall be determined for every child who is born, and it will be valid for all immunizations and their components.

In 2023, it was proposed to amend section (7) of the supplement to the Vaccination Victims Insurance Law, 1989, so that the law's provisions apply to every person who received a vaccine from 20 December 2020 to 21 December 2022. The proposal was accepted, and according to the new law today, its provisions apply to every person who received a vaccine against the coronavirus.

12. Possession and Use of Dangerous Drugs

a. General

82. The 1973 revised version of the Dangerous Drugs Ordinance regularized the use of dangerous drugs. The drugs listed in the appendix to the Ordinance are the substances whose use is restricted by its regulations. The appendix consists of two parts, of which the first contains two sections. The first section of the first part singles out six items that include cannabis, hashish, cocaine, and opium, while the second section deals with more than twenty items. The second part contains three sections, of which the first names over a hundred, the second ten, and the third approximately eight substances.

When a person wishes to refer to any of the Ordinance's Regulations, he or she must first ascertain which section in either part is applicable. It must also be borne in mind concerning any relevant dangerous drugs that the law refers to the pure drug and all its grains and the contents of prescriptions, compositions, mixtures, and solutions containing any of the listed substances.

b. Preparation, Manufacture, and Marketing

83. The Ordinance bans the cultivation of any dangerous drug, its manufacture, production, preparation, or formation from other basic elements without a permit from the Director General of the Ministry of Health.

84. In Amendment No. 16 to the Dangerous Drugs Ordinance, a new chapter was added concerning the use of Cannabis for medical and research purposes. This chapter stipulates that the director is authorized to grant a licence for cannabis cultivation based on his discretion, subject to security and protection measures to safeguard public safety and security, as determined by the Head of the Security Division and the Licensing Authority. The provisions of this clause do not limit the director's authority to impose additional conditions or restrictions for another purpose, and the licence conditions, including security and documentation requirements as per this ordinance, will be published on the Ministry of Health's website. Additionally, a committee was established under section 25D to review applications for Cannabis cultivation licences, composed of members appointed by the Minister of Internal Security, the Attorney General of Israel, the Minister of Finance, and the Minister of Economy.

c. Possession and Use

85. The Ordinance bans the possession and use of dangerous drugs without a permit, as specified in the Ordinance, or without a licence from the Director General. The Ordinance debars traffic with dangerous drugs.

The possession of dangerous drugs, detailed in the second part of the first section, is permitted in any one of the following cases:

(a) The possessor is a pharmacist who keeps the drugs on licensed premises.
(b) The possessor is one of the physicians, dentists, or veterinarians who have been given legal permits to keep drugs.
(c) The possessor can prove that a pharmacist has dispensed the drug in compliance with the Pharmacists' Ordinance directive or that it was acquired from a physician or veterinarian who is legally qualified to dispense the drug as required. For medical purposes, it is permissible to use dangerous drugs supplied by a pharmacist, physician, or veterinarian if they comply with the Ordinance's directives or to use drugs obtained by a special licence. The Ordinance is most prohibitive when a pusher supplies a minor with drugs. Still, the Ordinance exempts a person who provides a minor with a dangerous drug for curative purposes as prescribed by a physician or dentist. The 1979 Regulations for Dangerous Drugs permit a physician to supply hazardous drugs only to his or her patients and only for immediate, on-the-spot application. No physician may provide his or her patients with more than a ten-day quantity of drugs. A physician may sign a prescription for more than the daily number of dangerous drugs permitted by the regulations if intended for cancer patients as a painkiller. The 1978 Dangerous Drugs Regulations (Hospitals) decree that although a physician must sign the indent for dangerous drugs, custody over the drug supply evolves on the matron in every ward. For the Ordinance, the onus of proof in the form of the licence, certificate, or permit to supply drugs rests with any person who claims to do so.

The Dangerous Drugs Ordinance, 1979, has been supplemented by new regulations, the Dangerous Drugs Regulations (Amendment) 2023. These regulations specifically focus on cannabis. The aim of the new regulations is to change the previous situation so that in certain indications, physicians may prescribe cannabis products to patients for medical use, contrary to the previous situation where cannabis use, in all indications, required a licence. Transitioning to a prescription model will improve accessibility and significantly streamline bureaucracy for patients for whom cannabis can alleviate their conditions while maintaining health and medical considerations and addressing concerns about misuse of the substance.

d. Cancellation of Licence

86. If the Director General of the Ministry of Health is advised that a physician has released or prescribed a dangerous drug for him- or herself, for a patient, or some other person for any purpose other than the proper medication needed, the Director is empowered, after allowing the ample delinquent opportunity for self-defence, to disqualify the physician from possessing, acquiring, supplying, or distributing dangerous drugs as well as from using prescriptions for them.

Suppose a physician, dentist, veterinarian, or pharmacist commits an offence against the Ordinance mentioned above and if the court decides that he or she has done so in the performance of professional duties, in that case, the court may order that his or her licence be suspended for a period determined by the judge, provided that the latter is of the opinion that this decision is for the public good.

e. Institutions for Drug Addicts Treatment

87. The 1993 Law for Control over Institutions for Drug Addicts Treatment provides jurisdiction over institutions dispensing social treatment, medical treatment, or both social and medical treatments. An institution supplying social treatment proposes to provide purely social treatment to drug addicts. An institution giving medical treatment provides or proposes to provide medical treatment to drug addicts. A combined institution, for outpatients or inmates, supplies or offers to supply its addicts with medical and social treatment. Neither the proprietors nor the managers of any of these institutions may operate without a permit.

f. Treatment of Drug Addicts Accused of a Crime

88. Suppose a person is convicted of a crime and the court is informed that the person uses dangerous drugs, in that case, it may impose an ordeal by obliging him or her to accept communal treatment for a while, while the programme is being determined by the court. This kind of court order is permissible only under the following conditions:

(a) The guilty person agrees to be treated and understands the conditions and nature of his or her treatment.
(b) The state of his or her health justifies such treatment, and he or she is a suitable candidate for it.
(c) Preparations have been made for his or her treatment in accordance with a programme laid down by his or her probation officer, who has determined the type, nature, and period of treatment.

III. Suspension and Cancellation of Licence

A. Minister of Health's Powers

89. If by virtue of a complaint of the Director General or any injured party, it is brought to the notice of the Minister of Health that a licensed physician has perpetrated one of the following acts, the minister is empowered to sign an order cancelling the physician's licence, or instruct that it be suspended for a period specified by law; or reprimand, or caution him or her:

(a) The physician has been guilty of conduct unbecoming a licensed medical practitioner. The decision concerning the definition and nature of a physician's conduct will usually be assessed and finalized by a law court in each actual case. However, the legislator guided this subject. It is laid down, for example, that a licensed physician who assists an unlicensed practitioner as an anaesthetist, or in any other way, during such treatment of a patient, such attendance at a sickbed, or such surgery as requires the professional diagnosis and skills of a physician, shall be regarded as having behaved in a manner unbecoming a licensed physician. Similarly, a licensed physician who maliciously or carelessly has in his or her professional capacity signed or handed over a fictitious, misleading, or dishonest authorization, account, declaration, certificate, or other such documents shall be regarded as guilty of conduct unbecoming a licensed physician.

(b) He or she has obtained the licence by producing false evidence.

(c) He or she has demonstrated an inability or gross negligence in the practice of medicine.

(d) He or she has consistently contravened the rules of the Physicians' Ordinance.

(e) He or she has been convicted of a crime not covered by the Physicians' Ordinance.

(f) He or she has refused without good reason to show the diploma to the Director General of the Ministry of Health, despite the latter's repeated requests that he or she does so.

The minister will exercise authority after receiving the written findings of a committee appointed by him or her for this purpose. The committee will comprise, among others, the Director General and a representative of the Attorney General. Appeal against the minister's order will be directed to the Supreme Court, whose final decision.

Under Amendment No. 13 of the Physicians Ordinance, section 44D was added to regulate provisions regarding licensed physicians convicted of sexual offences or an offence under the Sexual Harassment Prevention Law shall be suspended from the date of conviction until a decision is made by the administrator under subsection (b) or by the Minister under section 41, whichever comes first. This suspension measure shall replace any temporary disciplinary measures taken against them under this ordinance if such measures were taken.

Additionally, a physician convicted as described in paragraph (1) must immediately report their conviction to the administrator and may request the administrator to revoke the suspension of their licence, shorten the suspension period, or impose restrictions on their professional activities in place thereof.

Moreover, if the licence of a physician is suspended under section (a), the administrator, based on the recommendation of a specially appointed committee (referred to herein as the 'special committee'), may decide to revoke the suspension, extend the suspension period for a specified additional period, or limit the physician's scope of practice for a specified period determined by the committee. A physician may request not to appoint such a committee in their case, and if such a request is made, the licence suspension shall remain in effect until a decision is made by the Minister under section 41.

Furthermore, the section defines the composition of the special committee, its members, and procedural provisions.

B. Director General's Powers

90. The Director is empowered to cancel a licence in one of two cases:

(1) When a licensed physician dies, his or her legal personal representative is expected to return the licence to the Director.

(2) When the licence holder has no legal right to prolong a stay in Israel, he or she is expected to return the licence to the Director.

Appeal against an order of cancellation must be addressed to the Supreme Court, whose decision is final. The Director is empowered to suspend or restrict a licence in the following two cases:

(1) The Director has reasonable grounds for suspecting that a physician's gross negligence has caused the death or the severe injury of a patient whom he or she has been treating. The Director may exercise his or her authority even if a verdict has not yet been reached in the case, or before the physician has been indicted, or before the police have initiated the investigation; however, the physician is still only a suspect.
(2) The physician has been brought to court, accused of a crime whose circumstances will leave a blot on his or her character. The evidence needed for such a decision by the Director will be provided by a committee formed by the Director for this purpose. The committee will consist of two physicians, one of whom will be chosen from a list submitted by the IMA and a representative of the Attorney General. The physician shall be given a convenient opportunity to defend himself at hearings of the committee.

C. Recommendation by Court for Cancellation or Suspension of Licence

91. A court that finds a person guilty of a crime against the Physicians' Ordinance has the right, in addition to imposing punishment, to recommend that the criminal be deprived of, or suspended from, his or her licence to practise medicine. It should be emphasized that this takes a recommendation for consideration by the Director or the Minister.

92. Regarding this matter, we must reference the ruling of the Supreme Court in the case of the physician who was photographed advising someone to claim back pain. The Supreme Court upheld the suspension of the physician's licence to practise medicine for one year. The Supreme Court determined that the district court president is authorized to deviate from the recommendations of the committee appointed by the Minister of Health to examine the complaint against the physician and suspend the physician for a longer period.

93. The physician reached a plea agreement with the committee, admitting to the facts and being convicted of a serious offence, and requested a sentence of reprimand. The Ministry of Health agreed to request a suspension of four months.

94. When the matter was brought before the Retired President Zeiler, who was appointed to decide on the punishment, Zeiler decided not to accept the plea agreement due to significant concerns and ordered the suspension of his licence for one year.

95. Justice Esther Hayut, who wrote the judgment, determines that the central consideration in this matter is protecting the public interest in maintaining the standard dignity of the medical profession and the public's trust in physicians.

96. Justice Hayut noted that the scope of intervention in decisions by the Minister of Health in such matters is quite limited and is restricted to cases where there has been a significant error in the decision-making process. In this case, there is no substantial flaw in Zeiler's decision that justifies intervention, she stated emphatically, highlighting that the public interest in suspending the physician's licence for an extended period was not adequately reflected in the reached arrangement.

D. *Loss of Licence*

97. As soon as a physician mislays his or her licence, he or she should notify the nearest police station. In addition, he or she must inform the Director General of the Ministry of Health through the agency of the District Health Officer. When the Director General has been advised, he or she is empowered to supply the physician with a copy of the licence or a ratification document, with whatever limitations he or she may see fit to impose.

IV. Medical Examinations

A. *General Rule*

98. Bearing in mind that the physician is likely, and may very often have, to come into physical contact with the person he or she is treating; the legislator has seen fit to act as guardian of the patient's health to prevent the latter's suffering more than his or her ailment warrants, in cases in which the physician is the victim of a 'dangerous disease,' such as one of the following:

(a) Mental illness.
(b) Any disease that may endanger the health of the patients being treated.
(c) An illness or diminished fitness that may completely deprive the physician of his or her ability to practise medicine, either temporarily or partially.

B. *Summons to Medical Examination*

99. Suppose the Director has a reason to suspect that an applicant for a medical licence is suffering from a dangerous disease. In that case, he or she is empowered to summon the applicant to appear before the medical board for examinations. The physician retains the right to ignore the summons, in which case the only sanctions imposed will be a deprivation of a licence until he or she is ready to be examined as demanded by the Director. As for a licensed physician, the fact that the Director 'suspects' that the physician has contracted a dangerous disease will not suffice. The Director is expected to obtain more substantial evidence. If the Director has a reason to believe that a medical institution or any physician possesses information that may shed light on an applicant's health for a licence, or of a licensed physician, after being treated, the Director is empowered to demand that such evidence be communicated.

C. Medical Committee

100. The Director General of the Ministry of Health is empowered to form a 'medical committee' either ad hoc or long-term. The committee will consist of three physicians; however, when mental competence is questioned, three psychiatrists. The medical committee is authorized to summon anyone as a witness. When the committee is faced with a refusal from a person summoned to testify or reveal information, the District Court may exert pressure, with the aid of a detention order or by any other suitable means to force such a person to comply with the committee's summons. During the committee's proceedings, the only person present, in addition to the committee members, will be the applicant for a licence, or the physician, and any other person whose presence has been approved by the chairman. An accurate record of the proceedings will be prepared, and the committee will submit its findings and reasoned decisions to the Director General. The committee's proceedings and research documents are confidential. Their contents are only revealed to the Director General, except for any part of the contents from which the committee chairman releases the ban of secrecy. Once the committee has decided that a dangerous disease disqualifies an applicant for a licence or a physician from practising medicine, permanently or temporarily, or that the disease limits or conditions the physician's sphere of medical activity, the Director will refuse to award the person a licence, will cancel or suspend the licence or will supply a special licence, as warranted by the circumstances of the case.

D. Appeal

101. The applicant for a licence to practise medicine or a licensed physician who defies the Director's demand for appearance before a medical committee, or any other person who feels injured by the Director's refusal to award a licence, or by the Director's decision to deprive a person of, or suspend, a licence or to supply with a special licence, there is a specific provision in section 44G regarding appeals concerning the suspension or restriction of a licence by the Director, the section specific that a physician whose licence has been suspended or restricted under section 44A, 44B, or 44D is entitled to appeal the suspension or restriction before a District Court.

102. However, section 38A of the Physicians Ordinance stipulates that an appeal against a decision on a licence application must be submitted in writing within thirty days from the date the Director's decision was delivered to the Appeals Committee as defined in the section.

E. Temporary Suspension

103. When it comes to the Director's notice that a licensed physician's dangerous disease causes such immediate threat to the public that delaying action before the medical committee reaches its decision or pending an appeal is inconceivable, the Director is empowered to suspend the physician's licence until the committee finally decides.

F. Obligation of Confidentiality

104. A person who happens to have received any piece of information connected with the activities of the medical committee or with the résumé of its relevant proceedings intended for the Director General, as detailed above, is required to observe silence and ensure that this knowledge is not divulged unless either the consummation of the committee's activities requires divulging; or permission has been given to do so by the law court, or either he or she is obliged to answer questions by an official with powers to investigate crimes that have been committed.

105. The Patient's Rights Law 1996 established the principle of the 'duty of care': Any information that has reached a physician or any employee in the health system, as part of his work, is information that must not be disclosed to anyone who is not qualified for it or does not need this information for the needs of the job. Keeping confidentiality is a necessary condition for the patient's trust, from the things that by their nature are usually given to the physician as part of training to keep them secret.

Chapter 3. Control over Practice of Medicine

§1. The Israel Medical Association

106. The IMA, an independent, professional organization that represents the physicians in Israel, includes, among its members, some 90% of the medical personnel working in Israel's health funds, hospitals, state institutions, and private clinics. The IMA functions in medical labour relations, the scientific sphere, and the ethical sphere.

107. The IMA is responsible for overseeing physicians' working conditions, clarifying and crystallizing the rules for medical ethics, establishing professional norms that guarantee the level of medicine in Israel, ensuring the quality and advancement of medical treatment, approving clinical guidelines, and establishing the basic qualifications that entitle health institutions to accreditation.

108. The Professional (Labour Relations) Committee deals with the relations between medical personnel and their employers.

109. The Scientific Council is responsible for maintaining the high level of medicine in Israel and establishing professional medical norms. The Council also oversees the various fields of medical specialization.

110. The Ethics Committee is responsible for establishing and maintaining the ethical regulations that apply to physicians.

111. The IMA issues two professional publications for its members; their circulation is numbered in thousands. *Mihtav LeHaver* (Letter to our Members) expresses the IMA's stand on professional, public, and ethical questions. *Harefuah* (Medicine) publishes professional articles. The IMA has started publishing a third journal, *'Jima-the Journal of the Israel Medical Association,'* and the *'Military Medicine'* journal.

§2. Professional Liability

I. Introduction

112. The law imposes different types of liability on mankind in other circumstances; people may become liable for crimes, contracts, quasi-contracts, and damages. Insofar as criminal law is concerned, its primary purpose is to protect the general public. When the liability is contractual, a person has made a promise to another person, or an agreement reached in writing between two parties, the Law of Contracts proposes to preserve the interests of an individual to whom another has made a promise that must be honoured. The law is effective in securing the keeping of promises, the implementation of agreements, or guaranteeing compensation for a person who has been promised something or for one who has been compromised so that the person must end up worse off than he or she would have been, had the promise or agreement been honoured. Liability for a quasi-contract exists when a person has come into unjustifiable possession of a fortune or has achieved some benefit claimed by someone else. Again, the principle of social justice guides legal considerations.

Liability for civil wrongs is of a different complexion from the three types of liability already defined. Liability for civil wrongs has sprung from a source that is closely related to liability. Still, the difference between them, which is poles apart, expresses itself, first and foremost, in the functions of the penalties imposed in each case. Lawsuits for civil wrongs enable the bench to make adequate restitution to the injured party. In criminal cases, there must be punishment for the crime.

II. Civil Liability

A. *Classification of Civil Liability*

113. The term 'negligence' may have different implications, such as:

(a) A particular state of mind.
(b) Careless behaviour.
(c) Breach of duty regarding the requirement of care ordained by law or decree.

1. Negligence Caused by a Certain State of Mind

114. The facts of life demonstrate that in numerous instances, a person, because of an action or inaction, has caused damage to another by failing to anticipate the results of behaviour. However, anyone capable of logical thought in a similar situation would have realized that danger was imminent. A person's state of mind, which prevents the realization of the result of the action or inaction, may lead to what may be classified as 'negligence.' Such a person should be distinguished from the possessor of the 'criminal mind' (*mens rea*), a dominant feature of whose make-up is in fact, a realization of what the future will bring. Negligence rules out the possibility of action deriving from a calculating state of mind; an action should be defined or calculated when purposeful and performed to create an anticipated effect. With similar consequences, an action must be classified as negligent if it results from the absence of mind, carelessness, or recklessness of the performer of the said action.

2. Negligence as Careless Behaviour

115. Negligence is the omission to do something that a reasonable person, guided by those considerations that ordinarily regulate the conduct of human affairs, would do something that a prudent or reasonable person would not do.

116. The test for determining negligent behaviour is the 'reasonable person' test, meaning whether a person from the community could have taken into account the existence of that fundamental factual element. In one case, the Supreme Court even used studies from Scandinavia to determine that certain behaviour would not have been undertaken by a person from the community and that the defendant, who behaved without the required caution according to the research, was negligent.

117. Section 36 of the Torts Ordinance establishes the foreseeability test as the criterion for the existence of a duty of care. The test distinguishes between two types of foreseeability specifically related to the reasonable person test: technical and substantive. The technical foreseeability question asks whether the reasonable person could have foreseen the occurrence of harm, whereas the substantive/normative foreseeability question asks whether the reasonable person should have foreseen the occurrence of harm.

3. Breach of Obligation to Be Cautious

118. The civil wrong described in paragraph 35 of the Civil Wrong Ordinance (New Version) is also classified as negligence, stating:

> If a person committed an act that a reasonable and prudent person would not have committed in the same circumstances, or, in the performance of his occupation, has not used the skill or exercised the degree of caution which a reasonable person qualified to act in that occupation would have used or exercised in the same circumstances, that constitutes neglect and a person who, by his negligence, causes damage to another, commits a civil wrong.

By this interpretation, negligence is failure to take the precautions that the law obliges persons to exercise in their relationships with other persons. Negligence is, in fact, conduct that is below the standard essential for protecting one's fellow person against the threat of unreasonable damage. This type of wrong is founded on three basic elements: the existence of one's duty of care, the breach of this duty, and the damage resulting from the breach. In its third implication, negligence constitutes a breach of the duty of care. The duty of care may be binding by law or created by contract. Consequently, the three grounds for a charge of negligence are based on:

(1) The requirement for the maintenance of the duty of care by the defendant in his or her dealings with the plaintiff. This duty, recognized by law, obliges a person to adjust his or her conduct to the level that will safeguard other people against unreasonable dangers.
(2) A breach of the defendant's duty to rise to the standard required by law.
(3) Such damage to the plaintiff may legally be worthy of compensation, but such grounds for the charge must prove a feasible connection between the defendant's action and the damage it has caused.

The current model of duty of care in Israeli law is known as the conceptual model, contrasting with the previous casuistic model. Under the casuistic approach, recognition of a duty of care was intricately tied to the specific circumstances of each case, leading to the gradual development of case law from one instance to another. In the conceptual model, the determination of types of injuries, harms, and their causation. This model incorporates two cumulative tests: the conceptual duty of care and the concrete duty.

Israeli case law's framework for negligence liability is distinctive and differs from other jurisdictions. The rationale behind this distinction lies in the court's intent to establish the principle that a duty of care may generally exist between parties, yet in specific instances, such a duty may not arise. Notably, there are no clear precedents in Israeli case law where the court outright denied the existence of a conceptual duty of care; rather, the duty is typically assessed at the concrete stage. This framework empowers the court with a robust tool to determine the presence of a duty of care in any given case, ensuring legitimacy and consistency in judicial decisions.

B. Analysis of Physician's Duty

1. General

119. The decision that the duty of care prevails is an expression of judicial opinion that provides for a plaintiff whose interests have been infringed to obtain legal backing for a case against the negligent conduct whose negligence relates to his or her duty to the plaintiff. The person who damages cannot be considered liable for the wrong unless he or she is duty-bound to the damaged party. In Israel, the legislature has constructed the overall framework by expounding the principles and has left it to the judges to fill in the details during their day-to-day jurisdiction in the law courts.

2. Source of Liability

120. For many years, the law has imposed liability on physicians for negligent treatment of patients. Such a damage claim has derived from the interest of public policy. Similar liability may also evolve from the Law of Contracts. But from the moment a physician commits to treating a patient, his or her duty is clearly defined by a procedure independent of all sources. The physician must exercise care and skill of a requisite standard based on the physician's closeness to the patient. Duty may not be regulated because services cost the patient nothing or the physician is employed by a third party, which means that he or she has no contractual relationship with the patient. Although the physician is not expected to volunteer to treat the patient, once he or she has committed to the treatment of that patient, he or she is obliged to exercise such care and skill as necessary. The source of this liability may be found in the Laws of Torts. As soon as the physician has undertaken the treatment, the patient can sue him or her directly, without any regard to contractual links.

3. Duties of Conceptual and Concrete Care

121. Israel's court decisions differentiate between the conceptual duty of care and the concrete duty of care. The former is dominant when questions of principle are involved, relating to whether care should usually be exercised concerning a specific danger. Israeli judges' decisions are guided by the view that the exercise of the conceptual duty of care consists of analysing expectations. The questions demanding answers are:

- Was a reasonable person bound to anticipate the occurrence of the damage?
- When there was a conglomerate of the party who was to cause the damage, the party who was to suffer the damage, plus the nature of the action and the damage it was about to create, should the alarm have been sounded and special care was taken?

In deciding the issue, the courts may use their juridical policy.

The existence of a physician's duty of care towards a patient is examined in medical malpractice claims.

In the legal assessment of the duty of care, two cumulative conditions are considered:

(1) *Conceptual Duty of Care:* The court examines whether there is a general and principled duty of care between the group to which the harm-causer belongs (the physician) and the group to which the harmed belongs (the patient), in relation to the type of harm caused and its manner of occurrence. In physician-patient relationships, generally, there is a clear conceptual duty of care. This conceptual duty of care is discussed in court in various borderline cases, such as whether there is a conceptual duty of care between a physician and a passerby encountered randomly.
(2) *Concrete Duty of Care:* Refers to the specific case. Here, the court asks whether, in relation to the specific harm suffered by the plaintiff, under ordinary and specific circumstances, there exists a duty of care on the part of the harm-causer (the physician) towards the harmed (the patient). In cases of medical negligence, the court examines whether there is a concrete duty of care towards the patient in the circumstances at hand. The approach generally holds that once a physician begins medical treatment, a concrete duty of care toward the patient arises.

This distinction helps clarify the legal obligations and responsibilities in medical negligence cases, ensuring that both general principles and specific circumstances are considered in determining whether a duty of care exists and has been breached.

4. Expectancy Analysis

122. By Israel's law-court standards, the care demanded from a person must be logical and protective of any person at all who, in the ordinary course of events, might be injured if the duty of care is disregarded. Thus, the relationship, which of necessity links a physician with a patient, is neither transient nor local; rather, the connecting link in a chain of cause and effect, leading from an act of commission or omission to the damage.

123. The basic duty of a physician is to provide reasonable and accepted medical treatment to the patient. The Torts Ordinance stipulates that failure to exercise reasonable care and/or reasonable level of skill in the practice of medicine (as in any other profession) constitutes negligence. If this negligence causes harm to the patient, they are entitled to compensation from the physician.

124. However, the patient also has obligations within the framework of medical treatment, such as following the instructions given by the physician. Otherwise, it may be argued that the treatment failed due to the patient's fault for not following the physician's instructions.

125. However, the relationship between the physician and the patient is not equal. The physician possesses knowledge and access to literature and guidelines, while the patient typically relies on the physician's explanations, which are not always conveyed clearly. The patient may not pay adequate attention to the importance or urgency of the instructions provided.

126. This asymmetrical relationship underscores the complexities in medical negligence cases, where the responsibilities and expectations are distinct for both parties involved.

5. Duty to Third Party

127. Side by side with the physician's loyalty to the patient, the law court recognizes the duty to protect society against the negative influences of the patient's condition. 'The protective privilege ends where the public peril begins.' This contemporary approach expresses itself, first and foremost, in anything connected with infectious diseases. Consequently, physicians have been ordered to compensate people who have contracted contagious diseases even if they were not patients of those physicians. Furthermore, the 1997 Penal Code decrees that a person possesses information of another's intention to commit a crime. Still, it does not adopt reasonable measures to prevent the crime, or its completion may be sent to prison for two years. This principle, firmly established by law, cancels the physician's obligation of confidentiality concerning any patient who contemplates the commission of a crime.

6. The Volunteer's Duty

128. Society does not usually impose or compel voluntary activity. However, a physician who volunteers, whether in dealing with an emergency or working for nothing in return, must accept liability for carelessness or lack of skill. The source of liability appears in the Law of Torts. By the very act of undertaking the treatment of a patient, a physician forges a specific link with the patient so that lack of care or skill in treatment, resulting in the risk of damage to the patient, makes the physician liable.

129. Not every case in which a person's conduct causes damage to another causes that person to be responsible for the damage. However, a person must take concrete precautions against the risks. The person whose duty is to be careful cannot guarantee the safety of all those who turn to him or her, nor is the role of an insurance broker, who must repair a person's damage, whatever its cause may be. The person responsible for the damage is duty-bound to exercise reasonable care, and his/her responsibility becomes actual only if failing to do so. The reasonability of preventive measures is determined by such objective assessment as may be expressed by the rule that the person who may cause damage is expected to behave as any reasonable person would act in similar circumstances. The reasonable party is none other than the law court, empowered to determine the requisite degree of care determined by juridical policy. No one will ask what care that will physically prevent damage. The question to be answered is, 'What is the requisite care required in the specific circumstances?'

The law makes a distinction between an act of commission and an act of omission. A negligent action is interpreted as active, improper conduct causing damage to a second party; an act of omission implies failure to take positive steps to the advantage of a second party or avert the danger that looms over the second party.

7. Treatment of a Person in the Spirit of the 'Neither Shalt Thou Stand Against the Blood of Thy Neighbour' Law

130. The 1998 'Neither shalt thou stand against the blood of thy neighbour' Law imposes the duty of lending helping hands to other persons on every person in Israel under conditions detailed in the law, which decrees that a person must go to the rescue of another, whose life, body or health is in serious and immediate jeopardy, and with whom he or she is confronted as the result of a sudden occurrence.

A person is obliged to render the aid of which he or she is capable without risking him- or herself or other people. In further clarification, the law states that a person who informs the authorities or enlists the help of another capable of treating the casualty shall be regarded by the law as having rendered aid. Offenders against this law will be fined. Furthermore, the law decrees that the law court is empowered to oblige the creator of the danger mentioned above, including the injured person, if he or she is the source of the crisis, to compensate any person who came to the aid of the endangered party 'for any reasonable expenses he or she has incurred or payments he or she has made'.

On 5 January 2021, an amendment to the National Insurance Law was approved, allowing the Minister of Labour and Social Affairs to enact regulations, with the consent of the Minister of Finance and approval of the Labour and Welfare Committee, to grant additional rights to family members of an individual who lost their life to save a person in imminent danger. The law applies retroactively to cases that occurred from the beginning of 2018.

C. The Basis of Liability and Burden of Proof

1. Fault

131. As has been mentioned above, a fault is the primary basis of a malpractice claim. This claim concerns the breach of the physician's duty. The violation of duty is the failure to conform to the standard of conduct demanded. Deviation from the professional standard is considered a fault. The plaintiff has the burden of alleging and proving the facts of the case, which, in the given circumstances, constitute the defendant's fault.

132. A negligent breach of duty by a physician may express itself, among others, by the following acts of commission or omission:

(a) Failure to use standard procedure, use of the antiquated practice, or omission of regular tests.
(b) Negligent diagnosis.
(c) Negligence in preparing prescriptions.
(d) Negligence in the documentation and registry of documents.
(e) Negligence in guidance, advising, and recording.
(f) Negligence in anaesthetization and surgery.
(g) Negligence in causing burns or the non-prevention of falls.
(h) Negligence in giving medication or injections.
(i) Negligence in the observation of patients.
(j) Negligence in exposing patients to infectious diseases.
(k) Negligence in not referring patients to specialists.
(l) Negligence in neglecting or abandoning patients.

2. Damages

a. Causation

133. The wrongdoer is liable only for damage that is the natural and reasonable result of the wrong. Namely, the consequence that the wrongdoer, had he or she been a reasonable person, in full consciousness of the medical proficiency, would have anticipated and could have averted.

The onus of proof of the cause-and-effect process concerning the fact of the wrong and the fact of the damage rests with the plaintiff. As for the legal aspect of causation, Israel's law courts have adopted the expectancies analysis, which means that if the person responsible for the damage, being a reasonable person, did not and could not anticipate that the commission or omission of action would lead to any damaging consequence to a person for whom it was his or her duty to exercise care, he or she is not liable to pay for the damage that has been incurred, even though the act in the physical sense was the fundamental cause, or the *sine qua non*, of the damaging effect. When several factors have caused the physical condition of the injured person, and there is difficulty in singling out each of these factors, all of them, individually and collectively, will be seen as liable for the whole damage. Therefore, the law courts do not impose the burden of proof on the injured party concerning each injuring party's share in the damage. The onus of proof rests with the persons whose actions caused the damage.

Law cases have tangled with situations where pinpointing the causation problem was not easy, not to say difficult, from an objective point of view. These cases have been described as the 'hazy causation'. These cases have involved natural factors that might have been the reason for the damage, yet there is no way to know to what extent they have been the only reason for that damage. In these cases, recent judgments show that despite the complication involved in deciding on the causation questions, courts were unwilling to let plaintiffs leave the courtroom with empty hands; yet these were diminished damages only.

The additional provision in the Penal Law where the legislator expressed their position regarding causation in omissions in section 309 creates the statutory causation. This section outlines five scenarios in which the causation remains intact despite the involvement of external factors:

(1) The defendant caused bodily harm requiring medical or surgical treatment resulting in the victim's death, and there is no break in causation if the treatment was erroneous, provided it was done in good faith and with ordinary skill, such that if not done, the outcome wouldn't have been seen as causing the victim's death.
(2) Failure of the victim to minimize the harm.
(3) Escape or flight of the victim.
(4) The defendant's act or omission hastened the death of a person suffering from a disease or injury that would have caused death even without his act or omission.
(5) Complementary external factors: This is very inclusive; whenever there is intervention by a complementary factor, the causation is not served. The issue is that it can be argued that every intervening external factor is a complementary factor.

According to *Biton* case law, section 309 appears to only address the issue of causing death. However, in practice, its scope has been broadened. It has been determined to apply to a range of criminal offences. Section 309 does not attempt to cover all possible cases of causation. It is an open list of five cases, and there may even be cases not listed where causation still exists.

The attempt to move from a general standard of causation to specific rules is a well-known effort in law. Judges undertake this action. The legislator sought to formulate rules in a minimally simplified manner based on the general idea of causation, detached from specific cases.

b. Definition of Damage

134. A difference exists between pecuniary and bodily damage. Pecuniary damage includes all concrete damage, whether it is the expenditure of some kind of monetary loss resulting from a wrongful act, whether it takes place before and up to the court decision, or is expected to occur afterwards.

Bodily damage includes any physical loss incurred by the injured party, whether it is the actual loss of an organ of the body, the loss of any of the body's normal functions, the loss of a person's recovery to good health, or even loss of life. Loss may also consist of deterioration in one's physical or mental well-being. A distinction is made between special damage, which is financial, and general damage.

Damages and losses incurred from the wrong done until the day of judgment are termed *special damage,* and those incurred after judgment are termed *general damage.* Another difference relates to the nature of the proof. Special damage requires a specific proof, whereas general damage requires an estimate based on general proofs.

c. Compensation for Special Damages

i. Estimate of Future Damage

135. The objective of compensation is to make restitution to the injured party to revert the person to the condition in which he or she would have been. Such compensation includes loss of earnings and pension. A person's potential earning consists of his or her ability to make money from activities in the business world. The claims courts have formulated three methods of dealing with the loss of future earnings concerning cases of general damage.

The first is the conventional assessment method of the injured person's expected financial loss, multiplied by the period the person is expected to work to calculate capitalization. In determining the loss of earnings until the date of assessment, the court must decide how much the injured party would have earned or gained. The basis of the court's reckoning will be the salary size and loss of emoluments. The court must draw a comparison or measure the distance between two situations before determining the injured person's loss of capacity due to the damage compared with one's previous ability. In doing so, the court measures the last potential by the side of actual competence. The second method favours the determination of lost ability to earn a living as measured by a person's degree of functional disability. A distinction must be drawn between functional and medical disability. Because a parallel does not necessarily exist between the two, the medical disability must signify a functional disability that will express the loss of competence to earn a living. However, the law courts are wary of adopting this criterion, and when they can put other components of the case together, they will prefer the use of different methods. The third method favours a lump sum award, which, however intuitive the law-courts assessment may be, must be based on calculations. The decision to award a lump sum will be made only when the lack of essential data rules out exact calculations. This may be compared, for example, with court orders in respect of compensation for a minor because of a lack of certainty about the assessment of his future losses. The source of the plaintiff's income loses all significance.

ii. Expenditure on Treatment

136. 'Treatment' implies medical, nursing, and psychological treatment, among others. In addition, such expenditures incurred by the injured party in efforts to recover are included in what is termed 'special damage' compared with 'general damage,' which will require monetary outlays for injury treatment in the future.

iii. Accommodation

137. The damage may have a significant economic bearing on the injured person's housing requirements due to the injury.

iv. Treatment and Observation

138. The damage to the plaintiff may involve complete or partial treatment in a person's home.

v. Accessory Appliances

139. The injury may lead to an accumulation of expenditure on accessory appliances.

vi. Transportation

140. As a result of the damage, the plaintiff may require means of transport that he or she did not previously own.

vii. Loss of Services

141. The widow or the widower of the deceased is entitled to compensation due to the loss of income by a dependent.

viii. Emoluments

142. It should be assumed that the person responsible for the damage should not pay more compensation than the cost of repairing the damage caused, even if a third party defends part of the compensation. But this principle does not apply concerning money awarded to the plaintiff as a gratuity or act of philanthropy or sums made to the plaintiff, either by the insurance company or as a pension from the employer. Any emoluments awarded by the Ministry of Finance will be deducted from the amount of compensation, in uniformity with the various laws for pensioners, which provide injured parties with emoluments.

d. Damages Without a Price Tag

143. Because the principle is that the compensation must be honest and reasonable, a just distinction must be drawn between more severe and less severe damage, and precedents from similar cases must be considered in the judges' preservation of uniformity.

i. Pain and Suffering

144. Pain is experienced when the impact of a blow on a body hits the nervous system, whereas suffering follows as the mental consequence of that blow. The law courts usually award conventional sums of money, considering the depreciation of local currency. The size of the compensation for both pain and suffering is as per the cost-of-living index on the day of the court decision. Damage of pain and suffering also includes mental damage that has no physical expression. In certain conditions, the plaintiff's mental anguish deriving from the blow inflicted on another person by the one responsible for the damage may be evident.

ii. Loss of Life Expectancy

145. Israel's court decisions provide for the award of damages to a living person who has been injured, in consideration of loss of life expectancy.

e. Monetary Damages

146. The plaintiff may sue for anticipated monetary damages and those incurred. The latter may include loss of earnings, medical and nursing fees, nutritional outlays, ruined clothes, and domestic help. In addition, future losses incurred after the court decision date include anticipated loss of earnings and accommodation expenses.

f. Interest

147. The legal framework for decisions on interest in Israel is supplied by the 1961 Law on Interest Decisions and its amendments and the third amendment of the 1978 Law on Interest Decisions. When litigants are awarded specific amounts of money, the law courts are empowered to readjust the sums to accord with changes in the Cost-of-Living (COL) index, plus interest from the date on which the reason for the suit arose.

g. Capitalization

148. Compensation awarded to cover future losses and expenditures and whose total amount is determined for immediate payment should be adequate for the present cost of those losses that will extend into the future for an extended period. However, because the injured party is to receive a sum of money in the present that will rightly be for losses in the future, payment in advance means that he or she will lose a certain amount. To deal with this problem, the courts use capitalization tables so that by calculating how much the person is likely to lose, they can increase the down payment awarded on the day of judgment.

h. Death of Injured Party

149. If the wrong that has been committed results in the injured person's death, dependants are entitled to compensation for the damage done to them by the person's death; furthermore, the deceased's legacy must by rights be supplemented by the compensation for which the deceased would have had the right to sue for the injury suffered. Both events are conditional on the deceased's having had a claim for pressing the lawsuit.

i. Payment by Instalments

150. The 1975 Law for Traffic Accident Casualties empowers the courts to decree payment by instalments for certain types of casualties.

j. Court Procedure and Proofs

151. The full claim for damages resulting from negligence must be presented to the court in one piece. Thus, even if it is later disclosed that the damage was considerably more significant than the first estimate, no additional claim can further be admitted to the court.

3. Causation

a. General

152. Causation is the relationship of a cause and effect between two events. The cause is the whole range of factors that must necessarily lead to the occurrence of the happening. A person treating another shall be considered liable for causing damage if his or her wrong is the cause or one of the causes of the damage. The term 'cause' applied to the civil wrong of negligence consists of two components: factual and legal.

The factual, scientific element is evident when the negligent behaviour that is physically the fundamental reason for the damaging consequences is under review. The legal component carries significance because the factual relationship between the conduct of the wrongdoer, namely the person who provided treatment, and the damage incurred by the patient is of a nature beheld in the eyes of the law as culpable enough for the giver of treatment to be charged with liability for fault. His or her liability may still be prevalent even when others have added contributory, wrongful factors to the cause of the damage.

When an action resulting from a combination of factors, even if each of them is independent, leads to a result whose components are inseparable, all the participants in the action will be deemed liable for the total damage. When each of the defendants creates part of the damage, and in practice, it is possible by analysing the total damage to attribute identifiable parts to each of the defendants, the liability for each separate part of the damage will be limited in the claim against each defendant.

b. The Extent of Liability Damage: Expectancy Criterion

153. The conception of 'lack of care' implies a duty to predict the future and a specific duty to adopt preventive methods in anticipation of the damage that the future may engender. The duty to take care arises when signs may be detected in advance of the following two contingencies; the action, or inaction, is likely to result in damage; and a particular person is expected to be hurt and suffer damage in consequence. The expectancy required of the person responsible for the damage consists of preconceiving a general idea of what may transpire in the future. Such expectancy is an attribute of a reasonable person. The remote possibility of the occurrence of damage will not hold water; there must be a fair probability of damage that should be anticipated in advance by the reasonable thinker. The rules of cause and effect are also valid for the determination of the scope of liability. If the plaintiff has suffered damage, compensation will be awarded only for the damage in the natural course of events and directly from the wrong committed by the defendant.

c. Expectancy Criterion Concerning the Scope and Type of Damage

i. Expectancy with Regard to the Scope of Damage

154. Because damage to the body or damage to the health of a person seems to be of a single type, if the person responsible for the damage expected any kind of physical damage at all, he or she is liable for the total damage, the concept being that he or she is responsible for damages aggravated by the unusual physical condition of the injured person. Such specific characteristics of the latter as being run down physically, or capacity for earning more than other people have no power in the eyes of the law to 'divorce' the damage from the wrong under court discussion, even if, in effect, they have a certain influence on the significance of the damage incurred by the plaintiff.

ii. Failure to Predict Rare Types of Damage

155. Lack of expectancy concerning the scope and proportions of the damage cannot be used to prevent the charge of liability; even the unpredicted extent of the damage will be attributed to the person whose negligence has caused the damage. But the law decides otherwise in the absence of a prediction of the type of damage to be incurred even if a damage claim has been made and its scope predicted.

d. Proof of Cause and Effect

156. A person who brings a civil suit to the court must prove the cause-and-effect connection between the negligence of the defendant and the damage incurred.

157. Regarding negligence, which is defined as a civil wrong in the Torts Ordinance of 1968, to succeed in a claim based on negligence, such as a medical malpractice claim, one must prove the existence of a 'duty of care' between the tortfeasor and the victim, breach of that duty (negligence), harm. And a causation between the breach of duty and the harm.

4. The Common Practice Rule

a. The Criterion

158. Failure of the treatment itself or damage incurred by the person under treatment is not always prima facie evidence of negligence. The physician cannot guarantee the results of treatment. The physician must treat but not promise a cure. He or she cannot commit to preventing mistakes, if they are not the results of a lack of skill or care. The court recognizes that physicians are humans, imperfect, and prone to errors and failures. Because the standard of care exercised by the physician is determined by social policy, much weight will depend on whether the defendant's conduct was tuned to standard practice recognized by other members of the profession as common and normal in similar circumstances. Failure to conform to common practice is usually the distinguishing sign of lack of care; in other words, the negligence claim may be rejected if it can be pointed out that the behaviour being judged is accorded with common practice. Choice of one method of treatment or another does not in itself constitute proof of negligence, even if the treatment results in damage. When two methods of medical treatment are available, the physician must use common sense and conscience in making a choice. When the physician has chosen and exercised reasonable skill in employing the method of his or her choosing, he or she will not be liable for a slip-up, even if it is due to the risks involved in the treatment chosen. When physicians are divided in their opinions with respect to the more suitable treatment, they must not regard a physician as guilty of misconduct if he or she has chosen the medical procedure preferred by the favoured few. The physician is obliged to employ a common procedure when it prevails. If there is a choice of methods, some more acceptable than others, the physician is free to choose any of them without having the choice labelled as negligence. It may happen that deviation from standard practice may not be evidence of negligence, for example, when a patient's condition or the nature of the illness makes a common procedure impracticable. If accepted practice does not improve the patient's health, the physician cannot be charged with negligence when resorting to less conventional treatment. A physician will be regarded as negligent if he or she does not anticipate hazards against which a reasonable physician's foresight would enable precautions to be taken.

b. The Reasonable Physician

159. It is a well-known principle that people are responsible for their negligence if committing to undertakings that they know, or ought to know, that they cannot carry out. A person who undertakes a mission requiring skills or specific knowledge is obliged to exploit those skills or knowledge required to accomplish the task. A person cannot demand that, because of inexperience, he or she be judged by lower standards than those of a practitioner who has sufficient expertise to do the job. The court will judge according to the standard of expertise required for the mission that the defendant undertook. The standard of measurement is because an action performed can be carried out safely only by the possessor of specific skills.

160. Consequently, operational intervention may be performed only by one who has been trained to operate, except in cases of a sudden, serious emergency. The standard of measurement is objective in its quality because it has no subjective connection with the physician, his or her knowledge, or experience. The required standard does not need to be exceptionally high, but a specific physician who feels any sort of handicap must find means to avert injury from his or her patient. The physician who is conscious of a *lacuna* in skill or expertise should obtain advice or assistance when feeling the need. A trained physician, recognizing the case beyond his or her medical education and expertise, will consult with a reputable expert or refer the patient to a hospital where the right treatment is available. The physician who does not anticipate the risks that a reasonable practitioner would foresee and provide for must be regarded as negligent. A matter for debate is that the courts have drafted the image of the 'favoured' physician as their criterion, from whose reasonable standard others must not fall short, in preference to the average physician in normal practice. The reasonable, as distinct from the unreasonable physician, is not determined by the dictates of reality, instead, by considerations of judicial policy, which fixes its eyes on public welfare insofar as judges' decrees can further it.

c. The Specialist Physician

161. A specialist physician concerns him- or herself particularly with one organ or one area of the human body and with the illnesses or injuries it may be affected. Specialization may also be defined as the concentrated treatment of specific diseases or a specific group of sick people. The specialist physician is expected to demonstrate a higher standard of skills than the general practitioner. The standard of expertise required to exercise must be equivalent to the normal standard of care taken by experts in this branch of specialization, considering medical development and attainment at any particular time.

162. Section 17G of the Physicians' Ordinance establishes the general rules for transferring responsibility for authorization between specialist physicians and physician assistants on a temporary basis. In order to affect this transfer, the specialist physician must fulfil the following conditions:

(1) The medical procedures performed under personal authorization must be within his speciality and constitute an active part of his medical practice.
(2) The specialist physician and the physician assistant operate within the same medical institution.
(3) Obtaining consent from the specialist physician who granted the authorization and from the physician assistant.

(4) Approval from the administrator of the medical institution where the specialist is employed.
(5) Written notification to the Ministry of Health including the required consents and approvals.
(6) The maximum period for transferring responsibility may not exceed forty-five days in a calendar year.
(7) The total personal authorization granted and received may not exceed four personal authorizations.

The transfer of responsibility for authorization is permissible under precise provisions outlined in this section, which came into effect after Amendment No. 16 to the Physicians' Ordinance.

d. The Medical Student

163. Any medical student who undertakes medical treatment of a patient will be expected to rise to the standard of a reasonable physician. The 1976 New Version of the Physicians' Ordinance empowers the Director General of the Ministry of Health to make medical students exceptions to the rules of the Ordinance.

e. The Young Physician

164. Lack of experience is no defence against the claim of negligence. A physician starting to practise, and is under the guidance of a specialist physician, may be forgiven, even if his or her mistake causes damage, in which the physician's instructor may shoulder case responsibility.

f. The Reasonable Nurse

165. The standard of care to be adopted by a nurse shall be that exercised by a reasonable nurse in similar circumstances.

g. The Layman

166. The unqualified person who renders voluntary aid will also have certain obligations to the patient. In general, it can be stated that non-medical standards will measure the action. Such a person will be expected to exploit whatever skill he or she may have, and the person may take whatever care in the street.

h. Alternative Medicine

167. Formerly, patients were treated in accordance with systems or schools of thought that were representative of diverse philosophical approaches to diagnoses and regimens. With time, most of these practices were unified and combined in the medicine of modern times. However, some systems and trends have preserved their identities. They are recognized today as osteopathy and chiropractic, to which have been added other accepted methods of treatment, known as 'alternative medicine' or 'supplementary medicine'. Israeli legislature has not been able to adopt a firm attitude regarding these systems and schools of thought and the juridical responsibility of their devotees. However, one can point to an underlying principle that guides the legal establishment insofar as the person who supplies treatment is assessed by those standards obtained in the branch of medicine with which he or she is concerned. It is assumed that a sick person applying for an alternative treatment to one who is not a licensed physician does so with eyes wide open and does not intend or have the right to demand that such a person will behave in accordance with the orthodox medical rules with which the qualified practitioner must comply. It should be obvious that the legislator is empowered to confine and condition the practice of unconventional medicine. In some contingencies, he or she may also determine the appropriate standard.

i. Updating

168. On principle, the physician is obliged to preserve a professional standard and keep in touch with scientific medical breakthroughs. Lack of contact with such development, causing the physician to give obsolete treatment, is liable to indicate deviation from the standard of reasonable care, which will prove the physician's negligence. It should be recorded that the reference is to scientific innovation that has already found its niche in the medical science structure and is currently going through a period of adolescence before it stands the test of time as medical practice, rather than some new novelty. The proof of the adoption of an innovation by a reasonable physician lies in the combination of several distinctive factors; a certain amount of time has elapsed since its publication; it has been allotted a place in the manuals of medical science; it has been adopted in the appropriate hospital wards, and there may be other factors. A person who does not peruse some article or other in medical literature can be forgiven. Still, ignorance of a series of repeated warnings published in the medical literature is liable to demonstrate a physician's negligence. At the same time, the use of what was once a common practice, discarded when antiquated, will be regarded as negligence.

j. Deviation from Standard

169. It may be stated that, in general, deviation from the required standard may derive from the physician's negligence, professional ignorance, or explicit determination to act differently. Deviation from the exercise of accepted practice does not necessarily constitute proof of the physician's negligence. If this is not clearly understood, medicine will come to a standstill and lose every development prospect. However, a physician who deviates from accepted standards must account to the bench for doing so to avoid being branded as negligent because of that deviation if no explanation is forthcoming. It should be noted that the judge always has the last word. At the end of the court hearing, the question to be answered is not 'Did the physician's conduct accord with common professional practice?' but 'Did his or her conduct accord with the standard of reasonable treatment, as required by law?' Authority for such a decree is lodged solely with the law court, which cannot leave it to expert witnesses or transfer it to the medical profession.

k. Proof of Standard

170. The non-professional's ignorance of medicine requires an expert witness' testimony concerning negligence in diagnosis and treatment. However, it should be evident that the judge has the privilege of the last word and the casting vote concerning the calling of witnesses. The expert witness need not necessarily be summoned from the defendant's environment, nor need he or she to support the same school of medical thought as the defendant if there happen to be different schools of medical opinion in the area. When it sets about permitting the evidence of an expert witness and weighing its value, the court must be guided by its answers to two questions. First, is the witness satisfactorily skilled and professionally knowledgeable? Second, is the witness acquainted well enough with the standards required of physicians in similar circumstances?

171. In the ruling of *Assuta Ashdod* issued on 20 June 2023 by the Supreme Court, it was determined that in a medical negligence lawsuit where the issue of liability (not just damages) is at stake and pertains to medical matters, the plaintiff must substantiate their claims with an appropriate expert opinion. However, the court has the discretion to exempt a claimant from attaching a medical expert opinion to the statement of claim, pursuant to Regulation 87(d) of the Civil Procedure Regulations. This authority is exercised under exceptional circumstances based on the unique circumstances of each case.

172. Further anchoring the court's authority, Regulation 93(a) allows the court to permit a claimant to substantiate a medical claim even if the conditions stipulated in Regulations 87(a) and (d) are not met, if a medical expert opinion is not attached to the statement of claim and exemption is not granted due to 'special reasons.' Granting an exemption from attaching a medical expert opinion under Regulation 87(d) occurs in exceptional circumstances. The court's use of Regulation 93(a) under the new regulations is rare and initiated by the court itself, without the claimant's request, making it an exceptional case among exceptions.

173. Another source of authority, which allows the court to exempt a claimant from attaching a medical expert opinion, can be found in the general directive established in Regulation 176(a) of the regulations, stating that the court may give instructions at any time on any matter within the rules of law and also correct any defect or error in any proceeding, including matters decided under Regulation 33(d) if it deems it necessary to achieve the purpose of these regulations.

174. Therefore, the court's authority to exempt a claimant from attaching a medical expert opinion is grounded in various regulations and is exercised judiciously based on the specific circumstances of each case.

l. Res Ipsa Loquitur

175. The New Version of the Civil Wrong Ordinance decrees that if an action is brought for damage and it is proven that the plaintiff had no information, and could not have known, of the actual circumstances that led to the event that caused the damage and that the damage was caused by an asset over which the defendant had complete control and that it appears to the court that the occurrence of the event which caused the damage is more consistent with the conclusion that the defendant did not take reasonable precautions, rather than with the conclusion that he or she took reasonable precautions, the defendant shall bear the burden of proving that in respect of the event that caused the damage there was no neglect for which he or she is liable.

176. The principle of 'Res Ipsa Loquitur' is an evidentiary rule anchored in section 41 of the Torts Ordinance under negligence, which shifts the burden of proof to the defendant in cases where factual ambiguity regarding the circumstances leading to the harm. Its role is to place the plaintiff, who lacks specific knowledge of the negligence that caused the harm, on equal footing with the defendant, who does possess such knowledge.

177. Although originating from English Law, the Israeli version of the principle and the interpretations given to it in rulings imbue it with unique significance within Israeli jurisprudence. The principle consists of three conditions:

(1) Ignorance Condition: the judgment in the *Perezker* case, one of the earliest Israeli judgments addressing the principle, established that the ignorance condition pertains to the victim's subjective lack of awareness. This view was also adopted by the majority opinion in the *Noyman* case, where Justice Zilberg expanded it to include a subjective-objective test. In other words, the examination of ignorance focuses on the victim's subjective knowledge but is objectively assessed.
(2) Control Condition: The significant expansion of this condition was seen in the *Israeli-lift v. Hindley* case, where the judge found that 'control should be assessed based on the apparent ability of the defendant to best prevent the occurrence of harm.'
(3) Probability Surplus Condition: Unlike the general evidence presented by the plaintiff, the defendant can also present general evidence to counterbalance theoretical negligence. This approach, adopted by the majority opinion in the *Solan* case, constitutes the current law.

178. The true innovation introduced by the Israeli ruling is that the third condition allows the plaintiff to base their claim of negligence solely on statistical evidence. In other words, the third condition is fulfilled when it has been proven that statistically, in most cases, the damage was caused due to negligence.

5. The Standard Rule: General

179. Although the standard of treatment constitutes a legal issue, whether, in a specific case, the standard of treatment was satisfactory is a matter of fact to be determined by the court after consideration of the circumstances of the occurrence.

The legal standard of conduct is external and objective. The law courts fix standards of general validity. A specific norm of behaviour demanding the disregard by a person for certain tendencies and characteristics is obligatory in human society when the common good has priority. As a rule, a physician is expected to respect the standard of professional conduct that is customary in medicine. The two components that determine the standard are knowledge and skill. The latter is capability, or a particular skill, expressed in developing a person's talent because of practice and experience. People who engage in healing are obliged not only to exercise reasonable care but are also compelled to rise to the standard of accomplishment achieved by their fellow practitioners.

180. Several factors that influence the determination of the standard level of care to be taken depend on the dimensions of the danger: the more serious the danger, the higher the standard of essential caution. The second factor is the degree of the actuality that the danger of injury presents. If there is little danger of injury, few or not, precautions must be taken. If the danger is considerable, precautions must be taken to eliminate it. The severe nature of the consequences is another factor that must be taken into consideration. The more serious the consequences of a fault, the higher the level of safety precautions. Another factor to be taken into consideration is the expense of the precautions that must be taken. The importance of the action under discussion is also a relevant factor. When it is the concern of a local authority, the action's benefit to society must also be evaluated. Finally, an assessment and determination of standard must be calculated regarding medical know-how at the time of the treatment. This does not mean that there can be fluctuations in the level of the skilled and careful physician's behaviour, but rather, the standard of treatment is dictated by the circumstances surrounding every case. The medical standard requires court recognition. The law court yardstick, being objective, disregards such subjective factors as ignorance, diminished mental capacity, disability, or thoughtlessness. A physician may be exonerated from liability in a situation where extraordinary conditions prevent the physician's anticipation of, or ability to safeguard against, dangers that demand care, for example, during emergencies.

6. Defences

a. Contributory Negligence

181. As a rule, the defendant will not be regarded as the one responsible for the damage to the plaintiff by a fault if the fault of the plaintiff is the decisive cause of the damage. If the damage incurred by the plaintiff is due partly to his or her fault and partly to that of the defendant, the compensation to be paid to the plaintiff will be reduced by the court to a sum representing the judge's fair and accurate assessment of the defendant's participation in liability for the damage. Contributory negligence may be a plaintiff's act of commission or omission that substantially contributes to the damage incurred and whose nature may be described as negligence or careless behaviour. The term 'contribution' is applied to anything that is the direct cause of a happening. It should be recorded that it is not a question of any dereliction of duty, so much as a person's failure to use such reasonable care for his or her protection, as it shows partial responsibility for the wrong created. The standard of care in a case of contributory negligence is identical to that of ordinary negligence. The onus of proof when contributory negligence is claimed rests with the defendant.

182. Contributory Negligence also appears in section 309 of the Penal Code, which deals with situations involving third-party intervention. Section 309(2) addresses the failure to mitigate damages by the victim. The section deals with the medical treatment of injuries sustained by the victim, here, the victim is the causal agent. The intervening party in this case is the victim himself/herself, who, for various reasons, refrains from taking action to mitigate the damage inflicted upon them. Their refusal to accept treatment ultimately leads to the fatal outcome. Thus, the victim brought about the result upon themselves. However, the causal connection between the action and the outcome remains intact. It is important to note that physicians should expect the victim to refuse medical treatment. Therefore, the intervention of a third party should be evaluated based on a reasonable expectations test in each case.

b. Volenti Non Fit Injuria

183. A person who has reached a specific or implicit agreement with a second party to accept liability for the risk of damage caused by that second party cannot be compensated for the damage suffered because of taking that risk. However, the New Version of the Civil Ordinance decrees that if a claim for a wrong is brought to court, a legitimate defence may be that the plaintiff knew how to estimate the lie of the land that caused the danger and exposed him- or herself to the situation voluntarily.

c. Inevitable Accident

184. A plaintiff should not be deemed to have caused damage by his or her fault if an unusual, natural event caused the damage that a reasonable person could not have foreseen when even reasonable caution could not have prevented the results. The defendant is obliged to prove the occurrence of an untoward event over which he or she had not the slightest control and whose results could not have been averted by the application of care and skill. The onus of proof that an unavoidable accident has occurred rests with the defendant.

d. Period of Prescription

185. The 'period of prescription' implies that the claim of a right may become obsolete. If an outdated claim is brought to court, when the defendant presents a plea of termination of prescription, the action will not be heard. However, the right itself cannot be eliminated. The period of prescription begins on the day the grounds for the claim arise. When a physician's negligence is concerned and a claim has not been brought to court, it will become obsolete after seven years. The new version of the Civil Wrong Ordinance decrees that when the claim is for the damage created by an act of commission or omission, the date on which the claim is made shall be the date the damage is discovered. Still, the claim will become obsolete if it is not brought to court within ten years of the date when the damage was incurred. In determining the period of prescription, any period before the patient reached the age of 18, or during which he or she was mentally ill and had no guardian, will not be considered. The 1958 Law of Prescription decrees that if the plaintiff, for reasons that are no fault of his or her own, or that no amount of reasonable care can prevent, is unaware of the facts of his or her claim, the period of prescription will begin from the date on which he or she becomes possessed of the facts. The burden of proof that the claim is obsolete rests with the defendant.

186. As a result of the war, the Constitution Committee approved the proposed amendment to the Statute of Limitations Law (Amendment No. 9-Temporary Provision), 2024, extending and reinstating the statute of limitations for filing civil claims. Section 15A was added as an amendment to the statute of Limitations Law, prolonging the expiration period. According to the amended text, the statute of limitations periods for civil claims will be preserved from 7 October 2023 to 6 April 2024. This period will not be included in the 'statute of limitations race' calculation for the general population. The law will apply, among other things, to compensation claims for medical malpractice, compensation for victims of traffic accidents, violations of Labour Law, breaches of contracts, and more.

e. Mitigation of Loss

187. It is a matter of principle that the plaintiff must do all he or she can to keep the damage as small as possible, nor will the plaintiff have a right to compensation for damage that he or she could have prevented by taking reasonable steps.

The burden of proof that the plaintiff did not act to confine the damage rests with the defendant. If the plaintiff has taken reasonable measures whose failure has not lessened the damage, he or she will be fully compensated by the defendant. A person is entitled to recover only those damages that he or she has incurred while acting reasonably. If acting reasonably, he or she could have minimized or reduced the damage sustained to a smaller amount, and only that smaller amount can be recovered.

f. Obligation of Operation for Injured Party

188. The consequences of the injured party's breach of duty to reduce the damage expresses itself in the sum of money awarded, which will be reduced by the assessed cost of the damage he or she could have prevented. When an operation considered by a reasonable person to involve no risks is suggested, the injured person's refusal to be operated on will be seen as a breach of duty to lessen the damage. When the plaintiff acts to decrease the damage by consenting to medical treatment, the defendant is obliged to pay all the expenses. If the patient has succeeded in reducing damage, he or she will receive no payment for any damage that has been prevented. The criterion for analysing the conduct of an injured party who refuses an operation must be decided by a reasonable person.

D. Aspects of Vicarious Liability

1. Liabilities of Hospitals for Acts of Medical Staff

189. The doctrine of vicarious liability is firmly planted on a base of social convenience and elementary justice. Because society has accepted the principle that a person is responsible for his or her own actions and not another's actions when responsibility is transferred to one person for another's actions, special conditions must exist that justify the imposition.

2. Liability of Employer for Employee's Wrongs

190. An employer is one whose relationship with another gives him or her complete control over how the second party does a job or work. In contrast, he or she is not similarly dominated by someone else concerning the performance of that job. An employee is one whose work is controlled by another, as described above. An employer is liable for an act of his or her worker if he or she has permitted or approved it, or if the worker has performed the action while working for the employer. An act shall be regarded as having been done during a person's work if he or she performs the act as an employee carrying out normal tasks, or other jobs related to work, even if the employee's action, permitted by the employer, was clumsily performed. However, any act performed by the worker for his or her benefit, and not in the employer's interest, must be regarded in a different light. The employer-employee relationship is determined in Israel by the test of 'uninhibited control.' This means that every employee's action is controlled by the employer, who is permitted to direct the employee's activities. Concerning unskilled labour, this uninhibited control takes the form of instructions on how the work should be done. For skilled labour, the extent of the employer's control must depend on the professional nature of the work. The more experienced the work, the less technical would be the control of the employer, who would confine himself/herself to the management of procedural matters in the sphere of the organization. A worker's employment consists of the worker's normal chores, which include specific and general jobs and functions inseparable from normal tasks. The employer is permitted to debar the worker from the performance of activities. If the employee does a job beyond the scope of his or her functions as defined by the employer, the latter will be exempt from responsibility for any wrong the employee commits while doing so. A physician's liability for a nurse's activity may be personal or vicarious. His or her liability may find expression in the inappropriate choice of a nurse, inappropriate instructions to a nurse, failure to prevent his or her commission of an inappropriate act, or inappropriate supervision of a nurse's work. Vicarious liability exists when a physician who is not a government employee is responsible for the actions of a nurse who is virtually an employee if he or she carries out activities in the ordinary course of work or if the physician has approved of or endorsed the actions.

191. The law courts are wary of imposing liability on physicians when the act of commission or omission is purely in the nursing sphere. The surgeon is not ordinarily liable for the anaesthetist's negligence. Nowadays, the hospital's operating theatre is the scene of a complicated business involving the ever-increasing specialization of different functionaries. Responsibility for the anaesthetization of a patient and keeping a check on the physical condition during surgery has been substantially transferred from the joint supervision of the surgeon and the anaesthetist nurse to an anaesthetist who is a specialist physician. The business of counting the instruments and sponges has been transferred to a particular nurse under the supervision of the matron. This development frees the surgeon from concentration on the operation itself and forgives him or her considerably from liability and supervision of the whole team of participants in the surgical intervention. The physician is not liable for a pharmacist's negligence in preparing the prescription if it is written down properly.

3. Liability of Pharmacist for His Assistant's Acts

192. The revised version of the Pharmacists' Ordinance empowers the owner of a pharmacy to engage licensed assistant pharmacists for work in a pharmacy if they work under the supervision of a pharmacist. Such supervision does not entail the owner's presence during their activities.

4. Vicarious Liability of Hospital

193. A hospital, first and foremost, is directly liable for all its inmates. But it is additionally liable vicariously. Moreover, the Directorate of a hospital is liable for any act of negligence committed during such treatment as a patient is given by the hospital because it, the hospital Directorate, is obliged to provide a patient with a suitable treatment.

5. State Liability

194. The 1952 Law of Civil Damages (State Liability) decrees that the state's liability concerning civil wrongs is like any corporate body. The state is liable for the commission of damage due to negligence. Thus, a physician who is a public employee, including all civil servants, is liable for any wrong committed, while the state shoulders vicarious liability for the physician's action. A physician employed as a civil servant bears no liability for a wrong committed by his or her appointed deputy or some other civil servant unless he or she has expressly permitted or approved the wrong.

6. Indemnity Between Wrongdoers

195. Any wrongdoer liable for damage may obtain a portion of the amount of compensation from another who is jointly liable or could be made liable for the same damage if a claim was made against him or her, either as joint wrongdoer or otherwise. The court will determine the amount of his or her share of the damage in accordance with the true deserts of justice by assessing his or her share of liability for the damage. An employee whose negligence has caused damage involves him- or herself and the employer in liability for the damage to a third party, who may sue both employer and employee, individually or together. The plaintiff may sue the employer alone, who may claim that the employee pays his or her share of the compensation. A distinction must be drawn between a worker and a master contractor who works independently and plans his or her methods of operation. The employer is not liable for damage caused by the master contractor or by the latter's workers or agents. An agent is a person who has been authorized to act on another's behalf. A person who has authorized an agent to commit a wrong is jointly liable for the damage.

7. Physician's Liability for Others' Medical Activity

196. The master contractor plans his work programme alone with no right of intervention from the person who orders the job and to whom he or she presents the results of labour as ordered. A private physician will normally assume the status of a master contractor. He or she who makes a contract with another, who is not his or her employee or agent, to have an act performed by him or her will not be liable for a wrong that springs from the performance of that act. This ruling will not be valid for a person who has behaved as follows:

(a) He or she was negligent in choosing a partner for the contract.
(b) He or she interfered in the contractor's work to a degree that caused injury or damage.
(c) He or she permitted or approved the act that led to the injury or damage.
(d) He or she was legally responsible for doing the job whose performance he or she committed to the master contractor.
(e) The work for which he or she hired the contractor was illegal.

197. A person who utilizes the services of an agent who is not his or her employee to act, or series of actions, on his or her behalf, will be liable for anything the agent does during the performance of the action, or series of actions, and for the method of execution. The criterion for defining an agent as distinct from a master contractor is the test of whether he or she is a 'representative' or 'the long arm.' The agent is characterized by the fact that he or she completes a mission on behalf of, and instead of, somebody else so that something in which his or her controller is interested may materialize.

III. Criminal Liability

198. Paragraph 300(c) of the Penal Code decrees that a person who causes another person's death by a reckless act will be charged with involuntary manslaughter. The punishment is imprisonment for twelve years. A punishment of twenty years imprisonment is imposed on a person who persuades, advises, or assists another to commit suicide. In paragraph 304, the code decrees that a person whose negligence causes another's death will be imprisoned for three years. A physician shall be regarded as causing a person's death if his or her act of commission or omission shortens the life of a person suffering from an illness or injury that would have been terminal, even without the physician's action or inaction.

The amended version of section 218 of the Penal Code stipulates that a physician who negligently commits an act that may spread a dangerous disease is liable to imprisonment for three years; if he or she does so intentionally, he or she is liable for a seven-year sentence.

Medical negligence can become a criminal matter in certain cases, particularly in instances involving fatalities due to negligence. In such cases, the state will assess whether it wishes to pursue the case and stand behind it within the criminal law framework.

It should be noted that not every case of treatment failure can be argued as negligence, nor does every instance of negligence necessarily lead to criminal charges. There are many cases in which the state may decide not to intervene and leave them under civil law.

In principle, the state will decide to act especially in severe cases, such as cases resulting in death or cases where patients have become disabled or incapacitated due to treatment, and in cases of repeated incidents. That is, if it is found that the same entity is repeatedly accused of these offences, then the state will decide to intervene.

§3. Quality Assurance

199. The 1996 Patient's Rights Law deals with establishing control and quality committees. The Director General of the Ministry of Health and Israel's Sick Fund Directors were empowered to set these committees, whose purpose is to improve the quality of health services. The hospital Directors were empowered to set up committees to evaluate medical activity and raise the quality of medical treatment. Paragraph 22 of the law stipulates that the contents of the proceedings of a committee, the minutes of its meetings, evidence prepared for those meetings, and distributed among committee members, the summing-up and conclusions may not be divulged to anybody, including the persons whose cases are dealt with; nor may the material mentioned above be used as evidence for any legal suit. However, summaries and conclusions are referred to the persons who formed these committees. Suppose a hospital Director or Sick Fund Director feels that there are patent reasons for disciplinary measures to be taken against a physician. In that case, he or she must inform the Director General of the Ministry of Health. Suppose a committee unearths actual findings concerning a patient's condition. In that case, the treatment and the consequences will be recorded in a medical register, and the ethics committee has the right to record such details in the register if the quality committee has refrained from doing so.

§4. MEDICAL ETHICS COMMITTEES

I. General Remarks

200. Ethics committees have been active in several of Israel's public hospitals for many years. These committees have worked voluntarily without any legal recognition. Committee members have met at intervals to discuss relevant ethical problems. Their decisions have had no legal validity or compulsive effects.

II. Ethics Committees in Hospitals

201. The 1996 Law of Patient's Rights authorized the Minister of Health to set up ethics committees. The minister established ethics committees in Israel's government and public hospitals by virtue of the authority vested. An ethics committee consists of five members.

The chairperson must be someone who could aptly be appointed judge of a district court; two physicians each specializing in a different sphere of medicine; a psychologist or social worker; and a representative of the public or a minister of religion. The ethics committee's broad powers will be described later.

A. Approval of Treatment Without Consent

202. Paragraph 15(2) of the Patient's Rights Law decrees that if a patient is in danger and objects to medical treatment in circumstances in which it must be given quickly, the treater has the right to render that treatment despite the patient's wishes, provided that the ethics committee, after hearing the patient, approves treatment on condition that it is satisfied that:

(a) The patient has been supplied with information to give his or her informed consent.
(b) It is expected that the medical treatment will materially improve his or her medical condition.
(c) There are reasonable grounds for assuming that the patient will consent retroactively after treatment.

203. The 1996 Patient's Rights Regulations (Methods of Nomination of Ethics Committees, Duration of Tenure, Work Procedure) oblige the committee to deal with a physician's request and deliver its decision within forty-eight hours after its receipt of the request unless the chairperson directs otherwise for the special reasons that are recorded. If the committee cannot deal with an urgent request within forty-eight hours, the committee's secretary will refer the physician to the district court.

204. Section 15 of the Patient's Rights Law specifies exceptional cases where medical treatment may be administered without consent, provided all conditions are met. It should be noted that following Amendment No. 16, which came into effect on 17 January 2024, the conditions according to the new amendment:

(1) The physical or mental condition of the patient does not allow obtaining their consent.
(2) The physician is unaware that the patient, their legal guardian, or temporary decision-maker opposes the medical treatment.
(3) It is not possible to obtain consent from the legal guardian, appointed guardian, or temporary decision-maker.

205. These conditions outline the circumstances under which medical treatment can be administered without consent, as amended by the recent legislation.

B. Approval for Denial of Information to a Patient

206. The Patient's Rights Law obliges the physician to supply the patient with the necessary medical information to obtain informed consent to the treatment proposed. But the physician may suppress certain information about the patient's medical condition if the ethics committee has certified that the divulging of such information may cause severe physical or mental damage to the patient. In addition, recent law cases have emphasized the scope of the information that ought to be provided before the patient delivers informed consent. Courts have clarified that all required information, as broad as it may be, must be spread out before the patient.

207. As a rule, the person under treatment has the right to be given medical information by the person who treats him or her or by the medical institution from the medical record dealing with the case. However, if the physician who treats him or her decides not to give the patient complete or partial information about the case, under the assumption that such information may cause severe physical or mental damage or endanger the patient's life, the physician must immediately inform the ethics committee of the decision, detailing the information he or she has concealed from the patient and the reasons for such concealment. The ethics committee can approve, cancel, or amend the physician's decision. In addition, the committee has a right to give a hearing to the patient or anybody else before deciding. If, as stated above, the patient has not been given the medical information, the ethics committee is empowered to decide whether someone else should be supplied with the information. The committee's decision must be handed down within thirty days after receipt of the physician's request.

C. Approval for Dispensing Information to Another

208. The ethics committee is empowered to provide the patient with a hearing before deciding that divulging medical information about the case is essential for protecting his or her and society's health and that the need to divulge information is superior to the interests of silence. The committee's decision will be handed down within thirty days of receipt of the request.

209. After amendment No. 15 to the Patient Rights Law, which occurred on 19 December 2023, subsection 20(a)(3a) was added. This subsection stipulates that a medical institution or healthcare provider is authorized to disclose information, for the purpose of identifying a body or part thereof or determining the cause of death, to one of the following: the National Institute of Forensic Medicine, including a physician associated with the institute, or another qualified healthcare provider authorized by law to perform such actions. For this purpose, the disclosure of information for identification or determination, as described, is considered akin to disclosing information for the purpose of patient treatment.

D. Objection to Item in Medical Record

210. Suppose a patient is of the opinion that factual findings have not been recorded in the medical register by the control and quality committee set up in accordance with the Patient's Rights Law. In that case, he or she can object to the ethics committee. If the latter decides that the factual findings have not been documented as required, it will order their insertion in the medical register and inform that patient accordingly. The committee's decision must be handed down within thirty days of receiving the application.

211. The committee's written decisions will be made known to the applicant as closely as possible after the conclusion of the proceedings. Decisions will be made unless the committee has decided not to state the reasons for the decision or will state the special reasons why it refrains from doing so.

212. The proceedings of the ethics committees will be on camera, although any ethics committee may allow an outsider to attend a session.

213. Suppose an occasion arises for an urgent decision of an ethics committee, although for some reason, it cannot be convened within the required short space of time. In that case, the district court will be endowed with the powers of an ethics committee.

III. The Dying Patient Act

214. The Dying Patient Act was enacted in 2005. The act purports to address multiple dilemmas concerning the dying patient situation. The act affixes a rule of establishing ethics committees that are empowered to determine whether a patient is a 'dying patient' for the purposes listed in the act. The act allows a patient or his or her physician of a patient or a patient's relative his or her guardian or the patient's caregiver or a social worker to apply to an institutional committee to seek the committee's decision on a dispute over a dying patient situation. The committee comprises three specialist physicians, a psychiatrist, an authorized nurse, a social worker or clinical psychiatrist, a legal scholar who is qualified for the position of a district court judge, and a religious figure to be chosen from the religious community to which the patient belongs. The institutional committee's decision is subject to appeal procedures before a national committee.

215. First, Amendment No. 2 to the Dying Patient Law, which came into effect on 9 February 2023, changed the process for obtaining approval previously required by the Labour, Welfare, and Health Committee for actions specified in section 33 (providing advance medical directive), 38 (obtaining power of attorney), 60 (setting regulations by the Minister), 62 (amendment to additions). As of today, following the amendment, the Minister must obtain approval solely from the Health Committee to exercise the authorities listed in the sections.

216. Second, on 3 June 2024, a bill titled the Dying Patient Law (Amendment-Validity of Advance Directives) 2024 was placed on the Knesset table. Essentially, the bill seeks to amend the rules regarding the validity of advance medical directives under Chapter E of the Law, respecting them when an individual is diagnosed as terminally ill and expresses a desire not to receive treatment.

217. The premise is that when a patient decides to sign the 'Advance Medical Directive' form, they do so knowingly and competently. The bill is motivated by concerns that the requirement to extend the validity of directives every five years, as stipulated in section 34, may adversely affect patients who may not be in a medical condition to renew their request.

218. The bill proposes changing the wording so that the directives' validity starts from the moment of signing and continues until altered by the signer unless a shorter period is specified beforehand. Additionally, the bill clarifies that the signer has the authority to revoke or modify the validity of the advance directives at any time at their discretion. Furthermore, the bill suggests adjusting the initial addition to explicitly state that the signer acknowledges the directives' unlimited validity and enables them to set a different timeframe.

IV. Ethics Committees of the IMA

219. The IMA has established and runs a central ethics committee and local ethics committees. The central committee comprises seventeen members. It is empowered to establish local committees and is authorized to debate appeals against decisions of local committees. Ethics committees discuss complaints from physicians, institutions, the public, or individuals. They may also submit complaints against institution members concerning issues involving ethical behaviour. Ethics committees may enforce the following penalties: warning, severe warning, reprimand, severe reprimand, temporary, and/or permanent expulsion of a member from the Medical Association. They may also impose fines and publicize their decisions.

§5. The Society for Medicine and Law in Israel

220. Professor A. Carmi founded the society he has been President of for thirty-two years in 1972. Its headquarters are located at Petah Tikva in central Israel, and its membership is 1,000.

221. The aims of the society are to:

- Dispel the professional tension existent between the representatives of two worlds, that of law and that of health.
- Research and comprehend the problems concerned with health and medicine in their reflection on the legal sphere and every aspect of the issues involved, to endeavour to resolve all those problems.
- Deepen the general public's awareness in Israel of the problems linking health with law and confronting medical law.
- Study and teach the issues of health and law for the improvement of groups of specialists in various fields of knowledge.
- Campaign for appropriate legislation concerning matters of debate among physicians and lawyers.
- Promote the interest of experts and society in subjects concerning health and law to raise the level of their quality.
- Keep the social activity of the Society's members alive.

222. The society's activities comprise:

- The publication of a journal in Hebrew twice per year.
- The organization of symposia and professional conferences.
- The holding of open forums on medical law subjects for the public at large.
- The establishment of research committees.
- The management of comprehensive social affairs, including visits to places of interest in Israel and abroad and participation in sundry social happenings.

Members of the society are active participants in the World Association for Medical Law congresses.

§6. United Nations Educational, Scientific and Cultural Organization Chair in Bioethics

223. In 2000, the United Nations Educational, Scientific, and Cultural Organization established its Chair in Bioethics at the International Centre for Health, Law and Ethics at Israel's University of Haifa (described below). It accredited it with responsibility for the advancement of education and research in Bioethics. Its main activity concentrates on creating modernized ethics syllabuses at schools for doctors and nurses worldwide.

224. Haifa University's International Centre maintains and activates several departments and institutions. The chair operated between 2001 and 2021 under UNESCO's auspices, and since May 2021 it has become an independent organization under the name 'International Chair in Bioethics,' it publishes *Medicine and Law*, an international circulation. This quarterly, which was founded in 1980, has printed more than 2,000 original articles and serves as a unique international forum for the most prominent members of the world's medical and legal professions, who are able to disseminate the fruits of their scientific research.

The library, housing thousands of books on medicine, law, and ethics, is probably one of the largest of its kind in the world.

Additionally, the centre's other departments organize symposia and conferences and promote international research. Members of the medical, legal, educational, ethical, and nursing professions in Israel and many other countries participate.

Part II. Physician-Patient Relationship

Chapter 1. General Description

§1. Duties of Physicians and Patients, Rights of Patients

I. Introductory Remarks

225. In Israel, the relationship between patient and physician has been regulated by specific legislation. Different pieces of legislation contain rules relating to patients' rights and physicians' duties. In addition to these rules, the Israeli legislature followed the example of its Finnish colleague and enacted the Patient's Rights Law in 1996.

The Knesset passed the law on 1 May 1996, to be effective from 12 August 1996. The proposal for the law was conceived during the Twelfth Knesset and was an incorporation of five private bills by different members of the Knesset: the proposed 1986 Law for a person's rights over his or her own body; the suggested patient's rights Law of 1989; the 1989 proposal for amending the Physicians' Ordinance (Medical Confidentiality); the 1990 bill for the defence of the patient; and the 1990 proposal for a patient's rights. All this led to the appointment of a mediation committee that combined the five proposals into one bill, taking into consideration, among other matters, the committee's assessment of the WHO's Lisbon Declaration on Patient's Rights.

226. The Knesset passed another law on equal rights for the disabled in 1998. The law determines the rights of all disabled persons. Israel's responsibility for those rights is based on the principle of equality; the recognition of the value of a person born in God's image; and respect for human dignity. The law purposes to protect the dignity and freedom of the disabled and cement their right to equal and active participation with others in every walk of life. The law determines a disabled person's right to make decisions concerning his or her own life, in accordance with his or her wishes and preferences.

227. The Disabled Persons Regulations (Medical Treatment) of 1954 was amended in 2020 to include detailed regulations concerning medical treatment to be provided to disabled persons upon a decision made by a medical commission. Such medical treatment includes financial funding that is accompanied by the treatment.

228. The Investigation and Testifying Procedures Act (Compatibility to Mental or Psychological Disability) of 2005 displays exceptional rules of procedures. Upon establishing a reason to believe that the interrogatee by a police officer is a mentally disabled person, the officer ought to refer the interrogatee to a special interrogator who is authorized to hold such an investigation. These rules apply to a mentally disabled person being interrogated as a witness, victim, or complainant. The Act aims to guarantee the fairness of the investigation proceedings and protect the rights of the mentally disabled interrogatee.

II. Duty to Care

A. *National Health Insurance*

229. The 1994 Law on National Health Insurance decrees that every Israeli resident has a right to the health services detailed in the package of services listed in the law. The 1996 Patient's Rights Law declares that anyone needing medical treatment has the right to obtain it in accordance with every law and subject to the conditions and procedures that are current at different times in Israel's medical infrastructure. Furthermore, in any medical emergency, in a matter of life and death, or when there is an imminent risk of severe and irreparable disablement to a person if he or she is not given urgent medical treatment, he or she has the right of such immediate treatment, unconditionally. Consequently, a public hospital or clinic must supply its services to a person who requires them, under conditions detailed in the laws. The duty of a physician who gives private treatment to a patient will be determined in accordance with the general laws of contracts.

230. At this point, mention should be made of the 1998 'Neither shalt thou stand against the blood of thy neighbour' Law, which obliges the physician, like anyone else, to lend a helping hand to a person with whom he or she is confronted, and who, as the result of a sudden occurrence, is in danger of losing life, limb, or health, provided that the physician has the means of supplying aid without risk to him- or herself or to other people.

231. The Transport Regulations oblige a physician driver involved in a traffic accident with a casualty to administer medical aid. Furthermore, a physician driving a car who passes a place where a traffic accident involving a casualty is obliged to stop and render aid to the injured person, even if his or her car is not involved. Jewish Religious Law (*Halacha*) emphasizes the physician's obligation to give medical service to anyone in need, even if occasionally it is without or against the consent of the injured party.

232. The 1977 Penal Code determines a prison sentence for a person who refuses to render such aid as he or she can give in a public disaster if a public official asks him or her to do so.

233. The IMA's code of professional ethics states that in emergencies, or cases of life and death, a physician is duty-bound to proffer medical assistance. If a physician has agreed to treat a patient, he or she is to continue treating as long as there is mutual trust and cooperation between him or her and the patient.

B. Emergency Care

1. General

234. It would seem proper to be liberal in assessing a physician's conduct when he or she is working during an emergency, and the law is indeed lenient in its judgment of a physician's activity in special circumstances. However, such considerations cannot detract from the validity of the general rules for professional behaviour. The obligation to observe common practice holds, as always, for treatment under conditions of emergency.

Emergencies face the physician with the possibility of, or even the necessity for, deviating from the practice that is normal when there is no emergency because, in an emergency, several such factors as a temporary shortage of manpower or medical instruments may occur. However, the medical profession should cope with such dilemmas by expanding its branch of medical treatment in emergencies, with anticipatory planning for crises, keeping medical personnel and facilities on call, and consolidating its common practice for emergencies. Emergencies may impose difficult missions on the physician where there is no standard drill for the situation in which his or her intervention is required.

The emergency in Israel following the outbreak of war led to significant operational changes in the country's healthcare system. As a result, the Ministry of Health, medical institutions, and health funds collaborated to expand the medical treatment sector. In addition, dozens of senior emergency doctors from around the world volunteered in Israel and assisted medical teams in emergency departments during the war days.

Initiated by the Ministry of Health in collaboration with health funds, efforts were made to ease public access to healthcare services tailored to emergency situation emergencies. They worked to establish specialized community clinics near shelters in the southern and northern regions of the country, offering medical treatment to beneficiaries of all health funds.

2. Emergency Treatment Standard

235. It is a well-known principle that people are responsible for their shortcomings if they commit to an objective they know or ought to know that they cannot achieve. Conversely, the person who commits to an objective requiring skill and speciality know-how is obliged to use the requisite skill and expertise to achieve the objective. In these circumstances, it is fit and proper that the law should expect the physician to demonstrate a reasonable standard of expertise and care. It would, therefore, be unfair to expect the same legal standard of efficiency in the conduct of a physician who, having no alternative, performs an urgent operation back or beyond, or in the patient's home, as distinct from the performance of his or her counterpart, working in a modern hospital with modern equipment and with specialist advice at his or her disposal. In addition, the standard of safety precautions in the emergency ward must be as high as the efficiency of similar wards serving the same purpose. In emergency patients and injury cases, the physiological changes are more abrupt and unexpected than among other patients, and it is occasionally difficult to diagnose such changes. Therefore, the physician is required to make continual estimates of the conventional changes. There is proof positive of such physiological changes in emergency wards and others that are exceptional to, and distinct from, the textbook changes. New, life-saving techniques, until recently unknown, are being researched and implemented. When new treatment methods become part of the common practice, they are added to the legal schedule of standard, compulsory treatments.

3. Lack of Patient's Consent to Treatment

236. The Patient's Rights Law decrees that in the event of a medical emergency, urgent treatment may be given to the patient even without the latter's informed consent if, in the circumstances of the emergency, which may include the changed physical or mental state of the patient, his or her informed consent is unobtainable. Serious treatment will be provided by consent of three doctors unless the emergency circumstances make this impossible.

237. The Knesset approved Amendment No. 16 to the Patient Rights Law, 2024, according to which, in case where urgent medical treatment is necessary and the patient lacks the capacity to consent, a social worker in a medical institution may authorize a temporary decision-maker for the patient. The rationale behind the proposed law emphasized that the proposed arrangement will apply only if no guardian has been appointed for the patient's medical affairs and there is no valid power of attorney regarding the patient's health matters, as in such a case, the decision-maker for the patient will be the guardian or the appointed attorney, as appropriate.

4. Resistance of Patient

238. The Patient's Rights Law decrees that when the patient objects to a treatment in which circumstances require that he or she receive it immediately because of the danger to his or her health, the physician is allowed to disregard the patient's opposition and treat him or her, provided that the ethics committee, after hearing the patient, has authorized treatment, having been convinced that:

(a) The patient was properly briefed when his or her informed consent was requested.
(b) The medical treatment is expected to lead to a considerable improvement in the patient's health.

(c) There are reasonable grounds for the assumption that the patient will give his or her retroactive consent after treatment.

239. In 2015, the Prison Ordinance was amended, thus allowing the establishment of special procedures to force prisoners who exercise hunger strikes to receive medical treatment, even if the hunger-striking prisoner opposes this treatment. Such a decision should be made only by the Chief Justice of the district court or his deputy, upon receiving an application by the Commissioner, who has consulted with the Attorney General, which is based on a professional medical opinion that provides that there is a real possibility that because of the hunger strike the prisoner will die or an alternative irreversible severe disability will be caused to him. Chief Justice of the district court may not make this decision but only upon being persuaded that all required efforts have been made to get the prisoner's consent, but the latter refused to consent. Before making his decision, the Chief Justice must request the ethics committee's opinion and give standing to the prisoner himself.

5. Emergency Treatment for the Mentally Deficient

240. In a civil assault action, if the plaintiff is of unsound mind or is mentally or physically deficient, the physician's best defence is that the force he or she applied without prejudice or malice aforethought was, or appeared to be, reasonably dictated by the need for self-defence and the safety of others. The district psychologist is empowered to order immediate, compulsory hospitalization of a person who, because of his or her illness, has lost much power of judgment or ability to appreciate realities, provided that he or she is liable to cause immediate physical injury to him- or herself or to others.

6. Emergency Treatment of a Backward Person

241. A 'backward' person is one who, because of the arrested or perverted development of mental faculties, is incapable of coping with the environment and requires treatment. If a welfare officer believes that the backward person is a source of immediate danger to him- or herself, or to other people, or that he or she requires medical or other, treatment that does not admit to delay, that welfare officer has the right to take all the necessary steps to supply the urgent treatment and avert what he or she considers the danger, even before the backward person's case is presented to a diagnosis committee and even without the consent of the backward person or his or her guardian.

7. Emergency Treatment of a Handicapped Minor

242. Suppose a welfare officer has a reason to believe that a minor is handicapped, in immediate danger, and in need of treatment that cannot be delayed. In that case, he or she has the right to adopt any means he or she sees fit to remove the danger or to apply the treatment, even without the consent of the adult who is responsible for the child.

8. Emergency Treatment of a Soldier

243. When two physicians make a written statement to the effect that a soldier's life will be saved, or a serious and immediate deterioration in his or her condition prevented, or other dangers to his or her health forestalled if he or she is given the treatment needed, he or she may be given the medical treatment, even against his or her will. However, a soldier may not be forced to undergo an operation except under battle conditions or similar emergencies. Therefore, during a period of hostilities, in battle conditions, or similar circumstances, the treatment mentioned above may be given with the signed authority of only one physician or even by word of mouth, provided that he or she puts it in writing as soon as conditions permit. Medical treatment of a soldier authorized as above will be regarded in the eyes of the law as having been given with the soldier's consent, even despite his or her objection.

9. Emergency Treatment by a Layman

244. Even if he or she is not professional, anyone is permitted to treat an injured or sick person, provided that if he or she does so on the spur of the moment and without pay or other compensation or acts under the direct, personal control of a licensed physician. The Penal Code decrees that a person who undertakes and gives medical or surgical treatment *where there is no emergency* must possess adequate medical expertise and exercise reasonable precautions during treatment.

245. This issue is currently governed by the Health Professions Regulation Law, 2008. Recently, the profession of physician assistant was formally regulated under Amendment No. 8 to the law, scheduled to take effect on 7 August 2024. According to this law, physician assistants will be authorized to perform a range of various medical procedures as determined by specialist physicians, specified in a personal authorization granted to them.

10. The 'Good Samaritan' Rule

246. The 1998 'Neither shalt thou stand against the blood of thy neighbour' Law imposes the duty of supplying another with aid in conditions as detailed in the law. The law decrees that anyone is obliged to render aid to a person with whom he comes into chance contact as the result of a sudden occurrence that poses a severe and immediate danger to that person's life, body, or health when he or she has the means to render aid without hazard to him- or herself or to anyone else. In further detail, the law states that anyone who informs the authorities of the occurrence or calls upon another person to supply such aid as he or she is capable of giving shall be regarded as having supplied the aid specified by the law. The court may fine any person who contravenes this law. Furthermore, the law ordains that the court may require the person responsible for the occurrence, whether the injured party or anybody else, to reimburse the Good Samaritan to the tune of the costs and reasonable expenses of the treatment.

III. Respect for the Patient's Privacy

247. The Basic Law for Human Dignity and Liberty determines that all persons possess the right to privacy and liberty.

248. The Law for the Protection of Privacy makes it illegal for a person to invade other people's privacy unsolicited. Such unsolicited invasion of privacy includes the spread of information about such matters connected with an individual's health or about the intimacies of one's personal life. Further privacy breaches include a violation of the duty of confidentiality concerning one's personal affairs as determined by law or agreement, as well as the use of information about one's private doings for a purpose unintended by the giver of such information. Thus, breach of privacy comprises a wrong as defined by the New Version of the Civil Wrongs Ordinance and a criminal offence.

The recording and use of data about a person's medical condition for an information bank and any use of such data require official approval. The keeper of the information bank is responsible for the security of his data and preventing leakage. Any person has the right to study particulars about him- or herself in the information bank. Still, the keeper is free to withhold information regarding one's physical or mental health if he or she believes that such knowledge might cause severe physical or mental damage to the enquirer or might endanger his or her life. In such a case, the bank keeper shall supply the information to a physician or psychologist as designated by the person who has requested the information. When a criminal or civil case of breach of privacy is brought to court, if there has been such a breach by a physician in circumstances that made it the physician's legal, moral, social, and professional duty to break the silence, his or her will be a legitimate defence.

249. A recent law legalizes the internal 'body search' in special circumstances and under special conditions. A 'suspect' is a person against whom there are reasonable grounds of suspicion that he or she has committed an offence. A 'body search' includes a blood test, photography of the body's contents with the aid of ultrasound instruments, or any kind of scan observation of the inside of the body by means of radiological instruments and gynaecological tests, including the withdrawal of fluids. A police officer is empowered to order an internal body search after obtaining the suspect's consent. In the case of the suspect's refusal, a law court may order the process if it feels that the need to elicit evidence is more vital than the breach of privacy attendant on the internal body search. An expert technician will search with a photographic instrument or camera; a gynaecological probe will be performed by a specialist or a person specializing in gynaecology or obstetrics. No court permit for an internal body search will oblige any member of the medical profession to act in the face of the suspect's refusal to grant his or her consent for said action.

250. An Amendment of the Criminal Procedure Law (Enforcement Powers – Data Communication) was made considering the Coronavirus pandemic, which states that a qualified officer may, at the request of a police officer, permit the receipt of location data from a database of a holder of a *Bezeq* licence, without a court order, to enforce the isolation orders of active COVID patients. However, this emergency regulation was extended four times in amendments. Nevertheless, Amendment No. 4 to the emergency regulation changed its expiration to 22 April 2020. In addition, as part of Amendment No. 2 to the Criminal Procedure Law (Enforcement Authorities-Communication Data) 2022, the definition of a holder of a Bezeq licence provider was removed from the law. In its place, the definition of an authorized provider was added as defined in the Telecommunications Law.

IV. Informed Consent

A. *Right to Information*

1. General Rule

251. A person's fundamental rights in Israel are soundly established on recognizing human status, the inviolability of life, and the fact that the person was born, and always will be, free. This central premise expresses itself in the fundamental law of human dignity and liberty. The second section of this law states that 'There shall be no violation of the life, body or dignity of any person as such.' A human being's status asserts itself, among other things, in a person's freedom to reveal his or her ambitions and choose how to realize them without the risk of heavy-handed suppression. The right of a patient to make his or her own decisions regarding medical treatment and behave accordingly is fortified by Israel's legislature; this basic, social, humanitarian principle lies at the root of 'informed consent' rulings and guides the concept that a decision to treat medically can only be determined by cooperation between the treater and the treated, both parties being linked together by mutual trust and reciprocity. The purpose of the informed consent principle is to achieve several objectives. It asserts the patient's autonomy; it protects his or her status as a human being; it prevents coercion and deception; it encourages the physician's self-criticism; it supports the process of rational decision-making; and it educates the public.

252. The statutory expression of informed consent was in the 1996 Patient's Rights Law. Section 13(A) of the law determines, 'Medical treatment will not be given to a patient unless his informed consent has been obtained in accordance with the chapter of the Law.'

253. The twenty-eighth ruling of the IMA's ethical code lays down, 'Every medical action, apart from normal, daily treatment, requires the patient's informed consent.'

254. Section 13(A) of the Patient's Rights Law makes it illegal to provide a patient with medical treatment without obtaining his or her consent. Section 13(B) conditions the receipt of informed consent on dispensing the requisite medical knowledge to the person to be treated. This seems to indicate that the directive in section 13(A) is intended for qualified personnel rather than for the unqualified. Section 2 of the same law defines 'a person who provides treatment' as 'doctor, dentist, intern, male or female nurse, midwife, psychologist, or any other professional singled out by the Director-General as involved in the health services'.

255. However, the Knesset approved Amendment No. 16 to the Patient Rights Law-2024, allowing a social worker in a medical institution to authorize urgent medical treatment for an incapacitated person unable to provide consent. This decision applies only in cases where there is no appointed guardian for the patient's medical matters and legal decisions regarding their health.

2. Criminal Responsibility of Supportive Staff

256. The Penal Code defines and determines the criminal responsibility of the assistants of a physician who is accused of committing illegal action. If there has been a crime, every one of the following will be considered an accessory:

(a) The person who committed the crime as well as his or her partner in crime or any perpetrator by proxy.
(b) The instigator is the one who caused another to commit the crime by using persuasion, encouragement, demand, request, or coercion.
(c) Before or during the commission of the crime, the accessory performed any action that made the crime possible, facilitated its commission, covered it up, or prevented detection of the criminal or the crime.

3. Medical Treatment

257. The rule of informed consent in Israel is operative concerning what is termed 'medical treatment'. In its widest sense, this term is defined in section 2 of the Patient's Rights Law as 'including diagnostic actions, in addition to preventive medication, psychological activity, and nursing treatment'.

4. The Giving of Consent

a. To Whom May Consent Be Given?

258. Paragraph 13(A) of the Patient's Rights Law, as amended at the end of 2010, provides that consent ought to be delivered to a medical treater, who is primarily defined as including physician, dentist, intern, nurse, midwife, psychologist, occupational therapist, physiotherapist, speech therapist, dietician, clinical criminologist, podiatrist, podiatrist surgeon, chiropractor, and any professional recognized by the Director General of the Health Ministry as a therapist of the health services. And after Amendment No. 18 to the Patient's Rights Law, an additional profession was added to the definition of medical treater, which is Medical Imaging.

b. When Must Consent Be Given?

259. The Patient's Rights Law decrees 'Medical treatment will not be given unless the patient has given his informed consent. And according to Amendment No. 16, a social worker in a medical institution is authorized to approve urgent medical treatment for an incapacitated person unable to provide consent.' Ergo, when informed consent is required, it must be antecedent treatment.

c. Invalidity of Consent

260. Consent, even when given, is invalid or comprises no defence to the physician who has 'assaulted' when the action to which the patient has consented is illegal; when an unauthorized person gave the consent; or when the patient was misled into giving his or her consent.

5. Supply of Information

a. General

261. Paragraph 13(B) of the Patient's Rights Law decrees: to obtain informed consent, the treater will supply the treated with the facts of his case as reasonably as possible, which will enable him to decide if he should consent to the proposed treatment. Such medical data must include:

(a) The diagnosis and prognosis of the patient's medical condition.
(b) A description of the quality, procedure, aim, desired benefit, and prospects of the proposed treatment.
(c) The hazards involved in the prepared treatment, inclusive of after-effects, pain, and discomfort.
(d) Prospects and risks of medical treatment by other methods, or of no medical treatment at all.
(e) The fact that the treatment may be innovative.

b. The Aim

262. The law expressly clarifies the purpose of the communication of the medical data by the treater to the treated, using the words, 'to give the patient an opportunity to decide whether he or she should consent to the proposed treatment'. This ruling concentrates on two components. First, the decision rests with the patient, whereas the physician is the counsellor. Although a partnership is formed between both parties in the business of the patient's return to health, in the choice of medical treatment it is the patient whom the law empowers to decide. Second, the decision with which the law is concerned is to be made essentially by the patient concerning the treatment proposed by the physician, giving the patient no right to force on the physician a method of treatment to which he objects. Just as the treated person is endowed with the right to consent to or refuse a treatment method, the treater is entitled to suggest his or her preferred type of treatment. The patient who does not consent to the physician's proposal may, of course, suggest substitute treatment on which the physician should express his or her opinion, but the final professional decision on any treatment method rests with the physician.

c. Definition of the Term 'Informed'

263. The issue concerns the mental process required for a choice between options. The process must be conscious insofar as the decision is reached by a person who is alert, willing, reflective, purposeful, and using common sense and intelligence. Consent will be valid only if the patient is willing because consent given by a patient under the influence of anaesthetics, narcotics, or alcohol cannot be classified as due to the patient's will. The same applies to consent obtained by unethical pressure brought to bear on the patient by compulsion or manipulation. An opinion that is reliable and feasible cannot be formed without evaluating information. Because the layman patient does not possess medically professional knowledge, the physician is required to supply it. These matters are dealt with in paragraph 13(B)(1–5) of the Patient's Rights Law. The information communicated to a patient should describe the current state of his or her health requiring the change that the proposed treatment will supply, a description of the change itself, and the consequences deriving from it or the alternative medical treatment. The physician's recommendation, namely professional opinion, will accompany the information given to the patient, who should consolidate his or her decision based on the data and advice directed to him or her.

264. The scope of the disclosure obligation is based on the 'reasonable patient' test. According to the Supreme Court ruling in the *Kadosh* case, to obtain informed consent, the medical treater must provide the patient with the medical information reasonably required for them to decide whether to consent to the proposed treatment.

265. However, it should be noted that in the *Herman* case, the Supreme Court established that the risks that require disclosure are only real and significant risks. There is no obligation to disclose information about rare and minor risks. Another example related to vaccines and the scope of the disclosure obligation is found in the *Alturi* case, where it was determined that there is no requirement to disclose information about a rare and minor risk associated with receiving a regular vaccine to the patient.

266. Moreover, section 18(C) of the law limits the disclosure obligation intentionally to protect the patient's mental, physical, and emotional well-being. The section stipulates that a medical treater is allowed not to disclose medical information to the patient if such information could cause serious harm to the patient's physical or mental health or endanger their life.

d. Who Is the Informant?

267. The duty of briefing the patient on his or her treatment is the physician's responsibility who will treat him or her. However, suppose treatment is to be given by a person who is not a physician. In that case, he or she is authorized to supply the patient with the information he or she needs for the treatment, within the limitations laid down in paragraph 18(B) of the law, which states, 'a member of the medical team may transmit medical information relating only to his field of expertise in coordination with the head of the team'.

6. The Information to Be Supplied

268. Paragraph 13(B) of the Patient's Rights Law details five bundles of information with which the treater must supply the treatment.

a. State of Health

269. The first information package refers to the description of the patient's health, 'the diagnosis and prognosis of the patient's medical condition'.

b. Treatment

270. The second package relates to the proposed treatment, stating, 'a description of the nature, procedure, purpose, expected benefit and prospects of the proposed treatment'.

c. Risks

271. The third package relates to the proposed treatment, with notes on its deficiencies, in words, 'the risks involved in the proposed treatment, including aftereffects, pain, and discomfort'. The policy consolidated by Israel court decisions is that the patient must be informed of the significant risks whose importance a normal person in the same situation would take into account before deciding to consent to treatment.

d. Pain and Discomfort

272. Suppose the proposed treatment is accompanied by pain. In that case, the physician must inform the patient of the pain, its nature, its severity, and its duration, to enable him or her to decide whether to consent. The physician is also expected to warn the patient against any phenomena accompanying the treatment proposed.

e. Alternatives

273. The fourth information package relates to alternative treatment methods, stating 'the prospects and risks involved in alternative treatment methods or no treatment at all'.

f. Innovative Treatment

274. The fifth package of information relates to the treatment of an innovative character.

7. Depriving Patient of Medical Information

275. Paragraph 13(D) of the Patient's Rights Law states:

> despite the Regulations in Sub-Section (B) the treater is entitled to refrain from supplying the treated with certain information concerning his medical condition, if the ethics committee has confirmed that such information is likely to cause serious damage to the physical or mental health of the person undergoing treatment.

An ethics committee comprises five members: a person who is qualified to be appointed to a district court bench, as chairman; two specialist physicians; a psychologist or social worker; and a representative of the public or minister of religion.

As mentioned above, the scope of the disclosure obligation is based on the 'reasonable patient' test. According to numerous rulings of the Supreme Court, the medical treater must provide the patient with the necessary medical information reasonably required to decide whether to consent to the proposed treatment. However, according to the Supreme Court's determination, the duty to disclose applies only to real and significant medical risks, and there is no obligation to disclose information about rare risks.

Additionally, section 18(C) of the law restricted the disclosure obligation so that the medical practitioner is permitted not to disclose medical information to the patient if there is a risk that the information could cause serious harm to the patient's physical or mental health or endanger their life.

8. Time of Briefing

276. Paragraph 13(C) of the Patient's Rights Law decrees 'the treater must supply the treated with medical information as early as possible'.

9. Explaining the Information

277. Paragraph 13(C) of the Patient's Rights Law states:

> The treater will supply the treated with the medical information … in a manner that will afford him the highest possible comprehension of the information and equip him to arrive at a decision willingly chosen and independently.

10. Ways and Means of Consenting

278. Paragraph 14(A) of the Patient's Rights Law, amended in 2016, decrees that 'informed consent may be written, oral or by behaviour'. However, this general authorization of consent is restricted in the following six cases of special treatment, which require written consent: (1) operations, apart from minor surgery, (2) catheterization of blood vessels, (3) dialysis, (4) radiotherapy treatment, (5) in vitro fertilization, and (6) chemotherapy for treating malignant growths.

11. Medical Treatment Without Consent

279. Paragraph 15 of the Patient's Rights Law details three contingencies that legalize the treatment of a person without receipt of informed consent. All three cases share the common principle that a patient's right to medical treatment assumes priority over his or her privilege of independence in exceptional circumstances.

280. Paragraph 15(I) of the Patient's Rights Law decrees:

> a treater may render medical treatment which is not listed in the Appendix, even without his patient's informed consent, if all the following conditions prevail: the physical or mental condition of the patient makes it impossible to obtain his informed consent; the physician is unaware that the patient, or his guardian, objects to the patient's treatment; it is impossible to obtain the consent of the patient's representative if a person has been appointed to represent him in accordance with Para. 16; or the consent of his guardian is unobtainable if the patient is a minor or legally incompetent.
>
> After Amendment No. 16 to the Patient Rights Law-2024, the legislature added new sections which define the "temporary decision-maker." Currently, section 15(1) states: The treater is authorized to administer medical treatment that is not subscribed to, even without the patient's consent, under the following conditions: The patient's physical or mental condition does not allow them

to provide consent, or it is unknown to the treater that the patient, their guardian, or their decision-maker are opposing the treatment. The third condition in the section specifies that consent cannot be obtained from the patient's guardian, decision-maker, or temporary decision-maker.

281. Paragraph 15(2) of the Patient's Rights Law decrees:

in circumstances where a person to be treated is in danger, although he objects to the treatment that his condition demands that he receive within a short amount of time, the treater is empowered to render treatment even against his patient's wishes, after the ethics committee, having heard the patient, approves the treatment to be given, provided that the committee is satisfied that the following conditions obtain:

(a) The patient was informed as required when his consent was requested.
(b) The medical treatment is expected to lead to a recognizable improvement in the patient's health.
(c) There are reasonable grounds for supposing that his retroactive agreement will follow the patient's treatment.

Paragraph 15(3) of the Patient's Rights Law decrees:

In cases of emergency,, the treater is entitled to render urgent medical treatment even without his patient's informed consent if the nature of the emergency, including the physical or medical condition of the patient to be treated, eliminates the possible receipt of informed consent in advance. Such medical treatment as is listed in the Appendix will be given upon the consensus of three physicians, unless the emergency character prevents it. A 'medical emergency' is defined in Para. 2 of the Patient's Rights Law as 'circumstances in which a person finds himself in imminent danger of death, or where there is an immediate danger that he will be seriously or irreparably disabled if he does not receive urgent medical treatment.'

12. Special Cases

a. Liability for Damages

282. If a physician is sued for assault, he or she will be able to justify it by proving that the plaintiff was of unsound mind or deficient in mind or body, that the force the physician exerted was, or seemed to be, reasonably adequate to defend the patient, him- or herself or others, and that the demonstration of force was in all innocence and not malicious.

283. However, there is a caveat to the assault, as emphasized in the Supreme Court rulings in the *Kadosh, Shtndel,* and *Da'aka* cases. It allows for the use of assault in cases of medical treatment without informed consent only in exceptional circumstances, such as when the patient was not provided with any information about the expected treatment or when the treatment administered differs significantly from the treatment information provided to the patient. Another scenario includes obtaining consent for treatment through deceptive presentation.

b. Criminal Liability

284. A physician who is an accessory to a patient's suicide may be sent to prison for twenty years. A physician will not be criminally responsible for an action required urgently to save a person's life, protect a person from injury, or prevent serious damage to the person's health, even if the circumstances prevented receipt of informed consent. A physician will not be criminally responsible for an action required urgently to avert a patient's illegal assault of dimensions that presented substantial jeopardy to the life, liberty, body, or property of the physician or other people. But the physician will not be regarded as acting in self-defence when his or her untoward conduct incites a patient to assault in a development that was a possibility the physician anticipated. A physician will not be held criminally responsible for an action urgently required to save life, liberty, body, or property, whether his or her own or another's, from tangible danger of serious injury in each situation when he or she is faced with no alternative but to act accordingly.

13. Treatment of Patient by Virtue of 'Neither Shalt Thou Stand Against the Blood of Thy Neighbour' Law

285. The 1998 Law of '[T]hou shalt not stand against the blood of thy neighbour' imposes on every person in Israel the duty of lending a helping hand to other people, in conditions stated in the law, which determines that a person is obliged to go to the aid of any other person with whom he or she is confronted and whose life is in serious, immediate danger, who may be in danger of losing a limb, or whose health may be impaired in consequence of a sudden happening, provided that he or she is capable of rendering aid without risk to him- or herself or to anybody else. Furthermore, the law explains that a person who informs the authorities or summons any other person capable of rendering the required aid shall be regarded as having lent a helping hand to the law.

Anybody who contravenes the law will be fined.

14. Appointment of Patient's Representative

286. Paragraph 16 of the Patient's Rights Law determines:

(a) A person undergoing treatment may appoint his representative, who will be authorized to consent as a proxy to medical treatment. His power of attorney will state the circumstances and conditions on which the representative is empowered to consent to medical treatment on behalf of the person who is to undergo medical treatment, and b) the Minister is empowered to issue instructions about the procedure for the granting of a power of attorney in accordance with this clause of the Law.

In Amendment No. 16 to the Patient Rights Law, the legislature revised section 16 regarding the appointment of a representative by the patient. The new section stipulates that the patient may appoint a representative authorized to consent to medical treatment on their behalf. The amendment added that the patient may do so through continuous enduring power of attorney for personal matters, which includes their health matters according to the legal Capacity and Guardianship Law, or medical enduring power of attorney as defined in section 32O of the law.

In addition, as part of Amendment No. 16 to the law, new Sections were added that establish new provisions, creating a new role to represent the patient as a temporary decision-maker. Section 14A stipulates that when the specialist physician determines that the patient lacks capacity or legal guardianship regarding their medical affairs, a social worker at the medical institution where the medical treatment is to be provided, with approval from the institution's director or an authorized person, and from the health fund or an authorized person, may issue written consent to act as a temporary decision-maker for the patient if the conditions specified in the section are met.

B. Competency: Minors

287. The patient's consent to be treated medically should be given by a legally fit person to consent. As a rule, every adult is legally fit to opt for medical treatment unless a court order has disqualified him or her because of insanity or mental deficiency. In respect of minors, the authority for valid consent to treatment is normally vested in their parents, who are their natural guardians. In contrast, for adult patients who are legally incapacitated, consent must be authorized by guardians appointed by order of the court. When a patient is disabled from opting for or against treatment due to a psychic condition, mental deficiency, or the temporary effect of illness or medication, the application should be made to such an authoritative body as the law court or welfare service to take the proper legal steps for the appointment of a guardian. Although the minor is not devoid of legal competency, the law appoints a guardian to protect the minor's interests because of his or her tender age, physical weakness, and inexperience. Because parents are natural guardians of their children during the latter's adolescence, a concerned authority requires parental consent before medically treating children. Both parents should normally act by agreement. Ostensibly, the person who is prepared to treat the child requires the consent of both parents. However, their consent may be specific or implied.

288. Moreover, it should be assumed that one parent's consent implies agreement with the other unless there is proof of a disagreement between them. In case of emergency, either of the parents may decide independently, and the consent of one of them will be legal, total, and adequate. If the parents have separated, they must decide who of the two will be the guardian of the minor and have their decision ratified by a court order. In the event of the death of one parent, the minor's surviving parent will assume guardianship.

289. The law court is empowered to appoint a guardian if the minor's parents have died, decreed incompetent, or deprived of their guardianship by court order. The court is also authorized to appoint a guardian in addition to a single parent, if the other parent has died, has been decreed incompetent, or has lost guardianship rights by court order, or is physically incapable of, or prevented from acting as a guardian, or is of unknown identity, or has not recognized a child born out of wedlock, or is handicapped in his or her duties as a guardian. The court may also appoint a guardian for an unborn child or a person not yet 'identifiable'. The court is empowered to supply a 'needy' minor with a mentor who will advise the minor's custodian. The judge may consign the minor to the care of a welfare officer. The judge may ordain rules for the treatment of the minor. Upon the assumption of guardianship, parents accept all the rights and duties involved in the care of the minor, including whatever medical treatment the latter requires. The performance of duties demands that the guardian acts for his or her ward's welfare as any devoted person would in similar circumstances.

290. The 1962 Law on Legal Competency and Guardianship states that a guardian is obliged to hear the opinion of his or her ward if the latter can understand a problem and if he or she can make an opinion articulate. However, a far more epoch-making regulation may be found in the 1996 Law for the Detection of the Acquired Immune Deficiency Syndrome (AIDS) Virus in Minors. Section 1(A) states:

> despite all legal regulations to the contrary, the examination of a minor to detect the AIDS Virus shall take place at the request of the minor even without the endorsement of his parent or guardian (henceforth his representative), provided that the examination takes place in a medical institution … and has been approved in writing by a physician on that institution's staff. Furthermore, the examination may be made only after compliance with the following conditions:
>
> (1) The physician has given the minor a complete and thoroughly understood explanation of each stage of the examination and its significance, of the ways by which the virus may infect a person and of the measures a person may take to avoid infection.
> (2) In a talk with the minor, although the physician has raised the possibility that the minor's representative be approached for his consent, the minor has refused.
> (3) The physician has become convinced that in keeping with the minor's age, his mental maturity, and capacity for knowing what he wants, the examination will be to his advantage. However, no application has been made to his representative for his approval.

The law also states:

(1) Despite Regulations in Sub-Section (A), an examination for the detection of the AIDS Virus will not be carried out without his representative's consent if the minor has not reached the age of fourteen, unless the probe has been approved by a board including a social worker and a physician.

Section 2 of the same law lays down:

(a) The minor will be notified of a negative result of his examination to detect the AIDS Virus by one of the following persons trained in this branch of medicine: a physician, a nurse, a social worker.

(b) (1) The minor will be informed of a positive result of his examination to detect the AIDS Virus by a board and in the presence of a welfare officer.

(2) The board, the welfare official, and the minor will discuss the possibility of making the result known to the latter's representative. Upon the minor's consent, the board will invite his representative to a meeting at which he will be told of the examination results and, together with his ward, be guided on how to act and how the minor should be treated. If the minor refuses to involve his representative, the guidance will be given to him alone.

291. Section 3(6) of the Youth Law (Treatment and Observation) lays down:

> where a welfare officer believes that a minor requires treatment and requires a court order to be treated and looked after ... (the court is permitted at his request) to order that a positive result of an examination for the detection of the AIDS Virus be handed over to the person whose charge the minor is.

292. Another law that attaches weight to a minor's wishes is the 1991 Law for the Treatment of Mental Patients as amended in 1995. Section 4(A) states:

> (C) A minor aged fifteen or above, shall not be hospitalized despite his guardian's consent, if he is unwilling, except by court approval, which will accord with the regulations of the Youth Law and the grounds which it lists for the compulsory hospitalization of a minor. (D) If it comes to the knowledge of a person treating a minor in a hospital that the minor has been hospitalized by consent of his guardian. Still, against his own will, he must inform the welfare officer as soon as possible. If the minor is aged fifteen or above, his case must be forwarded to the district psychiatric committee for children and teenagers.

Section 4B states that a minor aged 15 or older is permitted to apply for hospitalization of his or her own free will and may consent to hospitalization in accordance with section 4. However, in the absence of a guardian's consent, he or she may not be admitted to a hospital except by court order in accordance with section 3 of the Youth Law (Treatment and Observation).

An Israeli Law of 2001 ordained free education for minors with long-term ailments, whether hospitalized or residing in their own homes. In addition, the Law of 2000 for Endangered Children (at Day Centres) and the Law for Day Rehabilitation Centres of the same year guaranteed treatment and care for infants younger than the age of 3.

C. *Competency: Mental Patients*

293. Concerning the mentally deficient who are hospitalized, it should be noted that the 1991 Law dealing with their treatment states in section 35(H), 'A patient who has been voluntarily hospitalized will not be given medical treatment without his consent, except in cases of emergency.' The law further states (J), 'A patient must cooperate to the best of his ability in his own treatment' and (K) 'A patient is entitled to be informed of his condition at the discretion of his physician.'

294. A patient, upon hospitalization, is supplied with a pamphlet defining his or her privileges and liabilities, together with an oral explanation by the reception physician. Suppose the patient's medical condition hinders him or her from understanding the pamphlet's contents. In that case, the fact must be recorded in his or her personal file, and the contents of the pamphlet explained as soon as his or her medical condition permits. A copy of the pamphlet dealing with the patient's privileges and liabilities must be prominently displayed in every psychiatric ward. A patient must be associated to the greatest possible extent with the plan for his own or her treatment. A patient is entitled to such medical information about his or her illness as the physician decides he or she should receive. This directive, when reasonably applied, should be regarded as an addition to, rather than a substitute for, the requirements of the Law on Patient's Rights.

295. A mentally deficient person, as a human being and as a patient, is not denied the right to refuse treatment because of the mental illness. However, every case must be examined in the light of its circumstances and every patient's decision must be examined in the light of the person's illness, condition, and fitness at a relevant time.

296. Every human being is entitled to privileges and subject to liabilities. Everyone is subject to legal action unless he or she has been deprived of the entitlement or it has been modified by law or court order. A person who is termed incompetent is one whose insanity or mental deficiency deprives him or her of the ability to control his or her interests. Upon presenting a plea to a court of law, it may pronounce a person legally exempt after a hearing. As has been stated, legal action by the incompetent requires the consent of their representatives. It should be assumed that such legal action should include the incompetent's consent to medical treatment at least in certain circumstances and regarding specified subjects. Consent may be given in advance or retroactively. A court of law is authorized to appoint guardians for the incompetent. Their guardians must supply all their needs. Their duties will oblige every guardian to act in the best interests of their wards as any devoted person would serve a cause to which he or she is dedicated. Concern for the requirements of the incompetent includes providing them with whatever medical care is needed, which means that guardians are authorized to give their consent to such medical treatment as may be necessary.

297. Regarding guardianship, its possessor is obliged to comply with his or her ward's requests if the latter can understand the issue and make his or her wishes intelligible. Wards must be directed by their guardians in all matters relating to the latter's functions, as laid down by the court. The latter is authorized to instruct the guardians in all matters that appertain to the performance of their duties, whether it is requested by the guardian, the Attorney General, their official representatives, or judges. The court may always adopt suitable, temporary measures to protect the interests of the incompetent, at the request of one of the parties, or on its initiative.

298. The Law of Competency authorizes and obliges the law court to supervise the guardians' work and supply them with instructions in all matters that will enable them to perform their duties efficiently. When minors, legal incompetents, and others who cannot manage their affairs are concerned, the court is appointed to substitute for them in deciding whether the commission of some action or other will advantage one of them or whether he or she will benefit more considerably from the omission of that action. Regarding guardianship, when the question relates to the ward's person or property the court is empowered to provide the answer that best promotes the child's welfare. In every matter, the court must put itself into the ward's shoes and speculate on how the ward would decide if the ward were normal and not incapable of insisting on his or her rights or of realizing his or her inclinations.

V. Duty of Medical Secrecy

A. Legal Secrecy

1. Criminal Sanctions

299. The 1977 Penal Code lays down that a person who divulges confidential information supplied during the practice of a trade or profession may be sentenced to a prison stretch of six months unless the law has obliged the person to reveal knowledge. The 1981 Law on the Protection of Privacy lays down that anyone who divulges information of which he or she is the recipient by virtue of a position as a worker, director, or holder of an information store may be sent to prison for five years, unless the action is in the normal performance of duties, in implementation of the law mentioned above, or in the course of a law-courts proceedings. A person who maliciously publishes any detail of another's health may be sent to prison for five years.

2. Disciplinary Sanctions

300. The 1996 Law on Patient's Rights decrees that medical personnel or workers at a medical institution shall observe silence on all such information about a person who undergoes treatment as may reach their eyes or ears during their duties or work. The 1976 modern version of the Physicians' Ordinance lays down that the Minister of Health is empowered to cancel or suspend a physician's licence if the latter has contravened any of the Patient's Rights Law Regulations.

301. In addition, it is important to note that in the Patient Rights Law, in section 19(b), the legislator instructed the treater, and in a medical institution-the institution's director, to take necessary measures to ensure that employees maintain confidentiality of the matters brought to their attention despite their knowledge, while fulfilling their duties or during their work.

B. Contractual Duty

302. The medical worker who is pledged to secrecy regarding any information he or she may absorb during professional activity is duty-bound to silence also by the laws on contracts. Any agreement to render services includes an implicit condition requiring the factor to refrain from divulging information of the kind referred to above.

C. Unprotected Information

303. The Law on Patient's Rights lays down that the transfer of medical data from one medical worker to another for a patient's treatment is not illegal, nor is it illegal to transfer information about a patient's health to the medical institution that is treating the patient or to that institution's hospital worker whose task is to evaluate, record, or report on the medical data of the patient. It is also permitted to divulge medical information both for publication and scientific journals and for research purposes, provided that no details exposing the identity of a person under treatment are circulated.

304. Following Amendment No. 15 to the Patient Rights Law-2023, a Subsection was added to section 20 allowing the transfer of information after death for the purpose of body identification or determining the cause of death to one of the following: the National Institute of forensic Medicine, including a medical examiner assisting therein, or another qualified healthcare provider authorized by law to perform such actions.

D. Legal Exposure

1. General

305. Sundry pieces of legislation deal with functionaries who are the recipients of information because of, and during, the performance of their duties. Such legislation is of three types: (1) regulations that are not concerned with permitting or banning the spread of information; (2) regulations that permit information to be divulged; and (3) regulations that ordain that information be divulged. The first group of regulations comprises directives relating to security in various branches of medical activity. These oblige workers to be thoroughly examined medically. The results are all set before the employer; some are passed on to the District Inspector of Labour and even to the Labour Exchange. Suppose an employee exercises his or her right of refusal to present for examination. In that case, he or she is liable to face the consequences by being excluded from entrance to the labour force. The second group of regulations clearly states the circumstances in which specific information may be divulged. The third group of regulations, as has been stated, provides for the legal transmission of information. Many of the regulations oblige, empower, or allow a physician to pass medical information about a patient on to the authorities, to functionaries, or to other people apart from the patient. The axiom 'for the good of the public' is a motive for most relevant regulations that provide arrangements for extraordinary situations. The right to medical confidentiality is waived in these circumstances.

2. Information Gleaned from the Public Records Office

306. The 1965 Law for the Registration of the Population decrees that every member of the population is entitled to obtain information about himself from public records. Everyone is entitled to be informed of the name and home address of any registered person. If the person is an interested party, he or she may be given a registered person's date of birth or other statistics, such as the regulations' details. In performing their duties, the following officials have free access to the records: the ministers of the interior and defence, the Attorney General, the Inspector General of the police, and any other person authorized by a law court.

3. Medical Centres

307. The 1976 Public Health Ordinance (Preservation of Records) conditions the receipt of a written permit from the Director of a medical centre or from a person officially appointed to approve the removal of any type of record from a medical centre.

4. Release of Special Information

308. The 1940 Public Health Ordinance authorized the Minister of Health to issue regulations requiring the directors of medical centres and their physicians to supply government physicians appointed for the purpose with any medical reports or information that they demand. This official, or a member of the Minister of Health's staff who is the official appointee, is empowered to inspect the hospital register. Every member of the staff is enjoined to make this task easier. Suppose an informant or complainant apprises the Minister of Health that an action has been taken, or an error committed that gives grounds for the suspicion that a patient's rights have been abused in any way during hospitalization, or treatment at a clinic, or in consequence of said hospitalization or treatment. In that case, the government physician is empowered to examine the medical records of the patient's illness. The Director of the hospital or the clinic physician is obliged to furnish the government official with such information as he or she may demand, to further the enquiry, including such information in the medical records as concerns other patients, provided that the identities of the latter are not disclosed. None of those mentioned above regulations replace, or detract from, the injunctions laid down in any other directive of the Public Health Ordinance or any other regulations. They do not permit the exposure of patients' identities.

5. Reporting Irregularities

309. The Director of a medical institution or, during his or her absence, the senior medical officer in charge is obliged to report the following occurrences to the Director of Health Services in the Ministry of Health:

(a) faulty instruments, if, during medical treatment, an instrument has caused material injury to a patient or hospital worker;
(b) an external or internal state of emergency at the medical centre, affecting, or threatening to affect, its normal activity;
(c) a fault in the supply of electricity, gas, or water to all, or part, of the hospital;
(d) a fault or suspension in the working of any service that is essential to the hospital's normal functions;
(e) material damage to a patient, namely a major disablement or loss of a vital organ during, or because of, medical treatment.

6. Failure to Recover from Anaesthetization

310. The 1980 Regulations on Public Health (Failure to Recover from Anaesthetization) decree that the hospital Director, or the head of the ward in which a patient is hospitalized, must send an urgent report to the Director of Health Services of the Ministry of Health on any case in which a patient who has been hospitalized does not regain consciousness after he or she has been given an anaesthetic. The report must be forwarded within ten days after the incident.

7. Report on Cancer Illness

311. The 1982 Public Health Regulations (Report and Specific Information on Cancer Illness) decree that a hospital Director must forward a report to the government physician in charge of the registration of cancer illness in the Ministry of Health on every diagnosis of a malignant growth during a person's histopathological, haematological, or cytological examination, during a pathological eye probe, or the hospitalization of a person, if the phenomenon mentioned above develops while he is convalescing. It should be re-emphasized that the Ministry of Health must be given notice of every case of malignant growth, whether it is in the brain, the ovarium, the thyroid gland, or the urine bladder, whether the disease is detected in a person who is still alive or already dead. The report will be forwarded within thirty days after the patient has been examined. It will be forwarded in an envelope marked confidential medical to be opened only by the government physician, or under his or her vigilant eye. The government physician also has the right to order the hospital Director to supply him or her with the specific information to authenticate the diagnosis. This may be in the form of a microscopic slide, prepared during the histological, cytological, or haematological examinations, and an X-ray photograph. Authentication requests will be passed on by the Director General of the Ministry of Health to a committee of experts, who will deliver their recommendations to the government physician. The latter will not directly contact the person whose data have been discussed by the committee until the patient's physician has signified agreement in writing.

8. Notification of Birth

312. The 1965 Law on the Registration of the Population decrees that notification of birth in Israel shall be sent to the Officer of Records within ten days after the event. The proprietor must make notification of the institution where the baby has been born, or if the birth was elsewhere, by the baby's parents, the physician who officiated at the birth, and the midwife. An Israeli resident whose child has been born outside Israel is obliged to supply the Records Officer with the baby's vital statistics within thirty days after the birth. In addition, any person in charge of an abandoned baby is committed to oblige and inform the Records Officer of any of the baby's registration particulars that he or she may know and of any other details of the birth that may be in his or her possession.

9. Birth of Defective Babies

313. The 1982 Public Health Regulations (Notification of Births of Defective Babies) decree that a hospital Director is obliged to post a report to the Director

General of the Ministry of Health on every baby, alive or dead, who is born, or suspected of being born, with one of the following defects: Down's syndrome; any defect, patent or latent, in the central nervous system; lack of limbs; or lack of any part of a limb. This issue has been the subject of court litigations, especially in the context of negligence lawsuits. However, it is worthwhile mentioning that courts have been very reluctant to intervene in these cases.

314. In the draft Public Health Ordinance (Reporting of Births of Infants with Disabilities) (Amendment)-2023, it is proposed to amend the regulations to stipulate that the reporting obligations regarding the diagnosis of diseases and detailed disabilities shall also apply in cases where the disease or disability is diagnosed for the first time during pregnancy, on one hand, and if the diagnosis is made only after the birth has been discharged from the hospital, or during the infancy, adolescence, or adulthood of the diagnosed individual, on the other hand. Additionally, there is a proposal to expand the list of congenital diseases and disabilities that must be reported to the Ministry of Health.

10. Stillborn Babies

315. The 1940 Public Health Ordinance decrees that if a baby emerges stillborn from the mother's womb, after at least twenty-eight weeks of pregnancy, the father or mother, or the midwife, or anyone else who was treating the mother when she gave birth, or during six hours afterwards, is obliged to notify the District Health Office within fifteen days after the birth.

11. Report on Pathological Findings

316. Hospitals maintain tissue committees that are empowered to collect data on every operational removal of an organ or tissue, to examine organs and tissues and reach conclusions as to their nature, in accordance with the 1981 Regulations for Public Health (Removal of Organ and Radiation Treatment, in the Light of the Results of Pathological Treatment Alone).

12. Notification of Violence

317. The Public Health Ordinance empowers the Minister of Health to issue directives ordering all the directors of hospitals or clinics, which must be registered, and all their officials who are responsible for the intake of patients for treatment to take immediate steps to inform the nearest police station of the intake of any injured, unconscious, or dead person, reaching the institutions mentioned above, if there is a reason to suspect that such a person has been involved in an act of violence. The 1975 Regulations for Public Health (Notification of Suspected Violence) were promulgated to exercise these powers, specifying the form and contents of such notifications. They must be transmitted expeditiously and so far, as possible without delay, by telephone and in writing. They must contain as many details as possible about the names, I.D. numbers, and addresses of the people who brought each casualty to the hospital, the number on the licence plate of the vehicle that brought the injured party for treatment, or other details identifying the vehicle, the destination of the injured party after treatment, and the name and official capacity of the informant. If suspicion is aroused in the mind of the physician, or a physician being absent, in the mind of a nurse, after the injured party has been registered for treatment, that the latter has been involved in an act of violence, he or she must immediately inform the hospital Director. He or she will ensure that the police are urgently notified if they have not already been informed. Moreover, the Ordinance authorizes a particular medical institute manager to forbid a person from entering the institute, entirely or partially, if recidivism is proven against a violent person who acts against the institute and/or its staff.

13. Notification of Infectious Diseases

318. The Public Health Ordinance decrees that the incidence of infectious diseases must be reported. An infectious disease is described in the Ordinance. Therefore, a physician who is treating a patient or is called to a patient's home must notify the District Health Officer as soon as it becomes known that the patient's disease is infectious.

319. The 1930 Midwives Regulations obliged anyone who is a certified practitioner of midwifery to communicate with the District Health Officer at the earliest possible moment if he or she has revealed any possible source of infection.

320. The 1933 Quarantine Regulations decree that when a ship docks in an Israel port, the ship's physician is required to answer questions by the quarantine officials, to whom he or she must submit a written report on all the events of a public health nature that occurred during the voyage.

14. Notification of Death

321. The 1965 Public Records Law decrees that notification of death must be sent within forty-eight hours of the demise to the authority whose duty is to issue a burial certificate. Accordingly, such notification will be forwarded by the Administrative Director of the institution in which the death took place, or by the physician who pronounced the patient dead, or, in the absence of a physician, by any person who was at the deceased's bedside at the time of death.

15. Notification of Death to the Deceased's Relative and the Director of Health Services

322. The 1980 Public Health Regulations (Notification of Death and Unusual Occurrences) decree that if a person dies in a medical institution, the Director of the ward in which he has died, or the hospital's Director, will notify the deceased's relative as soon as possible. In the following seven cases also, the Director of the hospital must notify the Ministry of Health's Director of Medical Services:

(1) Death within twenty-four hours of admission to the hospital if the disease is not of long duration, consumptive, or chronic.
(2) Death caused by medication, transfusion of blood or blood products, or injection of any other fluid.
(3) Immediate death during an operation or any other intrusive treatment, or death within seven days afterwards.
(4) Death after the operation or intrusive treatment if the patient does not return to consciousness.
(5) The death of a woman during pregnancy or childbirth, or within forty-two days afterwards, or within a year if the cause of death is concerned with pregnancy or childbirth.
(6) Death as the result of a suicidal act.
(7) Death that determines the Director of the hospital or the Sick Fund to set up a committee of enquiry as detailed in the 1996 Patient's Rights Law.

16. Information about a Minor

323. The 1955 Welfare Law (A Series of Procedures Relating to Minors, the Mentally Ill, and Missing Persons) decrees that when a matter is pending law-court decision which may be affected by the judge's need or right to consider the immaturity of a minor, even if the latter is a party to the case, the court is empowered to order a welfare officer to make enquiries and deliver his or her opinion in writing. On preparing the report, the welfare officer has the right to enter any place where the minor is or is likely to be and examine any person believed to have information relating to the minor. The interrogated person is bound to give complete, sincere answers to the welfare officer unless, in doing so, any of the answers is liable to involve him or her criminally.

324. The 1953 Teenage Employment Law permits the employment of teenagers under the age of 18, with reservations, provided that a licensed physician has medically examined them. Suppose the examination reveals that a youth is unfit to work physically, or that his or her work will affect his or her health. In that case, the licensed medical institution will inform the District Inspector of Labour in writing. The latter will send copies of the notification to one of the youth's parents, the employer, and the local general labour exchange. These regulations also apply to a person under the age of 21 if employment poses a special danger to the person's health.

17. The Mentally Ill

325. The 1955 Welfare Law (Procedural Rules Relating to Minors, the Mentally Ill, and Missing Persons) decrees that when a case awaits a law-court decision depending on the judge's obligation or right to consider a mental patient's illness, even if the latter is not a party to the case, the court is permitted to order a welfare officer to investigate and present the conclusions in writing. While preparing the report, the welfare officer has the right to access any place where the mentally ill person is, or is presumed to be, and interrogate any person who may enlighten the officer with information about the person with a mental health condition. Anyone interrogated must answer truthfully and fully unless the information is self-incriminatory.

326. In accordance with the 1991 Law on the Treatment of the Mentally Ill, any person who, while enforcing the law, or committing an action connected with its enforcement, receives a piece of information concerning another person is obliged to treat the knowledge as confidential and may divulge it only in the following circumstances:

(a) The subject of the information has agreed to the exposure, knowingly and in writing if he or she does not cancel consent in writing.
(b) In the opinion of the physician treating the person with a mental health condition, the exposure is required to facilitate the patient's treatment, or essential to the dictates of the law and its regulations.
(c) The law decrees or permits exposure.
(d) He or she has a court permit to reveal the knowledge.
(e) He or she is required to reveal the knowledge to a police officer who is a Deputy Commander or of higher rank, or to any other person authorized by the Minister of Justice, during an investigation of crimes that have been committed, or for the prevention of a crime. In addition, such exposure of information requires the Chief of the Mental Health Services, a hospital Director, or the District Psychiatrist.

Physicians are allowed to use their judgment in supplying their patients, their patients' guardians, or their patients' relatives with information about the state of their patients' health. A hospital's medical Director is ordered to inform the head of the Mental Health Services when admitting a person with a mental health condition to the hospital when releasing the patient, when transferring the patient to another hospital, or when the person with a mental health condition die. The Chief of Mental Health Services is permitted to obtain information about a patient from any worker at a hospital or clinic.

18. Retarded Persons

327. The 1969 Welfare Law (Treatment of the Retarded) decrees that if a physician, or welfare, health, or education official, is of the opinion that a person with whom work has brought him or her into contact is mentally disabled, he or she must notify the welfare officer or a physician appointed by the Minister of Welfare for this purpose. The physician will purvey the information to the welfare officer, who will notify the person in charge of the retarded person. If a welfare officer hears of a retarded person, he or she has the right to demand information about the person from anyone who may help him or her in the performance of duties. The interrogated person must give complete and truthful answers, except insofar as the replies may be self-incriminatory. A judicial decree which provides that a person is incapable of being held on a criminal trial due to a mental disease or that the accused was insane at the time a criminal commission may serve the police forces to reach the accused in accordance with the decree, as well as the welfare officer if the accused was not under an arrest.

19. Firearms Permit

328. The 1949 Firearms Law decrees that a Records Officer who requests a firearms licence will forward it to the Director General of the Ministry of Health. Suppose the latter receives information that the applicant has been hospitalized by virtue of mental illness, real or suspected. In that case, he or she has the right to supply the Records Officer with details of the applicant's hospitalization. To make the report complete, the Director is authorized to use such knowledge about the treatment given to the applicant as is lodged with the Ministry of Health or with any of the branches of the defence establishment. When a physician or psychologist who is healing a person believes that the patient possesses a firearm or is given possession of a firearm that may endanger the patient or other people, he or she must notify the Director General of the Ministry of Health. A Records Officer is empowered to demand that an applicant for a firearms licence be immediately examined by a physician appointed by the Health Ministry's Director General. The results of the examination will be forwarded to the Records Officer.

20. Military Personnel

329. The 1967 Military Service Regulations decree that a hospital employee licensed to practise medicine, including the hospital Director, must provide the Enlistment Officer, a soldier licensed to practise medicine, with complete details concerning every military conscript admitted to the hospital. This information must include diagnoses, treatments, operations, and details of other medical data. This regulation is also valid for a psychologist, or any physician who is not a hospital employee, with respect to a soldier whom he or she has examined or treated.

21. Police

330. The 1927 Criminal Procedure (Evidence) Ordinance empowers a police officer, or a certified policeman, to conduct investigations of the commission of crimes. In the conduct of these activities, the police official is permitted to interrogate any person who is believed to know the facts of an offence and the circumstances in which it was committed. The interrogated person is obliged to give truthful answers to every question posed by an investigating officer except for such answers as may involve him or her in danger of being charged with a crime.

331. The 1977 Penal Code decrees that any person who, knowing that another is contemplating the commission of a crime, refrains from taking any reasonable measures against it before or during its commission may be sent to prison for two years.

332. The legislator has borrowed the principle of the 'Good Samaritan' in the Law of 1998, stipulating 'Neither shalt thou stand against the blood of thy neighbour,' which obliges a person to tender emergency assistance in the circumstances described in the law.

22. Statistics

333. The 1972 revised version of the Statistics Ordinance empowers the Central Statistics Bureau to collect, classify, analyse, re-edit, and circulate statistics concerning the population's activities in the sphere of health. A person from whom the Statistics Ordinance empowers the Central Bureau of Statistics or any other statistics authority to demand personal details must complete an official questionnaire, supplying his vital statistics to the best of his knowledge. Likewise, to the best of his or her knowledge and good faith, a person who treats patients is obliged to answer all the questions the certified authority addresses.

A certified statistician has the right to enter any hospital for a requisite interrogation that will enable him or her to complete his statistics.

23. Information on Physician's Health

334. The revised version of the Physicians' Ordinance provides for the medical examination of a licensed physician or a candidate for a licence to practice medicine if the Director General of the Ministry of Health has reason to suspect that either of the above-mentioned has contracted a dangerous disease. In such an event, the Ordinance authorizes the Director to demand information from an institution or a private physician if he or she has grounds for believing that medical data relating to the suspect's state of health may be lodged with either of them.

24. Social Security

335. The 1995 comprehensive version of the National Insurance Law authorizes the minister to determine directives in insurance against disablement, requiring every person, including a physician, to supply the establishment with any information he possesses connected with a person's disability. In addition, an injured person, or, in the event of death, his or her dependants, must provide the Institute for Social Security with a certificate of exemption from secrecy on the Institute's demand, before action is taken to deal with the insurance claim.

25. Testimony in the Law Court

336. The new version of the 1971 Ordinance on Evidence decrees that a person is not required to submit evidence containing an admission of guilt at the core of an offence of which he or she is accused, or likely to be accused. However, every witness must submit any piece of evidence which he or she possesses to the court. The 1977 Penal Code decrees that any person summoned to the witness box or to supply the court with information during a trial and refusing to give evidence may be sentenced to a two-year term of imprisonment.

337. The Contempt of Court Ordinance states that if a witness has refused to be examined, as required by law, or declines to answer questions during lawful interrogation, without providing any justifiable reason for refusal, the court can have him or her arrested forthwith and imprisoned for a maximum period of one month, unless, in the meantime, and before the conclusion of the trial, he or she consents to be examined and answer questions. In the context of the Laws on Evidence, the right of testimonial privilege means, in fact, the right or duty to abstain from giving evidence. This right may allow or compel a party to refrain from answering a question or to refuse to provide a document in the law court.

338. Furthermore, giving false testimony knowingly is a criminal offence in most countries worldwide. In Israel, section 237 of the Penal Law stipulates that the punishment for perjury is imprisonment for up to seven years: 'A person who testifies knowingly falsely in a judicial proceeding regarding a material issue in that proceeding, commits the offence of perjury, and the punishment is imprisonment for up to seven years. If the act was done for personal gain, the punishment is imprisonment for up to nine years.'

339. Perjury requires two central elements to prove the offence: criminal intent (*mens rea*) and the actual act of giving false testimony (*actus reus*).

26. Physician's Testimonial Privilege

340. A physician is not required to give evidence relating to a person who depends on his or her services, if he or she has acquired his knowledge while practising his profession and if his or her knowledge is such as is normally communicated to a physician, in a patient's belief it is confidential. However, if the patient waives the privilege of confidentiality, or if the court finds that the need to expose the evidence for justice supersedes the importance of suppression, the witness will speak out. The same ruling applies to any person who works on behalf of a physician, of a medical institution, or in the professional team working with a physician treating patients and has gleaned a piece of information intended for the physician's ear. The rules mentioned above remain valid even after the witness has retired from practice or medical employment. If the patient waives the right of silence, the physician is obliged to give clear and complete evidence.

341. The Evidence Ordinance was amended by Amendment No. 20; following the amendment, section 49(c) was added and divided into two subparagraphs:

(1) If an immunity claim is alleged under section 49, the hearing on the claim shall be conducted in closed chambers. If the court decides to hear the testimony, it shall do so in closed chambers unless ordered to conduct the entire or partial proceedings publicly.
(2) If the hearing, as described in subparagraph (1), is conducted in closed chambers, the court may permit a specific person or group of people to be present during the hearing, either in whole or in part.

VI. Right to Complain, Access to Medical Records

A. *Complaints*

342. The 1996 Patient's Rights Law ordered every hospital Director to appoint a staff member to look after the interests and rights of the hospital's inmates. It is that member's business, among other duties, to turn a hearing ear to patients' complaints, investigate them and deal with them. Complaints related to the quality of the institution's medical services shall be referred to by the staff member to the hospital's director. Following Amendment No. 16 to the Patient Rights Law, the role of the Patient Rights Advocate also includes receiving complaints from patients, examining them, and handling them, including complaints regarding temporary decision-maker approvals.

343. The Patient's Rights Law empowers the Ministry's Director General and hospital directors to appoint 'investigation committees' to examine patients' complaints. The findings and conclusions of an investigating committee must be presented to the official who appointed it and to the complainant. In addition, the Director General is empowered to initiate disciplinary action or address a complaint to the police when there is suspicion of a criminal offence.

344. In addition, following Amendment No. 12 to the Mental Health Treatment Law, a new section 24F was added, which stipulates that the Minister shall appoint, with the consent of the Chief Justice of the Supreme Court, a judge of a district court or a judge of the Supreme Court, in rotation, as the investigator responsible for complaints regarding the conduct of committee members in the course of their duties, including complaints regarding procedural management under this law.

345. The section also provides that if the investigator finds that a complaint was justified, he may recommend to the Minister to dismiss the committee member, suspend his appointment pending conditions set by the Minister, or recommend against reappointing him for another term.

346. For investigating the complaint, the investigator may review the minutes of the committee meeting and consult with its members and participants.

347. The investigator responsible for complaints shall not investigate complaints subject to appeal according to law.

B. Access to Medical Records

348. The Patient's Rights Law decrees that a patient has the right to receive the required information before being treated as a condition for his or her consent before treatment, and after treatment. The law orders the physician to document the progress of his or her treatment and make the documentation available to the patient for study. If the physician feels that knowledge of the facts is likely to cause serious damage to the patient's physical or mental health or endanger his or her life; the physician can refrain from supplying the patient with any or some of the information. Still, he *must* notify the ethics committee, which is empowered to ratify, modify, or cancel the decision.

349. The 1991 Law for the Treatment of the Mentally Ill decrees that a mental patient has the right to a physician's discretion.

350. The 1981 Law for the Protection of Privacy decrees that any person has a right to study information about himself or herself kept in a databank.

351. The Medical Association's ethical principles establish that the patient has a right to be informed by the physician as far as the patient can comprehend it.

VII. Medical Fees

352. A physician employed by a medical institution receives a salary in accordance with Israeli health establishment procedures, which vary from time to time. However, if the physician engages in private practice, he or she is free to determine his or her own tariff for medical services according to inclination and subject to the patients' consent and sundry directives, as laid down in the State of Israel's Contract Laws.

353. The Medical Association's ethical rules determine certain reservations with respect to physicians' fees. First, a physician is not allowed to accept any remuneration for sending a patient for an examination, for treatment, for a medical instrument, or for recommending a sanatorium or a convalescent home. Second, a physician must not share a gratuity or compensation for recommending other treatments. Third, a physician may not share the income from medical practice with anyone who is not a physician unless said partner is not authorized to interfere in anything connected with giving medical services. Fourth, suppose a physician is requested to issue a medical certificate. In that case, he or she has the right to charge for the document, but not to request or be given any compensation for profit that may accrue to the individual who requested the document., it is customary for a physician to treat his or her medical colleagues and their dependents, as well as medical students, gratis. However, he or she may accept compensation for any expenses incurred.

354. The 1979 Law of Enrichment without Recourse to Law determines that if a person, through kindness of heart, or as reason dictates, performs an action to save the life, body, or health of another, without being obliged, and expends, or commits to expending, a sum of money during this action, the beneficiary is obliged to compensate him or her for his/her reasonable expenditure. These directives are also valid for a person who is obliged to act in compliance with the 1998 'Neither shalt thou stand against the blood of thy neighbour' Law by giving aid to a sick or injured person with whom he or she is confronted and whose life, body, or health is in serious jeopardy as the result of a sudden happening.

Chapter 2. The Physician-Patient Relationship in Specific Terms

§1. The Minor Patient

I. Legal Provisions

355. Paragraph 1 of the 1962 Law on Legal Competence and Guardianship decrees that every person, from cradle to grave, benefits from civic privileges and is obliged by civic duties. A person younger than 18 is a minor and one who has reached the age of 18 is an adult, as per paragraph 3 of the law. A person's age is determined from the beginning of the date of birth, which, according to paragraph 11 of the law, begins with the sunset before the birth. Every person is competent for legal actions, in accordance with paragraph 2 of the law but a minor's legal action requires the consent of his or her representative, according to paragraph 4 of the law. Said consent may be in advance or retroactive.

356. Paragraph 14 of the law makes a minor's parents his or her natural guardians. As such, the parents are obliged to act in the minor's best interests just as devoted parents would act in similar circumstances, as stated in paragraph 17. Moreover, the law court is empowered to appoint a guardian of the minor even in an embryo state, as laid down in paragraph 33.

357. The court may order the performance of an operation or the adoption of other medical measures in the treatment of a minor if it is convinced by a medical opinion that the action to be taken is essential to the preservation of the minor's physical or mental health, as recorded in paragraph 68.

II. The Capacity of Minor Patients Concerning Medical Treatment

358. *See supra*-Part II, Chapter 1, §1, IV, B.

§2. The Mental Patient and Involuntary Placement

I. General: Patient's Rights

359. In 2000, Israel's Knesset passed a law to rehabilitate the mentally defective in society. It was intended that attention be paid to their rehabilitation and identification with society to facilitate their attaining the best possible degree of independent activity and quality of life. The law defines such invalids as members of society who suffer from mental disorders. The rehabilitation, with which the law deals, implies a process directed towards exploiting the potential and inclination of the mentally afflicted within the community's environment to enable them to reach the highest degree of functional independence and quality of life.

Any person older than the age of 18 who is mentally deficient and suffers from invalidity of 40% or more. Because of a mental disorder or such, a person's representative has a right to apply to a rehabilitation committee for recognition of entitlement to benefit from a rehabilitation programme. The application must be supported by a professional document from a psychiatrist. The law requires the establishment of a National Rehabilitation Council as an advisory body to the Minister of Health on matters concerning rehabilitation policy for the mentally deficient. For the subject under discussion, it should be taken for granted that a mental patient is a person who has been diagnosed as such by a certified professional who is none other than a psychiatrist. The 1991 Law on the Treatment of Mental Patients, which regulates the treatment of the mentally ill in Israel, also lays down their privileges. All sick persons remain possessed of their civic rights, of which they cannot be deprived by hospitalization. However, their ailments may prevent some of them from protecting their interests, necessitating the appointment of guardians who will care for them.

Additionally, one or another of their rights may have to be limited to further the purpose for which they have been hospitalized, or to protect the interests of other hospital inmates. Upon hospital admission, a mentally ill patient has the right to be given a printed list of his or her rights and obligations and an oral explanation of its contents by the physician in reception. If the patient's medical condition makes him or her incapable of understanding the meanings of the printed words, the facts must be recorded in his or her medical file, and the words must be explained as soon as the state of his or her health permits. A copy of the pamphlet on the rights and obligations must be prominently posted in every psychiatric ward. In general, a mental patient shall not be deprived of his or her privileges, nor shall any patient be conditioned in any way except in accordance with the regulations of the law. The essential purpose of hospitalization is to provide a patient with medical treatment; no patient shall be admitted to the hospital for the safety of society or of his or her body except as stipulated in the abovementioned law. A patient in the hospital has every right to obtain such treatment as his or her medical, physical, or mental condition prescribes, in accordance with the conditions and arrangements that are normal procedures in Israel's health establishments. A patient has the right to obtain such medical information about his or her ailment as his or her physician may see fit to impart. A patient will be associated with the programme of his or her treatment as much as possible. A person who has been hospitalized at his or her wish will not be given medical treatment except upon his or her consent unless it is an emergency treatment. If a patient, hospitalized at his or her wish, refuses to receive medical treatment prescribed by the hospital Director, the latter may terminate the stay in the hospital. A patient whose hospitalization is enforced or who has been ordered to accept treatment at a clinic will be given the treatment his or her health requires, even if demurring.

A patient who is a hospital inmate has the right to:

(a) Send and receive uncensored letters.
(b) Receive visitors at times and under conditions determined by the hospital Director.
(c) Communicate with people outside the hospital.

(d) Keep a reasonable number of personal belongings at the bedside and near his or her clothes under conditions decided by the Director.

The hospital's medical Director is empowered to limit these privileges, insofar as necessary for medical reasons. However, he may not deprive the patient of his right to send uncensored letters or communicate by any other means with his lawyer or guardian, with the district psychiatrist the district psychiatric committee, or the Attorney General. The hospitalization of a person does not deprive him or her as a patient of the right to continue to control his or her business, unless the hospital Director declares in writing that the patient is incapable of looking after his or her interests. However, the patient has the right to appeal to the psychiatric committee against such a decision. The law under discussion has empowered the Minister of Health to determine regulations for a patient's engagement in such activities as occupational therapy or a course of rehabilitation. However, during such activities or creating an employer-employee relationship between instructor and patient.

In addition, the Welfare Services for Persons with Disabilities-2022 aims to regulate and anchor the entitlement of every eligible individual to receive welfare services as part of the group of persons with disabilities. It supports their right to independent and autonomous living, freedom, equal participation and engagement in society and the community, and the safeguarding of their personal rights and security. The law specifies who qualifies as part of the group entitled to rights under its provisions and outlines the rights that beneficiaries are entitled to, such as health services provided within therapeutic-residential frameworks, support services for independent and autonomous living, therapeutic-residential care services, daily activity services including rehabilitation through employment and adapted occupation, and other services stipulated by the law.

II. The Mental Health Services

A. *The Head of the Mental Health Services*

360. The Minister of Health is empowered to appoint a psychiatrist employed by the government to Head of Mental Services. His or her duties will be as follows:

(a) to set up and manage all the mental health services and coordinate the activities of all the state's mental health centres;
(b) to inspect hospitals and institutions;
(c) to inspect and control the work of the district psychiatrists, ensuring that it accords with the regulations laid down in the law;
(d) to determine orderly methods of registering psychiatry reports and to inspect and examine arrangements made to preserve their confidentiality;
(e) to standardize procedures for transferring medical information as permitted or required by the law.

B. Authority for Receipt of Information

361. The Head of the Mental Health Services, or an official of the Ministry of Health appointed by the head in writing, is empowered to demand information about a patient from any hospital or clinic worker; to enter any medical establishment, as already noted; to examine any inmate and make any investigation he or she considers just. Furthermore, in the performance of duties, a district psychiatrist is empowered to enter any hospital or clinic in his or her district, to elicit information from any person, and conduct any investigation or examination in compliance with, or as a consequence because of, the regulations contained in the law. Any person to whom the Head of the Mental Health Services or the district psychiatrist applies during his or her activities is obliged to supply whatever information is required.

C. District Psychiatric Committee

362. The Minister of Health is empowered to appoint the district psychiatric committees and children's and teenagers' district psychiatric committees.

363. According to Amendment No. 12 to the Mental Health Treatment Law, 2023, section 24 specifies that the Minister shall appoint members to district psychiatric committees from the following list:

- A list of qualified lawyers eligible for appointment as judges in the Small Claims Court, as determined by the Minister of Justice.
- The Minister evaluates a list of psychiatrists in consultation with the Israeli Medical Association, provided that no district psychiatrist or hospital director specializing in psychiatric care may be appointed.
- In each district, the senior magistrate will determine the committee members and oversee pertinent matters. Each psychiatric committee will consist of three members: one qualified lawyer serving as chair and two psychiatrists.
- The term of office for a psychiatric committee member is five years, with the possibility of reappointment for one additional term, not exceeding two consecutive terms. The Director of Mental Health Services will monitor the regular operation of these psychiatric committees.

III. Legal Responsibility of the Mentally Ill

364. The 1977 Penal Code decrees that a person shall not be held criminally responsible for an act he or she has committed if, during its performance, a sickness of his or her mind or a deterioration of intellectual faculties considerably reduces the person's competence to:

(a) Understand what he or she was doing or the illegality of his or her action.
(b) Refrain from committing the action.

The Penal Code also decrees that a person shall not be held criminally responsible for an act he or she committed at a time when his or her lack of control over his or her physical movements made it impossible to choose between performing the act or refraining from doing it, for example, when the action is committed through physical compulsion that the performer cannot shake off, or it is caused by reflex or distorted response during somnambulism, automatism, or hypnotism.

365. The exemption mentioned above from liability may apply only when two elements exist: a mental disease and an uncontrollable or irresistible impulse. The onus of proving the existence of these factors falls on the defendant, who will be exonerated when it is the opinion of the court that the impulse was so strong that the defendant could not resist it in any circumstances because he or she was enslaved by such a dominant mental condition resulting from his or her mental illness as completely deprived the person of self-will.

IV. Hospitalization

A. *Hospitalization after Examination*

366. When there is a court order for hospitalization, a sick person will not become an inmate of a hospital until after a medical, mental, and physical examination at the hospital, determining the need for admission. If the patient is a minor, he or she must be examined by a children's and teenagers' specialist in psychiatry. If the latter decides to hospitalize the minor, his or her relative must be informed and a welfare officer of the hospital notified.

B. *Voluntary Hospitalization*

367. A sick person who wishes to be hospitalized will sign a form of voluntary hospitalization and consent to treatment. A patient who has been voluntarily hospitalized but wishes to leave the hospital will sign an application for release and be voluntarily released within forty-eight hours after signing the application.

C. *Hospitalization of a Minor*

368. A person in charge of a minor has the right to request the minor's detention at a medical centre and to consent on the minor's behalf to hospitalization and medical treatment. However, such a minor will not be hospitalized at his or her guardian's request if he or she has reached the age of 15 and objects to hospitalization unless a law court has approved his or her admission to a medical centre.

D. Compulsory Hospitalization

1. By Order of the Hospital Director

369. The hospital Director has the right to take a patient in for urgent hospitalization despite the latter's opposition, and without a hospitalization order, after the patient has been lawfully examined and in compliance with legal conditions for his hospitalization. The period of 'urgent hospitalization' shall be for no more than forty-eight hours. At the end of this period, the patient must be released unless, in the meantime, a hospitalization order has been obtained or the patient has given consent to hospitalization.

2. The Hospitalization Order

370. As a result of a psychiatric examination, if the district psychiatrist is convinced that a patient's symptoms accord with the law's rules for hospitalization, he or she is empowered to order that the sick person be brought to the hospital and admitted without delay. The period of stay in the hospital, in accordance with the order for hospitalization, shall be no more than seven days. However, the law allows the district psychiatrist and the psychiatric committee to extend this period.

V. Compulsory Examination

A. Urgent Compulsory Examination

371. A district psychiatrist has the right to issue a written order for the immediate summons of a person to psychiatric examination if he or she has been presented with proof that the person fulfils the following conditions:

(a) He or she is ill, and consequently, the power of judgment or ability to estimate realities is affected to a considerable degree.
(b) He or she is liable to cause immediate, considerable injury to himself or herself or other people around.
(c) He or she has turned down a psychiatric examination.

B. Less Urgent Compulsory Examination

372. The district psychiatrist has the right to sign a written order for a person to appear for a psychiatric examination if it has been brought to the psychiatrist's notice that said person fulfils the following conditions:

(a) He or she has contracted an illness due to which rational faculties and competency to estimate realities are defective to a considerable degree.

(b) His or her behaviour may cause him or her to act as follows:
  (1) He or she is liable to endanger him- or herself or other people around by inflicting physical injury at some time in the future.
  (2) His or her ability to supply his or her own basic needs is seriously impaired.
  (3) He or she is a source of such serious mental strain to other people, disrupting their regular way of life.
  (4) He or she vandalizes property.
(c) He or she has refused to be examined by a psychiatrist.

The district psychiatrist's order for an urgent, or less urgent, compulsory examination shall be valid for ten days after its presentation.

VI. Compulsory Clinic Treatment

373. When the district psychiatrist decides that a psychiatric examination has revealed the presence of conditions requiring the issue of an order for hospital treatment that a clinic can also provide, he or she is empowered to waive the hospitalization order in favour of an order in writing that the patient be given the required treatment at a clinic of the psychiatrist's choosing under conditions laid down by the psychiatrist, during no more than six months. However, suppose it comes to the notice of the district psychiatrist, by written referral from the hospital's Medical Director, that a patient whose hospitalization has been enforced requires further clinical treatment after release. In that case, the psychiatrist is empowered to order such clinical treatment for a maximum period of six months. In case this order for clinical treatment is ignored, the district psychiatrist may order hospitalization.

VII. Appeal Against Hospitalization or Clinical Treatment

374. Appeal against a hospitalization order, against summons for clinical treatment, or against denial of hospitalization may be addressed in writing to the psychiatric committee by any person. The respondent must reply within two days of receipt of the appeal. Suppose the respondent is of the opinion that knowledge of the decision is liable to affect the patient's condition. In that case, this must be stated in writing, so that the committee's chairperson may choose not to edify the patient. The committee must reach its conclusions no later than five days after the appeal has been lodged for a hospital patient and no more than ten days after it has been lodged for a patient to be treated at a clinic. Both parties can summon witnesses, including medical specialists, whose evidence will be heard during the proceedings. The committee may permit a medical expert to examine the patient; the district psychiatrist may voice an opinion at a committee session; the committee is entitled to ratify the decision, cancel it, or insert changes into it, as it may seem fit.

VIII. Implementation of District Psychiatrist's Directives

375. A district psychiatrist who has issued instructions for a compulsory, psychiatric examination, compulsory hospitalization, or compulsory clinic treatment has the right to:

(a) Appoint an executor.
(b) Order that the executor be given a permit to receive aid from the police if it is needed.
(c) Empower the executor and a police escort to enter the patient's house or any hospital; or any other premises detailed in the order, to implement the psychiatrist's objective and use reasonable force both to break in, to enter, and to carry out the order.
(d) Choose the hospital to which the patient will be admitted, the clinic where he or she will be treated, or the place where the patient will be examined, as well as the physician who will examine the patient.
(e) Determine the conditions of hospitalization, of the treatment at a clinic, or of the medical examinations.

IX. Hospitalization or Clinical Treatment of a Defendant

376. When the judges of a person charged with a crime receive information from someone involved in the case or about evidence disclosed by the initiative of the court, to the effect that the defendant's mental illness disqualifies him or her from being tried, the court is empowered to order that the defendant be hospitalized or be given treatment at a clinic. If, after a defendant has been hospitalized by court order, he or she is released by the decision of a psychiatric committee, the Attorney General is empowered to order the defendant to stand trial for the crime he or she allegedly committed. If the patient is hospitalized, he or she cannot be tried for the crime of which he or she has been accused.

377. If a person accused of a crime is brought to trial and the court finds that he or she committed the crime, but there is positive proof, attested by people involved in the case or revealed by the initiative of the court itself, that the defendant was mentally ill when committing the crime and therefore cannot be sentenced, and has not yet recovered, the court will order the person's hospitalization or treatment at a clinic.

378. If the defendant has not complied with the court order requiring clinical treatment, or that his or her mental condition has deteriorated to such an extent that he or she should be sent to a hospital, the district psychiatrist will order hospitalization.

X. Special Observation, Special Care

379. A hospital physician is empowered to sign an extraordinary order for special observation or special care. The order will be issued at the discretion of the physician, in accordance with the patient's condition upon medical examination, if he or she may be categorized as one of the following:

(a) A patient who may cause physical injury to him- or herself or to other people or may vandalize property.
(b) A patient whose physical condition is serious or unsettled.
(c) A patient who is being given treatment that may cause a sudden change in his or her condition.
(d) A patient who is passing through a period of recognizable psychomotor restlessness.
(e) A patient liable to break out of the ward or hospital.
(f) A patient who has requested special observation or care.

If an order for special observation has been issued, the nurse in charge must be always apprised of the patient's condition and whereabouts.

If the order for the special patient observation has been issued, the nurse in charge, who will attend all times and everywhere, may not leave the patient until a replacement appears. In addition, as soon as the order for the special care of a patient has been issued, the nurse in charge, or the appointed nurse, will remove any of the patient's possessions that may cause injury and ensure that similar objects do not come into the patient's possession.

XI. Methods of Enforcement

380. The application of enforcement methods to a patient in hospitals may be exploited only to the extent required for medical treatment or the prevention of the patient's use of violence against him- or herself or anyone else.

The physician will write an order to use force for a short, specified period. The patient will be isolated in a special room reserved for this purpose and containing suitable safety precautions.

The physician's order for tying the patient down will be valid for no more than four hours. The nurse in charge, or the appointed nurse, will examine the patient's condition under restraint at least every half hour. Upon a physician's orders, a patient will be tied to the bed by two or more limbs, only in the room specially prepared for the enforcement.

381. Electric shock treatment will not be given except under the following conditions:

(a) Three of the hospital's physicians approve.
(b) The patient has undergone a physical examination by a physician who has detected no medical reason to oppose the treatment.

(c) A patient whose hospitalization is voluntary, or his or her guardian has agreed in writing if the patient is legally incompetent.

Electric shock treatment will be applied to a patient only under anaesthetization if he or she is given relieving medication and if the necessary security regulations are in force.

XII. Release and Temporary Leave from Hospital

382. A hospital inmate, even one who has been admitted of his or her own free will, may not be allowed to leave the hospital except on the Director's approval if the patient's medical condition justifies release. The hospital's medical Director is permitted to use his or her discretion in deciding to release a patient or grant the patient's temporary leave, provided that the latter's hospitalization was not by court order. The Director may not release a patient who should be serving a prison sentence, but the latter may be granted leave if the Commissioner approves it of Prisons.

XIII. Transfer of Patient

383. A patient may be transferred from one hospital to another only by his or her consent and the mutual consent of both medical Directors. If consent is not unanimous, the district psychiatrist will make the final decision.

XIV. Confidentiality

384. Anyone who is the recipient of information about a sick person is obliged to keep silent and may not divulge the knowledge except in the following circumstances:

(a) The person who is the subject of the information has consented knowingly and in writing, that it be divulged.
(b) The officiating physician is convinced that disclosing the information will ensure successful treatment of the patient or implement the law and its regulations.
(c) The law ordains or allows exposure of such information.
(d) The informant has received a permit for disclosure from the law court.
(e) An authoritative body has ordered the informant to disclose the knowledge during an investigation.

The regulations contain no clause to prevent a physician from supplying the patient, his or her guardian, or relative with details of the patient's condition, subject to the physician's discretion. It should be added that nothing in the regulations prevents the revealing of information for research purposes or the improvement of medical services. However, a person who receives information for either of these purposes is forbidden to use any means to advertise details that may lead to the patient's identity.

However, according to Amendment No. 11 to the Mental Health Treatment Law, the provision allows for the disclosure of information for research or medical service planning purposes, subject to the approval of the Health Committee of the Knesset.

XV. Offences and Punishments

385. Any physician who issues a medical certificate attesting to a person's illness knowing that the person is malingering or who has not gone through all the procedures to decide whether a patient is ill or malingering may be sentenced to five years' imprisonment. Anyone who knowingly causes another to be unnecessarily or illegally hospitalized may also be sentenced to five years' imprisonment.

XVI. Gun Licences

386. According to the Weapons Law of 1949 and the amendments to the Law of 1978 and 2001, data are transferred between the Ministry of Interior and the Ministry of Health to verify the psychological fitness of persons applying for gun licences. The Department of Personal Weapons Licences sends to the Department of Information and Evaluation, Mental Services in the Ministry of Health, a computerized list of persons who have recently applied to receive or renew gun licences. The Department of Information and Evaluation then runs a computer check of the list against the information in the Psychiatric Case Registry that it maintains. The registry contains data about people who have had a psychiatric hospitalization or compulsory outpatient treatment. Finally, the Department of Information and Evaluation delivers its recommendation to the Department of Personal Weapons Licences based on two criteria: the date of the most recent hospitalization and the length of the hospitalization. Persons who have had compulsory outpatient treatment or whose treating physicians/clinicians have reported that they are not psychologically fit to carry weapons receive negative recommendations. An individual whose request to receive or renew a gun licence has been turned down may appeal, in which case a qualified psychiatrist will examine him or her.

387. Despite the above, in Amendment No. 24 to the Firearms Law, a subsection was added to section 11B, which stipulates that the provisions of the section regarding notification of hospitalization or danger by the Ministry of Health shall not apply to firearm-like licence.

§3. THE DYING PATIENT

I. Euthanasia and 'Comparable' Practices

388. Euthanasia is a term, meaning 'a good death' or 'dying well'.[1] The legal and moral problems attributable to the sick person or someone who tends towards death are the most complicated in modern medicine. There is no need to go further than to mention the intricate dilemmas that appear in circumstances in which treatment that will curtail life has to be administered, when there is a need to suspend the treatment of a terminal patient; when assistance to a patient who is bent on suicide may be desirable; or when a patient refuses to be treated, when such refusal will result in death. For examination of the issue, euthanasia will be considered the intentional curtailment of a sick person's life by a physician's act of commission or omission upon the instigation of the patient. A distinction is normally drawn between active, purposive euthanasia, a downright job intended to terminate life, and passive, unopposed euthanasia, which is brought about by the abstention from, or the cessation of, activities for the preservation of life. Occasionally, there is little to discriminate between these types of euthanasia. Israel's Supreme Court distinguishes an illegal act and a sin of omission. The former is always taboo, whereas only omission, which is a breach of a legal duty, is wrong. Active euthanasia is always illegal, whereas passive euthanasia, deriving from a medical omission, is not illegal if it does not breach any legal duty, if it is the result of a decision by a physically sick adult of a sound mind.

389. In Israel, there is an explicit and unequivocal prohibition on active euthanasia, even if requested by a patient.

390. To prepare for situations of incapacity, the legislature enacted the 'Dying Patient Act'. This law allows for an accepted balance to prevent suffering by outlining guidelines for patients to provide advance directives regarding acceptance or refusal of life-prolonging treatment. The law aims to regulate medical treatment for terminally ill patients, striking a proper balance between the sanctity of life, the autonomy of the individual's will, and the importance of quality of life. It is based on Israel's values in morality, ethics, and religion and has garnered broad support across various sectors of society.

II. Euthanasia

391. The idea and process of euthanasia have never achieved recognition in Israel's legislation. An attempt to pass a law in the Knesset in 1996 was a failure. Active euthanasia, even if performed by a qualified physician under the most compelling circumstances, falls within the purview of the following statutory felony. Paragraph

1. A. Carmi, *Euthanasia* (Springer–Verlag 1984), A. Shapira, *The Human Right to Die–Some Israeli and Jewish Legal Perspectives, in The Dying Human* (A. de Vries & A. Carmi eds, Turtledove 1979), A. Steinberg, *Encyclopaedia of Jewish Medical Ethics*, Vol. 4 (Schlezinger 1994).

300 of the 1977 Penal Code decrees that a person who causes another's death by premeditation shall be tried for murder and awarded a life sentence. A lesser homicide offence is involuntary manslaughter. Paragraph 300(C) of the Penal Code decrees that a person who, by commission or omission, causes another's death shall be charged with involuntary manslaughter and sent to prison for twelve years.

The *mens rea* features of this offence are referred to in terms of criminal negligence, recklessness, or indifference as to the outcome of the fatal consequences. Paragraph 309(4) of the Penal Code decrees that a person shall be regarded as having caused another's death if, by commission or omission of an act, he or she has caused the premature death of one who was suffering from an illness or injury that would have caused death, even without that act of commission or omission. No Israeli physician has been tried for murder or manslaughter due to euthanasia, active or passive.

III. Withholding or Withdrawing (Cessation of) Treatment

392. The statutory law does not forbid withholding or withdrawing medical treatment when such treatment has become therapeutically useless in the circumstances and is not in the patient's best interests.

IV. Refusal of Treatment

393. It is generally accepted that the physician must respect the refusal of treatment by a competent patient. However, the Law on Patient's Rights lays down in paragraph 15(2) that, in situations in which the patient is in danger and objects to the receipt of urgently required medical treatment, the physician may administer the medical treatment even against the patient's will, if, after hearing the latter, the ethics committee approves the treatment, provided that the committee is convinced that the following conditions prevail:

(a) The patient has received the necessary information enabling him or her to give informed consent.
(b) Medical treatment is expected to greatly improve the patient's medical condition.
(c) It may reasonably be assumed that the patient will consent retroactively after administering medical treatment.

It appears that the more serious the patient's medical condition is, the more reluctant the ethics committee becomes to approve treatment that is forced on the patient against his or her will, as is borne out by the wording of paragraph 15(2) of the law.

394. What should the law demand when a patient is unconscious and his or her condition makes consent to the required treatment unthinkable? There are two different sets of circumstances creating the dilemma. If the need is for light treatment without surgery, the physician may supply it even without the patient's consent, provided that:

(a) The patient's physical or mental condition does not permit him or her to signify informed consent.
(b) The physician is unaware that the patient may want to refuse medical treatment.

In a medical emergency, the physician may administer emergency treatment even without the patient's informed consent. If, because of the emergency, which may be partly due to his or her physical or mental condition, the latter's informed consent cannot be obtained.

Presumably, there is no resort to such an extreme when the patient, before deteriorating into a state that prevents him or her from expressing his or her wish and opinion, gives a clear and explicit voice to a refusal to be given medical treatment. However, no judgment on this subject has yet been handed down.

395. Concerning the 'living wills,' their validity is dubious. For the time being, it seems that they are without any binding legal effect, although they may serve as a basis for interpreting a patient's wish. A living will, requesting a physician to end a patient's life, would, without any doubt, be void. The Patient's Rights Law supplies a substitute for the judicial 'living will' arrangement by providing a representative. Paragraph 16 of the law determines that a sick person may appoint his or her representative with the authority to consent to medical treatment on his or her behalf. Ostensibly, this does not exclude the patients authorizing a representative to object to treatment, or the continuation of treatment, in certain circumstances. One may assume that in some circumstances this appointment and the representative's decision will be valid, but that in different circumstances the representative's decision will be turned down because of the public good or for other reasons, but, to date, there has been no court decision to provide a precedent.

396. According to Amendment No. 16, a patient may appoint, by his own consent, a reprehensive who is authorized to consent on his behalf to receive medical treatment through the continuous enduring power of attorney for personal matters, which includes his health matters under the Legal Capacity and Guardianship Law or medical enduring power of attorney.

V. Assisting Suicide

397. In 1966, the offence of attempted suicide was removed from the Israeli Criminal Code by the Knesset. However, paragraph 302 of the 1977 Penal Code decrees that a person who causes another's suicide by persuasion or advice or assists in the suicide of another person may be sent to prison for twenty years.

VI. Post-Mortem Examination

398. On a person's demise, if there are reasonable grounds to suspect that the death is from unnatural causes or the result of an illegal act or if the person was an inmate of a hospital for mentally ill patients or a closed institution for backward juveniles, the Attorney General, a ranking officer in the police, a physician, or an interested citizen, is entitled to apply to a judge for an enquiry into the cause of death. Upon presentation of the application, nothing may be done to the corpse except by permission of the judge, who is empowered to order a post-mortem and even an exhumation of the body for a post-mortem.

§4. Medical Treatment of Nazi War Invalids

399. Nazi War Invalids (Medical Treatment) Regulations regulate the invalids' benefit from privileges accrued to them in the sphere of medicine. It should be recorded that, in addition to these regulations, there are others about Nazi persecution victims (determination of percentage of invalidity).

§5. The Illegality of Discrimination Against the Blind

400. The law to prevent discrimination against the blind, when guided by their dogs, ordains that they cannot be denied their right of entrance to public places or use of public transport when guided by their dogs. The law also determines that the fact that they are bound to use the dogs cannot be a reason for their failure to obtain employment.

Chapter 3. Special Activities

§1. Termination of Pregnancy (Abortion)

I. Pregnancy, Examination of Amniotic Fluid

A. Right of Examination

401. In accordance with the 1980 Regulations for Public Health (Examination of Amniotic Fluid), a pregnant woman who has reached the age of at least 37, at an early stage of pregnancy, or whose embryo, in the opinion of a 'responsible physician' can reasonably be affected by such genetic disorders, diseases, or birth defects as it is possible to diagnose before birth, has the right to have her amniotic fluid examined at a hospital. The 'responsible physician' is an official specialist in childbirth and gynaecology, or medical genetics, appointed by a hospital Director to take charge of the medical centre.

B. Performance of Puncture

1. Monopolistic Nature of the Action

402. The puncture of a woman's amniotic bladder for the diagnosis will be performed only by a physician who is a qualified specialist in childbirth and gynaecology or is specializing to obtain the title under the control of a holder of the title. The diagnosis must take place in a registered and approved hospital.

2. Methods of Puncture

403. The regulations detail the various methods of puncture and include the following directives:

(a) Before the puncture of the amniotic bladder for the analysis is made, the woman's blood type must be ascertained; in every case of RH negative, if there is still no sensitization, Anti-D must be given to the woman.
(b) The physician making the puncture of the amniotic bladder for the diagnosis will check the embryo's heartbeat before and after every puncture.
(c) No more than three punctures of the amniotic bladder for the purpose of being made per visit.
(d) The puncture of the amniotic bladder for the diagnosis will not be made before the placenta has been mapped and before the possibility of multiple pregnancies has been explored by means of ultrasound equipment.

3. Date of Implementation

404. Puncture of a woman's amniotic bladder for the diagnosis will not be made before the sixteenth or after the twentieth week following a woman's last menstruation. However, the Director General of the Ministry of Health, or a person legally entitled by the Director to do so, may permit puncture of the amniotic bladder of a woman for diagnosis, even after the twentieth week of her last menstruation, if the Director has found that special circumstances warrant the belated puncture.

4. Informed Consent

405. The regulations lay down that the puncture of a woman's amniotic bladder for diagnosis shall not be made without her consent. Such consent will not be accepted before the hospital Director or the legal appointee has previously explained the nature of the examination to the woman, as well as the dangers to her and her unborn child. Her consent, as the regulations require, must be in writing.

5. Disclosure of Test Results

406. Suppose the amniotic fluid examination results have revealed no sign of genetic disorders, diseases, or natal deformities. In that case, the person appointed by the responsible physician will write a certificate containing the results and deliver it to the woman and the physician linked to her pregnancy.

If the results of the amniotic fluid examination indicate the possibility of genetic disorders, disease, and embryonic deformities, the responsible physician, or the appointee for the task, will explain the results to the woman and deliver them in a written certificate to the physician linked to the woman's pregnancy.

II. Prevention of Pregnancy (IUD)

407. The 1982 Public Health Regulations (Intrauterine Device [IUD]) introduced legal order into the process of inserting the IUD into a woman's body. The IUD is a medical instrument inserted into a woman's womb to prevent pregnancy. A gynaecologist, a physician with the title of a specialist in childbirth and gynaecology, is certified by the practice and title to bring the whole process to a successful conclusion. The insertion of this instrument into a woman's body by a physician who is not a gynaecologist requires a licence.

III. Abortion

A. Criminal Abortion

408. Abortion is criminal when it is the illegal removal of the womb's contents at any stage of pregnancy before childbirth. The criminal aspect of abortions is particularized in Mark 2, Chapter 10 of the 1977 Penal Code. This decrees that any person who knowingly prevents childbirth, either by medical action or in any other way, is liable to five years imprisonment or a fine. The law does not refer to any person or group of persons but lays down a blanket prohibition with certain exceptions specified in the law. It declares, for example, that a woman on whom an offence has been committed by a person who has caused her to abort illegally shall bear no criminal responsibility for the affair. No criminal responsibility attaches to a woman who terminates her pregnancy by her own decision. The law deals with a person who has terminated pregnancy 'on purpose'. If the person who causes the termination of pregnancy does so accidentally and unintentionally, he or she is not regarded as an offender in this section of the law. The law deals with 'medical treatment' and any other kind of treatment. 'Any other kind of treatment' may be that of a non-professional or a quack doctor.

B. The Gynaecologist's Sphere of Authority

409. The Penal Code decrees that no criminal blame will be incurred by a gynaecologist who terminates a woman's pregnancy under two conditions. First, the termination of pregnancy occurs in a recognized medical institution; second, written consent to the termination of the pregnancy has been made out before the event. The first condition is intended to safeguard the woman's health and well-being. A 'recognized medical institution' is a hospital or clinic that the Minister of Health has recognized as a medical institution for the law. A *proviso* for such hospital recognition is that it houses a gynaecological childbirth ward and an operation theatre.

A 'gynaecologist' for the Penal Code may be, first and foremost, a licensed physician who holds the title of a specialist in childbirth and gynaecology, or a licensed physician who is continuing studies for the award of the title of a specialist at a recognized medical institution, under the control of a physician who is a specialist.

The law lays special emphasis on the reservations of a gynaecologist who, for reasons of conscience or medical opinion, decides against abortion or abortion. The law specifies that even when official approval of the abortion has been given, such approval cannot compel a gynaecologist to terminate a woman's pregnancy if it is against his or her conscience or professional judgment.

The second condition requires receipt of approval from the committee appointed for this purpose. This is a committee appointed by the Director of the institution or the Minister of Health; it consists of three members: a licensed physician possessing the title of a gynaecology or childbirth specialist; another licensed physician, occupied either in childbirth and gynaecology, internal medicine, psychiatry, family medicine or public health; and the third member a social welfare official. At least one member of the committee will be a woman. First, there is an urgent need to terminate the pregnancy to save the pregnant woman's life or to deliver her from serious immediate injury. As for the nature of the risk to the woman, it is a matter of life or death, or, at the very least, danger of serious, irreparable injury, if the abortion is not performed. The damage may be either physical or mental. The urgency demanding immediate action derives from the physician's certainty that the circumstances and details of the specific case permit no alternative to abortion. Second, the termination of pregnancy occurs during the physician's treatment of a woman unconnected with the pregnancy the physician was previously unaware of, and that treatment dictates its termination. Unlike in the previous case, this regulation does not deal with a situation of extreme danger to the life or health but prefers to concentrate on the emergency when the physician faces a puzzling, or unexpected dilemma. While the physician is supplying a woman with medical treatment, which usually implies surgical involvement, upon discovering that the woman is pregnant, the physician suspects, or is of the opinion, that failure to terminate the pregnancy will nullify both the treatment for the woman's other condition and her consequent return to good health.

C. Committee Procedure

410. A woman who applies for the cessation of her pregnancy must supply the committee's secretary with laboratory evidence or a physician's certificate to prove her pregnancy. The physician will also notify the committee of the reasons for an opinion that the pregnancy should be terminated. The licensed physician will examine the applicant to determine her stage of pregnancy and explain, among other things, the hazards she will undergo during the abortion and its possible consequences. If the committee members are inclined to turn the request down, the applicant will be invited to plead her cause before the committee. The committee's consultations and all the information it acquires due to the requests of applicants for abortion will be confidential and restricted, and no word will be divulged except as required for the implementation of the law.

All these rules are specified in the Criminal Regulation (Cessation of Pregnancy).

Following the amendment to Penal Law Regulations (Termination of Pregnancy), section 13 was amended as follows:

(a) Prior to referral to the committee, the following documents must be submitted:
  (1) Identification details of the applicant and request details according to Form 2.
  (2) Physician's confirmation or ultrasound examination indicating the gestational age, location, and number of foetuses.
  (3) An informed consent form signed by the woman, following a detailed explanation by a physician as stipulated in the law, explaining the risks and possible outcomes of the abortion.
  (4) Any medical or other documents focusing on the request.
(b) The medical institution operating the committee shall offer the applicant the services of a social worker for counselling, support, and guidance before and after the abortion.
(c) If necessary, the applicant may submit a psychosocial report to the committee through a social worker.
(d) Committee members sign the committee's decision, which is then delivered to the applicant.
(e) If the committee refuses to approve the abortion, it provides reasons in writing.

(f) The committee refrains from deliberating on a request for a reasonable period that could interfere with the possibility of abortion unless approved by a committee member physician.
(g) Committee deliberations and information received are confidential and may only be disclosed as necessary for law enforcement.
(h) The Committee secretary promptly provides the applicant with a copy of Form 2 along with the committee's decision.

D. Informed Consent

411. The committee mentioned above is empowered to approve the termination of a pregnancy if it decides that it is justified by one of the reasons decreed by the law, provided that the applicant's informed consent has been received. The Penal Code gives a clear definition of 'informed consent'.

For this section, a woman's 'informed consent' to the termination of her pregnancy is 'her written consent, after the physical and mental hazards related to abortion have been explained to her'. Such informed consent may be given only by the pregnant woman. The Penal Code empowers the committee to approve the termination of pregnancy after it has received the woman's consent. From this affirmation, one can deduce a negation, namely, that the unborn child's father's consent is not required.

However, the Supreme Court points out that according to Jewish Law, the father should also be seen as one of the parties concerned and invited to express his opinion before the committee. However, the Supreme Court emphasizes that if there is an obstacle to hearing from the father, whether due to urgency or because it is not wise to decide without consulting him, the committee should make a decision without consulting him.

E. Justification for Abortion

412. The law specifies four reasons for any of which the committee is authorized to approve abortion.

1. The Woman's Age

413. The committee is empowered to approve an abortion for a girl younger than 17 or a woman older than 40. In this sphere, the committee's initiative is limited: Requirements are satisfied, and the application meets with the desired approval if it is made either by a woman who has reached or passed the age of 40 or by a girl who is not yet aged 17, whether she is healthy or sick, married, or single.

2. Source of Pregnancy

414. The committee is empowered to approve the termination of a woman's pregnancy if it is the result of a forbidden relationship (this includes, *inter alia*, pregnancy caused by rape), as defined by criminal law or from illegal copulation, or if the woman is unmarried.

3. Defective Baby

415. The committee is empowered to approve a woman's termination of her pregnancy if the baby is likely to be born deformed or mentally defective.

4. Danger to the Mother

416. The committee is empowered to approve a woman's termination of her pregnancy if its continuation is liable to endanger her life or cause her physical or mental injury.

F. The Physician's Reservation

417. The law decrees that even when official approval has been granted for the abortion, the approval itself cannot oblige a physician to perform any abortion in conflict with his or her conscience or professional opinion.

IV. Birth of a Defective Child

418. The Minister of Health has the right to enforce regulations requiring notification of the emergence or removal of an embryo or dead foetus from its mother's womb. In addition, after the expiry of forty-eight hours from the emergence or removal of an embryo or dead foetus from its mother's womb, a government physician may at any time demand that the person responsible for the notification supply information to the best of his or her knowledge and reliability concerning the details of the report that he or she is obliged to make and that functionary is bound to comply.

419. The 1982 Public Health Regulations (Reports on Births of Defective Children) decree that within ten days after the first month of birth, hospital Directors shall present the Director General of the Ministry of Health with a report on every baby born in their institutions, whether live or stillborn, if it possesses or is suspected of possessing, at least one of the irregularities recorded in the regulations, namely:

(1) Down's syndrome.
(2) Any open or closed defect in the central nervous system.
(3) Lack of limbs or lack of any part of them.

420. The 1980 Regulations for Public Health (Notification of Deaths and Extraordinary Events) decree that a hospital Director must inform the Director General of the Ministry of Health of every case of a woman's death during pregnancy or childbirth either within forty-two days of the date of birth or, if the cause of death is connected with the woman's pregnancy or childbirth, within a year after the event.

421. The draft Public Health Regulations (Reporting of Births of nannies with Disabilities) Amendment, 2023, proposes significant changes to existing law. The amendment aims to expand reporting obligations concerning diseases and disabilities found in newborns, among other things.

422. Diagnosis During Pregnancy or After Birth: Reporting requirements will apply even when a disease or disability is identified during pregnancy, not only after childbirth. This may include diagnoses made during prenatal stages or during childbirth.

423. Expansion of Disease and Disability List: The draft suggests expanding the list of diseases and disabilities that must be reported to the Ministry of Health. This will provide additional information on various congenital conditions and enable analysis of confirmed health risks.

§2. Sterilization

424. Israeli legislation makes no specific reference to an intervention in a person's body for sterilization. The Patient's Rights Law leads one to believe that the Law for Sterilization is like that for any other kind of medical treatment that demands receipt of consent from the person who wishes to be sterilized. The consequence is that the physician must comply with all the law's other directives. There is nothing in the law ordering the consent of one's partner in marriage. Every adult is competent for legal actions, and a husband or wife is competent to consent to sterilization without requiring the agreement of the other. The law is different for one acting as the guardian of another, who is a minor, or who is mentally deficient.

§3. Medically Assisted Conception

I. Removal of Ovum

425. The 1987 Public Health Ordinances (extracorporeal fertilization) lay down the rules for the reproductive processes when a woman's ovum is impregnated with sperm outside the body. The removal of the ovum, namely extracting the ovum from the ovary for reproduction, is permissible only for extracorporeal fertilization before its return to the woman. In addition, an ovum may be removed only from a woman who is undergoing medical treatment for defective health after a licensed physician has determined that the removal of the ovum will benefit her treatment.

II. Use of Sperm

426. To fertilize the extracted ovum, the physician may only use sperm that has already been set aside for the purpose and donated for fertilization by a person who is not her husband and to whom the identity of the recipient is not known; or by the husband of the woman from whom the ovum has been removed; or by the sperm bank. The 1979 Public Health Ordinances (Sperm Bank) direct that artificial insemination from a donor may be carried out only in a hospital with a sperm bank approved by the Director General of the Ministry of Health, and only sperm from the bank may be used. An ovum taken from a married woman for transplant may not be impregnated with the sperm of a donor or with sperm from the sperm bank unless consent has been obtained, in writing and in advance, both from the woman from whom the ovum has been removed and from her husband. Likewise, the ovum of a donor, namely the woman from whom it has been removed with her consent for transplantation in another woman, shall not be impregnated with the sperm of the beneficiary's husband unless the written and anticipatory consent of both the woman and her husband has been obtained.

427. Post-mortem sperm retrieval, preservation, and usage, the process is called 'sperm extraction' and it gained prominence during the Iron Swords War. It allows for the retrieval of sperm from deceased family members for reproductive purposes. During the Iron Swords War, hospitals have been advised that until 30 June 2024, they may approve sperm retrieval requests from deceased parents without requiring court intervention, provided they believe that a court referral could delay the process beyond the expiration of the retrieval window. Exceptions include cases where known family members oppose retrieval or when there is parental disagreement.

428. In recent months, the Health Committee of the Knesset has deliberated on the preliminary reading of the 'Post-mortem Use of Sperm for Reproduction' bill.

429. The legislative proposal aims to regulate the use of sperm from deceased individuals for reproductive purposes, either according to their expressed wishes or instructions left behind. In cases where no instructions exist, only the deceased's spouse or designated partner may use the sperm for pregnancy or fertility treatments.

430. In specific circumstances, a deceased person's parent may use their sperm for reproductive purposes through other women, subject to court approval. Any child conceived through post-mortem sperm use is considered the legal child of the deceased unless specified as an anonymous donation.

431. Special provisions are outlined for regular and reserve soldiers regarding the retrieval and use of their sperm for reproductive purposes, utilizing digital means for instruction writing.

432. The proposal balances the deceased's reproductive rights with family and legal considerations.

III. Transplantation of Ovum

433. The transplantation of a fertilized ovum is the insertion of said ovum into a woman's womb. As a rule, a fertilized ovum will be transplanted only into the woman's body who will mother the child. No ovum will be transplanted into a woman unless fertilized by her husband's sperm. In addition, no ovum will be transplanted into a woman who is related to its donor:

(a) A married woman may receive a transplant if the ovum is her own or that of a donor and if it has been fertilized in compliance with the regulations.
(b) A spinster may be the recipient of a transplant only if the ovum, which has been fertilized, comes from her own body and provided that her request for the transplant has been approved in the report of a certified social worker.
(c) If the possessor of the fertilized ovum becomes a widow before transplantation, the fertilized ovum may be returned to her body only a year or more after its fertilization, provided that the transplant is approved in a social worker's report.
(d) If the woman in whom it is intended to transplant the ovum is divorced, and the ovum was fertilized by her husband before their divorce, the transplant will take place only with her ex-husband's consent.
(e) No use shall be made of the ovum taken from a married woman who subsequently dies.
(f) An ovum taken from a married woman whose husband has died may be donated, with the widow's consent. Therefore, if the husband dies, the law for the widow shall be as above recorded; if the woman dies, the fertilized ovum may not be used.
(g) An ovum, including one which is fertilized and taken from a single woman who has died, shall not be transplanted into another woman unless, before she died, the deceased agreed to donate her ovum.

IV. Reproduction in a Recognized Hospital Ward

434. The removal of an ovum from a woman's body, its fertilization, refrigeration, and transplantation may be carried out only in a ward approved for the purpose by the Director General of the Ministry of Health.

An ovum that has been acquired and fertilized outside Israel may be transplanted in a woman in Israel under the following conditions:

(a) The transplant must be made in a recognized hospital department.
(b) The department head and the treating physician are confronted with authentic medical certificates as proof of the suitability of the fertilized ovum for transplant after the examination of the donor has been conducted in accordance with the terms of the regulations.
(c) The department head and the treating physician have been supplied with medical documents showing that every precaution has been taken to ensure the good health of the donor and the recipient.
(d) The department head and the treating physician have been shown the donor's certificate of consent to undergo any genetic test that may be required in the future and to the preservation of a blood specimen for any genetic test that may be required in the future.
(e) The treating physician will inform the recipient of the ovum that it will be most desirable for her to receive at least three ova to strengthen the chance that one of the fertilized eggs is productive.

Regarding an ovum taken from a woman and intended for transplantation when fertilized:

(a) The operation must be performed in a recognized hospital department.
(b) It must occur after the treating physician has examined documents certifying that the ovum was both drawn from a body and fertilized in an institution licensed by the country's government.

The Supreme Court received an appeal from a lesbian couple seeking to bring a child into the world through the following procedure: an ovum would be taken from one partner, fertilized, and then implanted into the uterus of another partner. The appellants argued that this procedure should be allowed either under the Surrogacy Agreements Law or under the Ovum Donation Law.

The Supreme Court rejected the appeal of the lesbian couple seeking to perform the ovum donation procedure in Israel, allowing only the first part of the procedure to take place domestically and the subsequent implantation abroad. The decision was made by a majority of four judges against three. The court determined that performing the entire procedure in Israel was not feasible and approved the partial solution following the Ministry of Health's regulations on the 'Export of Sperm, Ovum, or Embryos from Israel,' and the decision of the Exceptions Committee operating under the Ovum Donation Law.

Additionally, the court determined that the Ovum Donation Law does not apply to the appellants because the partner who wants to donate the ovum does not have a medical condition preventing her from becoming pregnant from her own ovum, as required by the law's provisions. The law primarily addresses cases where women suffer from medical conditions preventing pregnancy from their own ovum.

In summary, the court's decision reflects its approach to balancing legal definitions with evolving social norms, leaving room for legislative amendments to address equality issues in parental rights.

V. Refrigeration of Ovum

435. An ovum may be kept in refrigeration for no more than five years. The hospital is authorized to add five years to this period if a written request, signed both by the woman from whom the ovum was taken and her husband, is presented to the hospital. The refrigeration of an ovum demands that it be preserved at a low temperature to arrest all its biological processes; in a fertilized ovum, the splitting of the cells is suspended.

VI. Informed Consent

436. Every action connected with extracorporeal fertilization will be performed only after the responsible physician has explained the operation's sign to all the concerned parties and has received the informed consent of every one of them. In addition, every action involved in extracorporeal fertilization for a married woman shall be performed only after her husband has consented.

VII. Confidentiality

437. A recognized hospital ward for extracorporeal fertilization may not dispense information concerning the identity of a sperm or ovum donor.

438. According to Chapter G of the Ova Donation Law, which regulates the issue of anonymity and confidentiality, a person who receives information under this law during their duties or work shall keep it confidential and not disclose or use it except in accordance with this law or by court order.

439. The responsible and treating physician shall not disclose to the donor identifying information about the recipient, nor shall they disclose to the recipient identifying information about the donor, unless the donor has pre-designed the ova to be retrieved from her body to that recipient. However, the responsible physician and the treating physician may provide the recipient with non-identifying information about the donor if they believe there are justifiable reasons to do so.

440. Section 40 sets forth limitations on releasing information from the information registry and birth registry. First, waiving medical confidentiality regarding a medical record or information shall not be considered consent to release information from the information registry and birth registry.

441. Additionally, the section stipulates that despite the provisions of Chapter D of the Privacy Protection Law, information transferred from or released from the information registry and birth registry shall only be done in accordance with this law.

VIII. The Right of the Treated Persons

442. A 2001 amendment to the Women's Employment Law makes it illegal for an employer to terminate the employment of a woman who is undergoing extracorporeal fertilization or of a male or female employee undergoing fertility treatment as specified by the law's regulations either then or for 150 days after the cessation of absence from work.

443. In the National Labour Court, a dispute arose focusing on the interpretation of section 9(E)(3) of the Women's Labour Law, which stipulates that 'provisions of paragraph (1) prohibiting the dismissal of absent employees without permission from the authorized person shall also apply to a female employee or worker who has not been absent from work during the period of treatments or within 150 days from the commencement of fertility treatments or extracorporeal fertilization treatments, whichever is later'.

444. The National Labour Court ruled in a precedent ruling that an employer may not dismiss a female employee undergoing fertility treatments without obtaining permission from the authorized person under the Women's Labour Law, even if the employee has not been absent from work due to the treatments. The judges determined that protection against dismissal applies 'both during the treatment period and during the 150 days from the commencement of fertility treatments or extracorporeal fertilization, whichever is later'.

445. The Women's Labour Law is a central legislation in Israeli law, alongside other legislative provisions, serving as a legal mechanism to reduce inequality in society in general and in the labour market. Section 9 of the law, titled 'Limitation on Dismissals,' establishes a mechanism requiring permission for dismissals from the authorized person under the Women's Labour Law and prohibits granting permission for dismissals related to pregnancy or other protective matters. This mechanism is described as providing 'Intensive Protection'.

§4. Human Genetics

446. The 1999 Law Prohibiting Genetic Intervention (Cloning Human Beings and Genetic Changes in the Reproductive Cells) decrees that with effect from 1 January 1999 until 2020, no person shall perform any action of intervention in a human's cells with one of the following objectives:

(a) The cloning of a human, namely the creation of a whole human being who is completely identical genetically and chromosomally with another, whether he be a person or embryo, alive or dead.
(b) The contrivance of the creation of a live person by using such reproductive cells as sperms and human ova, which have undergone germ-line gene therapy. The law aims to fix a definite period of five years during which no type of genetic intervention into humans will be conducted. During this period, the moral, legal,

social, and scientific aspects of such types of intervention and their reflections on human dignity will be closely researched. The Supreme Helsinki Committee has been given powers to look into the developments of medicine, science, and biotechnology in the sphere of genetic experiments on human beings, to present the Minister of Health with an annual report, and to advise the minister in these matters. Despite the law's directives, the minister has been legally authorized to issue regulations for the implementation of certain genetic interventions which have no connection with human dignity upon the recommendation of the Supreme Helsinki Committee. The law specifies two years of imprisonment for any contravener of the law.

(c) Scientific research into genetics developed in recent years has enabled researchers to identify the genetic cause for various diseases that afflict or are liable to afflict mankind. This development carries with it the expectation of an improvement in the health of the world's population. At the same time, genetic information is liable to discriminate against or attach stigma to such people who carry genes that are carriers of several diseases. Genetic information differs from medical information as it is the knowledge of the potential and envisioning of the future. Genetic information may be used negatively against a person whose genes have been tested. The Genetic Information Law of 2000 was intended to protect persons from misuse of the gene test they have undergone. The law intended to regularize genetic examinations and counselling and protect the right of the examinee concerning genetic information that identifies him without prejudicing the quality of medical treatment, medical and genetic research, medical development, or the preservation of human health.

As mentioned above, the law was first enacted in 1999 as a temporary law for five years and has been extended thrice. Currently, the law's validity, which expired on 29 May 2024, prohibits human cloning-the creation of an embryo genetically identical to a living or deceased human or the transfer of a cloned embryo to a uterus or a human or animal body. It also prohibits using reproductive cells (sperm and ovum cells) and intentional genetic modification aimed at creating a person carrying a specific genetic alteration. Violation of these prohibitions constitutes a criminal offence punishable by up to four years imprisonment.

Amendment No. 5 introduces three major changes from the existing law: expanding the prohibition on performing targeted genetic modification to create a person only on reproductive cells but on any other cells as well and extending the law's validity for an additional five years until 31 May 2028. In addition, the law's name will be amended so that instead of referring to genetic modification in reproductive cells, it will refer to genetic modification in cells.

Genetic tests must be performed at a licensed genetic institution or in a laboratory authorized to do so. A genetic test is conditioned by the potential examinee's informed consent. The law determines the illegality of Deoxyribonucleic Acid (DNA) samples taken from a minor under the age of 16 or from a mentally unfit person unless allowed by law.

Under certain conditions, the law permits genetic physicians, clinical geneticists, genetic counsellors, and medical specialists to give genetic advice. However, any recipient of genetic information about an examinee during his or her functions or work is obliged to maintain secrecy and make no use of the knowledge without the examinee's consent.

It is illegal for an employer to demand genetic information from an employee or potential employee or ask the employee to take a genetic test. Nor may the employer take genetic information into account when deciding to employ a new worker, determine a new employee's working conditions, or dismiss an employee from service.

The law declares it is illegal for an insurer to ask an insured person or an applicant for insurance if he or she has taken a genetic test. Nor may the insurer request that a person take the test or supply the person with information obtained by the insurer or of a person's refusal to supply genetic information in the determination of the terms of insurance.

The 1998 Law on the Right of People to Be Informed preceded the Law on Genetic Information. The 1998 Law determines every citizen's right to be supplied with information by a public authority. The law also details those instances in which, or subject on which, it is not permissible or obligatory to deliver information. For example, it is illegal to supply information that may damage a person's privacy unless regulations permit it, and illegal to impart information that may trespass on the privacy of the dead. The regulations detailed in this law do not apply to any judicial authority appointed to investigate a person's medical condition that has a bearing on the procedures of that authority.

447. In 2005 and 2008, substantive amendments to the Genetic Information Act of 2000 were established. The amendments concern genetic examination, the authority to perform such examination, the rights and duties of the examiner and the examinee, methods of implementing the examination, and the limitations of such examination. As affixed by the Act, the general rule declares the impermissibility of performing genetic examination outside of a genetic institute or a laboratory for genetic examination. Genetic examination for research purposes may not take place unless permission for this research is first granted. Furthermore, DNA samples may not be taken without the informed consent of the examinee.

448. Furthermore, the provisions of the Patient's Rights Act apply to this examination, subject to the required adaption. In the case of performing a genetic examination in the absence of the examiner's informed consent due to courts for family issue decree, an explanation ought to be delivered to the examiner; such explanation must address the methods for performing the examination and its consequences on the examinee's body. The 2005 Amendment allows security authorities to use DNA samples if such samples were obtained legally in accordance with the provisions of the Act. This usage by security authorities is legitimate if committed for the listed purposes, including criminal identification and presentation of attacks against the state's security.

§5. Removal and Transplantation of Organs

I. General

449. The 1953 Anatomy and Pathology Law lists the circumstances in which it is permissible to cut up or operate on a body post-mortem: the dead person has consented; the body poses a threat to public health; an event has caused a large number of casualties; an embryo may be saved; an organ or organs will be used in transplantation; and a pathologist may have to determine the cause of death.

450. In each of these post-mortem operations, the following options are applicable:

(a) The deceased objected to the operation during his or her lifetime. Therefore, the corpse will be left intact.
(b) The deceased, while alive, agreed to be operated on. Therefore, a post-mortem examination of the body is permissible, subject to the issue of a death certificate as required by law, and notification of the death to a member of his family.
(c) The deceased gave neither written consent nor written refusal to an operation while alive. In this case, if the deceased had no living relations, a post-mortem operation would not take place. If the deceased's relations are alive, the deceased may not undergo an operation post-mortem, either to reveal the cause of death or for curative purposes, unless a relation has consented. Still, an operation to save lives is permissible, if the deceased's wife or husband, child, or parent has not objected.

II. Cure

451. The Anatomy and Pathology Law decrees that a physician is allowed to operate on a dead body to use a part of it to cure another person. However, the permit is subject to several restrictions:

(a) The operation may be performed only by a physician.
(b) To cure a person, only a part of a corpse may be used; this means that an operation may be performed only on a body that has been pronounced dead.

452. The permit to transplant is subject to several other restrictions. The first set of conditions concerns the time of the operation. The rules forbid such an operation before five hours have expired after a member of the deceased's family has been notified of the death. Israel's Sabbath and festivals, and with respect to a non-Jew, the Sabbath and festivals of his or her sect, will not be included in the count of five hours. The reason for this restriction is to enable the deceased's relatives to determine their stand and express it with respect to the post-mortem, as detailed below.

453. It should be noted that the law does not specify whose responsibility it is to inform the relatives. This general restriction divides itself into two sections. First, if the operation is required so that a part of the body may be used to cure a person, a relative of the deceased must be informed in reasonable advance of the post-mortem. But the operation will also be legal if it is not possible to inform the relative in reasonable advance, or at all, since the latter cannot be located, provided that rational attempts have been made to notify. The directive stressing the need to save a life is a medical obligation that a physician must observe in every decision he or she makes. However, without prejudicing the general application of his directive, the legislator has singled out certain parts of the body as instrumental in the saving of life. These are the cornea, which may restore a person's sight; any part of the body that may remedy a sight or hearing defect; the deceased's kidneys for transplant; and pieces of skin for skin graft.

454. The second set of restrictions relates to the deceased's consent or opposition to a post-mortem operation.

Accordingly, if a person has agreed to a post-mortem, the pathologist may conduct the operation despite any objection from the deceased's relatives. However, if, while alive, a person had objected to a post-mortem, he or she will not be operated on after death, even if relatives consent, and even if it is purposed to use a part of the body to save a living person's life. Furthermore, if any relative does not survive the deceased, there will be no operation on the corpse, unless the person consented to a post-mortem before dying.

455. The third set of restrictions relates to the consent or opposition to a post-mortem operation expressed by the deceased's relatives. It has already been shown that the law normally decrees a delay in a post-mortem examination for a certain period to leave room for communication with the deceased's family. In so decreeing, the legislator sought to emphasize both the right that relations must maintain the interest they once had in the deceased and consideration for the feelings of those relatives. Consequently, the legislator has decreed that if the deceased has any surviving relatives, and if there is no question of a post-mortem whose objective is to obtain parts to save other people's lives, there will be no anatomic-pathological post-mortem except in compliance with the following conditions:

(a) The deceased's lifelong partner has consented, or in his or her absence, his or her children, or in their absence, his or her parents or in their absence, his or her brother or sister.
(b) No written objection has been recorded by a person as closely related to the deceased as the one who consented, or by a next of kin in the order of relationships mentioned above.

III. Sanctions

456. Any person who conducts a post-mortem in contravention of the regulations mentioned above may be sent to prison or fined.

§6. RESEARCH WITH HUMAN BEINGS

I. The Helsinki Declaration

457. The Helsinki Declaration was approved by the Eighteenth World Medical Association meeting in Helsinki in 1964 and amended at the Twenty-Ninth World Medical Assembly convened in Tokyo in 1975. Israel law adopted the contents of the Helsinki Declaration giving it the validity of an inviolable decree in the 1980 Public Health Regulations (Medical Experimentation on Human Beings) supplying additions to every law and ethical rule in current Israeli practice.

II. Definition of Experimentation

458. 'Medical experimentation on human beings' is defined in the regulations as the employment of medication, radiation, or chemical, biological, radiological, or pharmaceutical components in contradistinction to such use of these materials as is statutory, or when the employment of the materials mentioned above is not acceptable in Israel for their present objectives or is applied to objectives not previously tested in Israel, and is intended to affect the health, body, mind, or genetic system of a person or worker, wholly or partly. Medical experimentation on human beings also includes performing any unconventional process or action upon, or examination of, any person. Israel imposes a ban on making any medical experiment on human beings in a hospital in contravention of the Regulations or the Helsinki Declaration.

An amendment to these regulations is concerned with three kinds of extraordinary medical experiments consisting of medical supplies and others, the main intention being to determine their degree of usefulness.

The amendment clearly defines the instructions in the report procedure and confirmation that the extraordinary experiment has been carried out. The hospital's medical Director in which the extraordinary experiment has been performed is obliged to forward a report on any extraordinary experiments that he or she has approved to the Director General of the Ministry of Health. The regulations do not allow the performance of extraordinary medical experiments on minors, women during pregnancy, patients who lack physical or mental power of discretion, and persons detained or in prison.

III. Licence for Experimentation

459. No experiment will be made on a human being at a hospital unless the Ministry of Health's Director General or an authorized official has approved the experiment in a document that stipulates the terms of the experiment. The Director is empowered to grant conditional approval, limit approval by adding additional conditions, and cancel approval. But no approval will be given without the following three conditions. First, the hospital's Helsinki Committee informed the Director in writing that the experiment had been approved. This committee is appointed by the hospital's Director and approved by the Minister of Health's Director General. It must be composed of at least seven members and must include:

(a) A representative of the public who is a minister of religion or a lawyer.
(b) Three physicians who are heads of hospital wards, or at least associate professors at recognized medical schools and one of whom is a specialist on internal diseases.
(c) a physician who represents the hospital's governing board.

It is the job of the hospital's Helsinki Committee to approve any experiment on human beings that is carried out in the hospital. Second, the Ministry of Health's Director General, or a proxy, must be convinced that the experiment does not contravene the Helsinki Declaration and the regulations. Third, advice has been obtained from the Medication and Food Directorate of the Ministry of Health whenever the regulations require that such advice be obtained. The Higher Helsinki Committee is appointed by the Ministry of Health's Director General. Of its ten members, a lawyer and a minister of religion represent the public; six are professors of recognized academic institutions, three of whom being physicians who are full professors; the other two are the Ministry's Director General if a licensed physician, or a representative who is a licensed physician; and the chairperson of Israel's Medical Association. Every application for approval of a medical experiment on a human being must be addressed in writing to the Ministry of Health's Director General or an appointee. The application must be signed by the hospital Director where the experiment will be carried out and by the physician who assumes responsibility for the experiment. A detailed plan of the desired experiment will be attached to the application, stating its objectives and the need for it, together with full particulars of tests, research, and experiments already carried out in that or a similar field of medicine, in, or outside of Israel.

IV. General Conditions for Conducting the Experiment

460. The experiment must be done by certified researchers who are capable and eminent physicians under the supervision of licensed practitioners.

461. The need for the experiment. This condition consists of three provisos:

(a) The experiment must be necessary and its aim curative.
(b) It must be determined that the patient's condition dictates recourse to experimentation.
(c) The physicians must be satisfied that the circumstances make the standard treatment method in current practice unsatisfactory.

462. The range of the experiment. This condition also consists of three provisos:

(a) The experiment must be made as safe as possible for the patient. Safeguards should, as often as possible, comprise previous experiments on animals or other scientific treatment methods.
(b) There must be as little exceptional departure from common practice as possible.
(c) Unnecessary damage to the patient must be avoided. No experiment may be carried out if it entails unnecessary danger to life or substantial deterioration of health.

Biomedical research into mankind will become possible only if the importance of the aim is in fitting proportion to the risks it raises. It is a basic principle that anxiety over a person's welfare when he or she becomes a human guinea pig, must always take precedence over the needs of science and society. Therefore, in addition to confining the scope of the experiment, the researcher must adopt sound working habits.

V. Briefing of Person Undergoing Experiment

463. The process of obtaining the patient's consent is complicated. His or her consent must be 'informed' consent, requiring free will, competence, knowledge, and understanding for it to be valid in the eyes of the law. For all research on a person's body, the subject of the research must be apprised of the aim of the research, its methods, and its expected advantages. Still, attention must also be drawn to the risks it involves and the inconveniences it may create. Moreover, it must be explained to the patient that they can refrain from participating in the experiment or terminate participation at any stage.

VI. Clinic Research

464. The best possible methods of diagnosis and treatment must be assured for the patient when medical research is combined with professional treatment. Therefore, priority must be given to such existent medical expertise as it is most applicable to the patient's condition. This ruling holds for the committee of supervision as well. The physician is permitted to combine medical research with commonly accepted treatment, if the aim is to acquire new, medical expertise, only on condition that its diagnostic or curative value justifies the medical research to the patient who is the subject of the experimentation.

VII. Research That Is Not Clinical

465. When the physician conducts purely professional research on people, he or she is also obliged to protect every person's life and health. It must be taken as a principle that when experiments are done on people for the sake of research, priority shall never be given to the interests of society and the general public at the expense of considerations connected with the well-being of any pho under experimentation.

VIII. Guardian's Consent

466. The Helsinki Declaration determines that if a patient is legally incompetent, the informed consent of his or her legal guardian must be requested and obtained according to Israeli legislation. When mental deficiency renders informed consent impossible, permission must be provided by a responsible relative in accordance with the country's legislation. The appointment of a guardian of a mentally retarded person shall accord with the country's legislation. The guardian is obliged to devote and protect the interests of his or her ward. No retarded patient may be invited to participate in medical research before his or her guardian has given consent. During the experiment, the researcher must report every significant development, every reaction of the patient, and every side effect, to the guardian. The appointment of guardians does not completely solve the problems. A guardian may fail badly in a misconceived estimate of the patient's condition or real interests. It is not always sufficient to obtain the guardian's consent even if the patient's consent reinforces it.

§7. Professional Freedom

467. As a rule, physicians enjoy professional freedom. This can be learnt from the fact that society endows them with the right to practise their profession under the licence awarded to them by the Director General of the Ministry of Health and in compliance with the list of directives that appear in the laws of the realm. Our Basic Law for Freedom of Occupation decrees that the freedom of occupation is inviolable and that every sovereign authority must respect a person's freedom to choose his or her occupation. As a professional combine, Israel's physicians are incessantly consolidating their rules and systems of common practice in the different spheres of medicine. Society is, for the most part, prepared to trust the reliability and professionalism of physicians and respects common medical practice. Only more weighty considerations of the public good can impel society to step in and sully professional freedom. A general directive may be found in paragraph 35 of the revised version of the Civil Wrongs Ordinance that authorizes, and obliges, every member of a profession to employ the expertise and care which any fit and proper member of his profession would use in specific circumstances. The Patient's Rights Law expresses this principle in paragraph 5 when determining that the patient's right is to be treated properly from the point of view of professional standards and medical quality. The ethical principles of the Medical Association decree categorically in paragraph 3, 'When giving instructions and undertaking activities in the field of medicine, the physician answers only to the dictates of his professional conscience.'

Part III. The Physician and the Healthcare System

Chapter 1. Relations with Other Healthcare Providers

§1. Pharmacists

I. Monopolistic Nature of Occupation

468. Legislation in the sphere of the licensing of medications in Israel is conservative insofar as it imposes thorough inspection at every stage beginning with manufacture, marketing, and retailing. These restrictions at every phase are intended to protect the consumers who are in vital need of medicines from misuse that may be calamitous. The law stipulates, among other things, that the retail sale of medicines may be made only at the pharmacies because of the importance of those being sold in establishments of the required standard and the need to enable experts' inspection of the retail sale of medicines.

The Pharmacists' Regulations (Medical Supplies) determines that advertisement for the sale of every medicine intended for the public requires the approval of the Ministry of Health. The Pharmacy Regulations stipulate that importing unregistered medicines in Israel for personal use requires a permit from the Ministry of Health. This will not be granted to import any medicine of an identical nature to one already registered in Israel. The 1981 revised version of the Pharmacists' Ordinance makes it illegal for a person to engage in pharmacy unless he or she has obtained a licence in accordance with the law.

469. In 2008, a special law was enacted 'The Act for Resolution of Health Professions.' The Act sets up a high-standard apparatus of conditions for granting degrees and licences for health professions. First, the Act limits the performance of several actions solely to authorized persons who hold degrees or licences in accordance with the provisions of the Act. Such limits intersect with the trend to affix high ethical standards to health professions. Second, granting such licences and degrees involves practical training, examinations, and specialization. Underlying this act is the desire to preserve the integrity of such provisions. Third, the Act provides a complete set of disciplinary felonies, commissions, procedures, and a system of enforcement. Additionally, the Act also establishes a supervision system over recipients of degrees in health professions. Finally, the Act's normative provisions are accompanied by penal sanctions over infringements of certain provisions, especially provisions that might also constitute disciplinary felonies.

470. The Physicians' Regulations (Impermissible Advertisement) were enacted in 2008. The regulations prohibit misleading advertisements and those that impede the integrity of the medical profession. They also prohibit other advertisements that insult the public, such as publishing tariffs or encouraging patients to receive medical treatment that is not necessary solely for financial advantages.

II. Application for Licence

471. An application for a licence must be addressed to the Director General of the Ministry of Health through the agency of the District Health Officer. The Ordinance stipulates that the applicant for a licence in pharmacy must re-enforce his or her request with proof of identity, moral character, fitness to practise pharmacy, and attainment of such skills as are laid down. In addition, the 1930 Regulations for Pharmacists oblige the applicant to attach documents to the application attesting to the following facts:

(a) He or she has reached the age of 21.
(b) He or she has successfully matriculated.
(c) He or she has studied pharmacy of an academic standard for at least three years at a university or a recognized pharmacy school and gained a recognized diploma in pharmacy.
(d) He or she is an Israeli subject or possesses a certificate of permanent residence in Israel.

Additional attachments to the application will be:

(a) A signed questionnaire as completed by all workers professionally employed in the health services.
(b) A certified copy or photograph of certificates attesting to training and ability to practise pharmacy.

472. The Director General is empowered to grant a temporary licence or the licence of an assistant pharmacist. Conditions for the award of an assistant pharmacist's licence are as follows:

(a) He or she has a good character.
(b) He or she has reached the age of 20.
(c) He or she is an Israeli citizen or the possessor of a certificate for permanent residence in Israel.
(d) He or she has been apprenticed to a licensed pharmacist at a chemist's shop for three years.

III. Loss of Licence

473. Suppose a pharmacist or assistant pharmacist mislays his or her licence. In that case, he or she must notify the police and the Director General who is authorized to replace the licence with a copy.

IV. Medical Inspection of Pharmacist

474. The Pharmacists Ordinance of 1981 was amended in 2005, thus empowering a special medical commission to re-examine the licence of an already-licensed pharmacist or licensed assistant pharmacist and to suspend his licence if it was reasonably established that he suffers from a dangerous disease, if such disease exposes the public to an urgent danger, to the extent that it is impossible to wait until the completion of the formal procedures before the medical commission.

475. Suppose the Director General of the Ministry of Health has reason to suspect that the applicant for the licence of a certified pharmacist or registration as an assistant pharmacist has contracted a dangerous disease. In that case, the Director is empowered to order the applicant to appear before a medical committee for examination. A 'dangerous disease' may be:

(a) An illness, including mental deficiency, which is liable to impair the health of a person requiring the services of the certified pharmacist or assistant pharmacist.
(b) An illness, including mental deficiency or diminished competence, is liable to deprive the certified pharmacist or assistant pharmacist of the ability to engage in pharmacy completely, partially, or temporarily.

The medical committee, appointed by the Director General of the Ministry of Health, consists of three medical specialists authorized to summon anyone to testify during their investigation.

476. Similar powers are vested in the Director General during dealings with licence holders. The Director is authorized to order persons, including physicians and workers at medical institutions, to supply him with information that they are legally bound to divulge concerning the health of applicants for licences of certified pharmacists and assistant pharmacists. When the Director General is convinced that the illness of a pharmacist or assistant pharmacist is such an immediate public menace that it is wrong to delay action until the conclusion of the medical committee's proceedings and any consequent appeal against the Director's decision, he or she is authorized to order the intermediate suspension of a licence. If a medical committee decides that a certified pharmacist, an assistant pharmacist, or a potential pharmacist is completely, partially, or temporarily incapacitated from engaging in pharmacy, by virtue of a dangerous disease, or if any of these three persons can perform pharmacy duties only within limitations, or in conditioned circumstances, the Director General will refuse to grant a licence, will cancel the licence or suspend it as applies to each case, or may grant the person a special licence. An appeal against the Director General's decision will be heard by the district court. Any person who is the recipient of information concerning the dangerous diseases referred to above must regard it as confidential and may not divulge any of it unless required to do so in the enforcement of the regulations mentioned above, or by permission of the court, or in compliance with an order to answer questions by an authority appointed to enquire into the commission of crimes.

477. Notably, the Pharmacists Ordinance of 1981 was amended also in 2017. This amendment concerned the imposition of a sharp prohibition on pharmacists to modify, alter, or change the kind and/or dosage of a medication as already prescribed by a physician. In addition, the amendment includes a further prohibition on hospitals, clinics, or any other likewise institute, which act voluntarily, as a matter of charity or for religious reasons, to provide medical drugs or any other medication but only upon issuing a legal prescription by an authorized physician or nurse.

478. In 2007, the Pharmacists' Regulations (Issuing Defending Chemical Preparations) (Temporary Order) of 2007 were enacted. The Minister of Health provides rules for the carriage and storage of defending chemical preparations and regulations for documentation issuance of such chemical preparations.

479. In 2005, the Pharmacists' Regulations Nitrogen Dioxide Gas (NO_2) were enacted. The regulations set forth rules for granting permission for importing and exporting NO_2 and its marketing.

480. In 2008, the Pharmacists' Regulations (Proper Manufacture Conditions for Chemical Preparations) were enacted. These include regulations concerning the conditions for permitting chemical preparation manufacturing and establishing a list of conditions for proper manufacturing of chemical preparations. In addition, the regulations include a very strict system of supervision.

481. In 2016, the Pharmacist Regulations (Condition for the Establishment and Administration of Pharmacies and Drug Rooms) was amended, thus requiring any pharmacist and other employees in a pharmacy to respect the patient's dignity, privacy, and medical confidentially. This requirement applies akin during consultation and other actions that are relevant to the pharmacist-patient relationship.

V. Cancellation and Suspension of Licence by the Ministry of Health

482. In the context of Amendment No. 24 to the Pharmacists Law, the Minister of Health appoints a disciplinary committee, tasked with adjudicating and deciding on disciplinary offences. The disciplinary committee, comprising three members, determines that a professional has committed one of the following:

(1) Behaved in a manner incompatible with his profession.
(2) Violated ethical principles established under section 56.

(3) Contravened a provision of this law imposing a prohibition or obligation.
(4) Breached directives under patient rights legislation.
(5) Fraudulently obtained a pharmacist assistant licence or registration.
(6) Demonstrated incapacity, irresponsibility, or severe negligence in the course of professional duties.
(7) Convicted in final judgment, either in Israel or aboard, of a criminal offence of such gravity or nature that he is deemed unfit to practice, with implications for his profession.

483. The committee is authorized to impose one or more of the following measures: warning, reprimand, fine, suspension of licence, revocation of licence, imposition of conditions, or restrictions.

484. The plaintiff or respondent may appeal the decision of the disciplinary committee to the district court within forty-five days from the date the decision concludes the hearing, or within forty-five days from the date of discovery if rendered without the parties present.

485. A district court's judgment on an appeal under this section may be further appealed to the Supreme Court if authorized by the President of the Supreme Court or another judge designated by the President.

VI. Cancellation and Suspension of Licence by the Director General

486. The Director General of the Ministry of Health is empowered to cancel the licence of a certified pharmacist or an assistant pharmacist if he is convinced that the licensee is dead or no longer a legal resident in Israel.

VII. Judicial Cancellation of Licence

487. A *licensee* found guilty of an offence against the Pharmacist's Ordinance may forfeit his or her licence by decree of the law court.

VIII. Prescription by a Personally Authorized Pharmacist

488. *In* 2014, the Pharmacists' Regulations (Prescription Delivery by a Personally Authorized Pharmacist) were enacted. The regulations grant personally authorized pharmacists the power to deliver prescriptions for continuance treatment. In addition, the regulations provide a list of conditions that must be met before those mentioned above. The authorized pharmacist may exercise this power, thus guaranteeing supervision for such exceptional power.

489. In addition, under the Pharmacists Regulations (Authorized Pharmacist Prescription) Amendment 2024, new provisions stipulate that if the Director General imposes a limitation on the validity period of a personal authorization under section 26(A1)(2) of the ordinance and it expires, he may renew the authorization for the authorized pharmacist without the need for additional training. Furthermore, if the Director General determines that the authorization will be granted without a limitation on its validity period, according to the provisions of the section, he shall specify in the authorization that its validity is unlimited.

§2. DENTISTS

I. Practice of Dentistry, a Legal Monopoly

490. The 1979 revised version of the Dentists' Ordinance lays down that only persons licensed to do so may engage in the practice of dentistry. The infrastructure of dental medicine as determined by the Dentists' Ordinance consists of dental operations, the regular treatment of teeth, advice on, or observation of teeth, gums and mouth routinely purveyed by the dentist to the patient, as well as work normally undertaken like the measurement, insertion, adjustment, and repair of dentures, and kindred activities. The Ordinance confines the practice of dentistry to a dentist and dental dispenser, who have been awarded licences to practise dentistry. A licensed physician is free to engage in dentistry insofar as it is involved in the practice of medicine.

The law makes it illegal for a dentist to advertise for any occupation that may mislead or show disrespect to his calling.

II. Conditions for Award of Licence

491. The *Ordinance's purpos*e is twofold. First, it standardizes the award of licences to dentists and prevents the infiltration of undesirables into the profession.

A licence to practise dentistry may be awarded only to an Israeli subject or to the holder of a permit for permanent or temporary residence in Israel.

The licence is awarded on three conditions:

(1) The applicant is an honest citizen.
(2) He or she has completed studies in preparation for the practice of dentistry.
(3) He has successfully passed examinations for dentists as laid down by the Director General of the Ministry of Health.

A person who has studied dentistry must have obtained a degree in proof of the completion of studies at an Israeli dental institution for higher studies recognized as such by the Council for Higher Studies or has pursued a course of study in dentistry at a foreign university or dental school of university status recognized by the Director General and has been awarded a diploma recognized by the Director General. A 'diploma' is defined as including, among other documents, confirmation in writing of any degree, certificate, status, authorization, or letter awarded by a university or other body, by the governing functionaries of a country or a territorial area, or by the representatives of the same governing functionaries.

III. Medical Examinations

A. General Rule

492. Because the dentist has physical contact with the patient, the legislator has seen fit to protect the patient's health, ensuring that he or she does not suffer more than his or her indisposition warrants if the dentist has contracted a 'dangerous disease'. A dangerous disease is one of the following:

(a) Mental illness.
(b) Any disease that may infect the people whom the licensed dentist is treating.
(c) A disability or incompetence that may deprive the licensed dentist of dental skills, completely, partially, or temporarily.

B. Summons to Medical Examination

493. Suppose the Director General has a reason to suspect that an applicant for a licence has contracted a dangerous disease. In that case, the Director is empowered to demand that the applicant present to a medical board for examination. Although the applicant retains the right of refusal, he or she may be penalized if objecting by being deprived of a licence to practise dentistry until changing his or her mind has been examined, as required by the Director General.

As for the licensed dental practitioner, the least suspicion that he or she may have contracted a dangerous disease will not suffice. The Director General must have more concrete evidence. The Director General is empowered to suspend any dentist's licence until the latter agrees to be examined.

C. The Medical Board

494. The Director General of the Ministry of Health is empowered to appoint a 'medical board' ad hoc, or permanently. It will consist of three physicians and, when there is a question of mental health, it will be a board of three psychiatrists. The medical board is authorized to summon anyone as a witness. Suppose a person who has been ordered to testify or produce evidence refuses to do so. In that case, the district court is empowered to compel the person to comply with the medical board's demand by ordering detention or any other means it may decide. The medical board's sessions will be on camera, with no person present except for the board members, the petitioner for a medical licence, the licensed dentist, invited witnesses, and any other person whose presence has been approved by the chairperson.

The board will ensure that the minutes taken at the meetings are true records of the proceedings and will deliver the findings and reasoned decisions to the Director General. The board's discussions and analysis of documents shall be confidential, and their contents made known only to the Director General, except for those parts that the board's chairperson may release for publication. Suppose the medical board has decided that the applicant for a licence or the licensed dentist cannot practise dentistry, at all, partially, or temporarily, because of a dangerous disease, or can engage in dentistry with limitations or under specific conditions. In that case, the Director General will refuse to issue a licence or cancel or suspend the licence, if the person has one, according to the circumstances, or may grant a special licence.

D. Appeal

495. In Amendment No. 7 to the Dentists Ordinance, section 22A was added, addressing the issue of appealing a decision regarding a licence application.

496. A person applying for a licence under subsection A must submit a reasoned appeal within thirty days of the decision made on their application. The appeal is submitted to an Appeals Committee appointed by the Minister, consisting of three members as specified in section C. Committee members include the Director-General of the Ministry of Health or their appointee, a legal advisor, and a public representative with relevant experience.

497. Subsection B specifies that the legal advisor to the Ministry of Health or their representative is authorized, at the applicant's request, to extend the period specified in subsection (a), for special reasons to be recorded, by an additional thirty days.

498. Furthermore, subsection E states that a member of the Appeals Committee may not adjudicate on an appeal concerning a decision they made. The Appeals Committee must determine the appeal promptly, within sixty days from the date of submission of the appeal as specified in subsection F.

499. In summary, the procedure for handling appeals and decisions within the Appeals Committee appointed by the Minister shall comply with the procedures set by the Minister or by the Committee itself.

E. Temporary Suspension

500. When the Director General realizes that the dangerous disease of a licensed dentist causes such immediate danger that it is unthinkable to delay action until the completion of the board's proceedings and the consequent hearing of the appeal, the Director is entitled to suspend the dentist's licence until the decision is finalized.

F. The Obligatory Nature of Confidentiality

501. Any person who is the recipient of information concerning the activities of the medical board or the Director General's synopses of relevant proceedings as detailed above is obliged to maintain silence and divulge no part of it, except insofar as necessary for the implementation of the board's directives; or if he or she has been permitted to do so by the law court; or if he or she is obliged to answer the questions of a functionary who has been authorized to conduct an enquiry into the commission of crimes.

IV. Application for Permit

A. The Application

502. An *application* for a licence to practise dentistry must be presented to the Ministry of Health's Director General. The application will be posted to the District Health Officer for transmission to the Director General, with the following attachments:

(a) A questionnaire that all professional workers must complete in the health services.
(b) A certified copy or photograph of a diploma as proof of the applicant's medical and dental education.
(c) A certificate attesting to the applicant's Israeli nationality or legal status as a resident in Israel.

If the applicant complies with all the conditions in the Ordinance, the Director General is obliged to grant the licence. In addition, the Ministry's Director General is authorized to award a temporary permit for the practice of dentistry for a period of up to six months.

B. The Advisory Licensing Board

503. As *already* stated, the Ministry of Health's Director General is empowered to issue licences and temporary permits for the practice of dentistry. In addition, the law provides the services of an 'advisory board' consisting of three members who are appointees, namely, a physician or dentist employed by the Ministry of Health and two licensed dentists of whom at least one is a faculty member or senior lecturer of professional status at a dental school. The latter two are chosen from a list supplied by the Dentists' Association.

C. Appeal Against Refusal of Licence

504. Amendment No. 7 to the Dentists Ordinance section 22A stipulates that the disappointed applicant for a dentist's licence who wants to appeal the decision can submit a reasoned appeal to the Appeals Committee appointed by the Minister within thirty days. Additionally, the legal advisor to the Ministry of Health or their representative is authorized, upon request from the appellant, to extend the aforementioned period by an additional thirty days for specific reasons to be documented. Section 22A aims to regulate all matters concerning the Appeals Committee to which an appeal can be lodged regarding decisions on licence applications.

V. Practice of Dentistry Without a Licence

505. No person who is unlicensed to practise dentistry shall do so or profess, in fact, or speciously, to practise, or be prepared to practise dentistry. Contraveners of this order may be sentenced to a year's imprisonment or be fined. A person who does not possess a dental licence may not be compensated by the law court for hours of work or be granted an honorarium for work completed or services rendered in the sphere of dentistry. The Ordinance debars a person from using the title of 'dentist' or 'dental practitioner' unless entitled to perform as such. A person who illegally uses the title of a licensed dentist may be sent to prison for three months; a licensed dentist who uses an illegal title may be fined.

VI. Suspension and Cancellation of Licence

A. *Powers of the Health Minister*

506. On *the* strength of a complaint made by the Director General or by an injured party, the Minister of Health may issue an order cancelling the licence of a dentist, or temporarily suspending it for a stated period, or reprimand, or caution a licensed dentist if it is clear that the dentist has acted as follows:

(a) He or she is guilty of conduct unbecoming a dentist.
(b) He or she has obtained as licence by false credentials.
(c) He or she has demonstrated an inability or gross negligence in performing dental activities.
(d) He or she has repeatedly contradicted the directives of the Dentists' Ordinance.
(e) He or she has been found guilty of any criminal misdemeanours not covered by the Dentists' Ordinance.
(f) He or she has refused, without reasonable cause, to exhibit the certificate that entitled him or her to the award of a licence.

The minister will exercise the authority mentioned above after receiving a written report from a committee that he or she has appointed. The committee will consist of at least three persons. Still, it must include the Director General, a representative of the Attorney General, and a spokesman who, in the minister's opinion, represents most licensed dentists. A person who feels aggrieved by the Minister's decision may appeal to the District Court within three months from the date they received notification of the order issued against them.

B. Powers of the Director General

507. The *Director* General is authorized to cancel a licence at its owner's request if the Director is informed that the licensee is dead, or if its owner is no longer eligible for temporary, or permanent residence in Israel.

C. Court Recommendation of Cancellation or Suspension of Licence

508. A *court* finding a person guilty of a crime against the Dentists' Ordinance is authorized to sentence the person and recommend the cancellation or suspension of his or her licence and the forfeiture of possessions by whose aid he or she committed the crime.

VII. Loss of Licence

509. If a licensed dentist mislays a licence, he or she must immediately notify the police and must also inform the Director General, through the agency of the District Health Officer.

VIII. Specialist Titles in Dentistry

A. General

510. The Dentists' Ordinance authorizes the Minister of Health, after consultation with the Israel Dental Association, to issue titles of specialization in various branches of dentistry; to award specialist titles to dentists in the various branches of their profession; to lay down the conditions under which licensed dentists may be allowed to call themselves specialists; and to stipulate those applicants for the title pass examinations whose format, the minister shall decide subject matter and dates. By virtue of duties, the latter promulgated the 1977 Dentists' Regulations (Approval of Title of Specialists and Examinations). These lay down that no dentist will be ratified as a specialist in any other subject than those listed in the appendix. A title will be awarded only after compliance with the regulations.

B. Application for Specialization

511. A dentist wishing to specialize will tender a request to be enrolled as a specialist student to the Scientific Council of the Israel Dentists' Association.

C. Specialization

512. The specialization will be at a recognized institution under the guidance and observation of an instructor who is a qualified specialist in the same branch of dentistry as the student aspires to the title. The period of specialization for each branch of dentistry shall be as specified in the appendix to the regulations mentioned above.

D. Examinations

513. Subject to the Director General's approval, the Scientific Council will appoint professional committees whose members will all be dental specialists, for the various branches of dentistry. Each professional committee will determine the examination procedure and format and appoint examination teams for all the subjects. Each committee will also determine the locations, dates, and times of the examinations. A dentist may sit for examinations after completing the period of his specialization. All matters connected with the examinations will be confidential and officials concerned with them will divulge nothing unless the law requires or permits them to do so. When the applicant has been examined, the Scientific Council will present the Director General with a survey of all its probes, together with the results of the applicant's finals.

E. Confirmation of Title

514. A dentist requesting confirmation of a title as a specialist will apply to the Director General through the agency of the Scientific Council, attaching the following documents to the application:

(a) The diploma attesting to the completion of studies at the dental school of an institution for Higher Education recognized by the Council for Higher Education, or at a university or dental school of university status outside Israel and recognized by the Director General.
(b) An unexpired permit to practise dentistry in Israel.
(c) A certificate attesting to the successful conclusion of the specialization.

The Director General shall decide on the award of specialist title only after receiving the Scientific Council's recommendation.

F. Cancellation or Suspension of Title

515. The Director General is empowered to cancel or suspend a title awarded in the following two cases:

(1) The Director has learned that the title was obtained by false evidence.
(2) The specialist has demonstrated gross negligence or incapacity in practising the type of dentistry in which he or she has specialized.

G. Specialist Titles

516. To date, there are nine roads to specialization:

(1) Mouth and Jaw Surgery.
(2) Paedodontics (Child Surgery).
(3) Orthodontics (Strengthening Teeth and Gums).
(4) Periodontics (Diseases of Gum Tissue).
(5) Endodontics.
(6) Public Dentistry.
(7) Mouth Treatment.
(8) Oral Pathology.
(9) Prosthodontics.

IX. Dental Hygienists

A. Dental Hygienists

517. The Dentists' Ordinance has empowered the Ministry of Health's Director General, subject to consultation with the Israel Dentists' Association and before Amendment No. 8, approval was required from the Knesset's Labour and Welfare Committee, however, following the amendment, approval must now be obtained from the Knesset's Health Committee, to lay down regulations according to which dental hygienists' competency and permitted sphere of activity is defined. Dental hygienists are authorized to practise as educators in dental hygiene and care for the mouth and teeth. By virtue of the Director General's powers, the Regulations for Dentists (Hygienists) were compiled in 1978. These regulations list the activities in which dental hygienists are permitted to engage for the cleaning and brushing of teeth, as follows:

(a) The removal of stones and other coatings from the teeth.
(b) The removal of superfluous lime from the external covers of the teeth.
(c) The polishing of the teeth's external coverings.
(d) The making of impressions for teaching models.
(e) The removal of stitches and bandages.
(f) The use of ointments for the removal of caries.
(g) The use of preparations for local anaesthetization.
(h) Advice and guidance on oral and dental hygiene.
(i) Examination of the mouth in preparation for dental treatment.

B. Qualifications for a Licence

518. An Israeli subject or resident who has reached the age of 18 is eligible for a licence after satisfying the Director General of the Ministry of Health that he or she has acquired suitable professional knowledge. In addition, such a person must have pursued a recognized course of studies for dental hygienists in Israel and passed government examinations or is the possessor of a recognized diploma attesting to the successful completion of a course of studies in the subject.

C. Application for, and Award of, Licence

519. An application for a licence must be addressed to the Director General through the agency of the District Health *Officer*. Attachments to the application will consist of certified copies or photographs of the applicant's professional attainments and proof of Israeli citizenship or residential status in Israel. The Director General will award the licence to applicants who satisfy the requirements.

D. Rejection of Application

520. In two cases or situations, the Ministry of Health's Director General is authorized to refrain from granting a licence:

(1) The applicant has been found guilty of an offence of a nature that indicates a lack of the necessary responsibility to do the work of a dental hygienist.
(2) Some other fact tends to demonstrate that the applicant is incapable or unworthy of working as a dental hygienist.

E. Cancellation or Suspension of Licence

521. The *Minister's* Director General is empowered to order the cancellation or suspension of a licence in any one of the following contingencies or situations:

(a) The licensee has no permit for residence in Israel.
(b) The licensee is guilty of conduct unbecoming a member of the profession.
(c) The licensee has obtained a licence by producing forged evidence.
(d) He or she has demonstrated inability, irresponsibility, or gross negligence in the performance of his duties.
(e) He or she has contravened the directives of the Dentists' Ordinance or its resultant regulations.
(f) The licensee is guilty of an offence that is a blot on his or her character, or which indicates irresponsibility in the practice of the profession. Appeal against the Director General's refusal to award a licence, cancel it, or suspend it may be directed to the Minister of Health.

F. Loss of Licence

522. Any person who mislays his or her licence must inform the police and the Director General, by whose authority a copy may be issued.

X. Dental Technicians

A. Legal Monopoly of Dental Practice

523. The Dentists' Ordinance authorizes the Director General of the Ministry of Health to formulate regulations with the approval of the minister, defining the spheres of activity in which dental technicians may engage and their working conditions. As a result of the authority invested in the Director General, the 1986 Dentists' Regulations defining the spheres of activity of dental technicians and their working conditions came into force. The regulations deal with four types of artisans: the practical technician, the certified technician, the master technician, and the specialist technician. In addition, the regulations illegalize dental technology practice by any person who does not hold a licence to practise as one of those mentioned above. Directives concerning dental technology are on such subjects as the construction and repair of partial or complete dentures, bridges, welded fillings, and the fabrication of other devices for the mouth or teeth – all if they do not require workmanship in the mouth of the patient.

524. Application for a licence will be addressed to the Director General through the agency of the District Health Officer, with the following attachments:

(a) A completed questionnaire intended for professionals in the health services.
(b) A copy or photograph of certificates testifying to the applicant's professional attainments.
(c) A document in proof of the applicant's citizenship of, or residence in, Israel.
(d) Confirmation of the applicant's experience, namely the years of practice in dental technology as the sole occupation.

B. Conditions for Award of Licence

525. The *Director General* will grant the applicant a licence, subject to the following terms:

(a) The applicant is an Israel citizen or a permanent resident of Israel.
(b) The applicant is an honest person.
(c) He or she complies with the conditions detailed in the regulations.
(d) He or she has passed the examination for which he or she was required to sit.

526. A committee sets the examination in dental technology. It consists of three parts: written, oral, and practical tests. Subjects for examination include dental morphology, elements of physics and chemistry, laboratory equipment and structure, materials including metals and tools for welding, fashioning and polishing crowns, bridges, and sets of complete and partial dentures.

A committee will determine the times and venues of an examination at least once a year. The committee will also assess each applicant's examination results. A failed candidate may appeal to the Director General, whose decision will be final.

C. *Loss of Licence*

527. If a dental technician has mislaid his or her licence, the Director General must be informed, who is authorized to supply the technician with a copy.

D. *Cancellation or Suspension of a Licence*

528. The *Director* General of the Ministry of Health has the right to cancel or suspend a licence in any of the following events or situations:

(a) The licensee has obtained credentials by forged evidence.
(b) The licensee has committed an offence contravening the Dentists' Ordinance.
(c) In the licensee's work as a technician, he or she has overstepped his authority.
(d) He or she has refused, for no reasonable cause, to produce certificates for inspection by the Director General.
(e) He or she has been found guilty of conduct unbecoming a dental technician.
(f) He or she has demonstrated incapability or gross negligence in performing duties as a dental technician.
(g) He or she has had recourse to illegal self-advertisement.

529. In 2009, the Minister of Health enacted the Dentists' Regulations (Impermissible Advertisement). The *Regulations* set out a high standard of professional ethics, thus prohibiting any advertisement that might mislead the public or insult the profession's integrity. Likewise, is prohibited advertisement that insults the public (e.g., publishing tariffs or encouraging patients to receive medical treatment that is unnecessary solely for financial advantages).

§3. Psychologists

I. Practice of Psychology

530. The 1977 Psychologists' Law describes the psychologist's occupation as a profession dealing with the diagnosis and evaluation of features and problems in people's mental, intellectual, and behavioural habits and with the consequent treatment, rehabilitation, advice, and guidance that only a psychologist normally supplies.

531. No person may practise psychology unless he or she is a psychologist, which means that he or she is listed in the official register of psychologists or has a permit to practise. A person who has a bachelor's degree in psychology awarded by a recognized institution has the right to practise psychology only under the guidance of a psychologist at a recognized place of work. Any chance action taken by a person or any haphazard advice by a person, unintentionally or in the course of normal duties, will not be regarded as the practice of psychology. No person may be called a specialist in psychology unless the Ministry of Health's Director General has approved the award of the title in compliance with the Psychologists' Regulations (Approval of Title of Specialist) of 1979.

II. Listing in Psychologists' Register

532. Those eligible to be listed in the Psychologists' Register will be inscribed by the decision of the registration committee appointed by the Ministry of Health. The committee consists of five members, comprising the minister's representative, three psychologists chosen by the minister from a list supplied by the Council of Psychologists, and another psychologist who is on the psychologists' teaching staff of a recognized institute of higher studies. Any person is eligible for listing in the Psychologists' Register, if he or she is an Israeli citizen, or resides in Israel and is one of the following:

(a) The holder of at least a master's degree in psychology from a recognized institute of higher education in Israel.
(b) The holder of a foreign degree of similar status and recognized as such by the registration committee.
(c) A person of long experience in the practice of psychology.

533. In the following cases or situations, the registration committee is authorized to turn down a request for registration:

(a) The candidate for registration has been found guilty of an offence that clearly reveals that he or she lacks the responsibility required by a practising psychologist and less than ten years have elapsed since that court decision or since the period of probation if such is decreed by the court.
(b) There exists some other fact that discloses the applicant's inability or unworthiness to practise psychology. If the registration committee has rejected the application, a person has the right to request that the case be reconsidered. The applicant also has the right to appeal to the district court if a request for registration is rejected.

534. The registration committee is authorized to issue a temporary permit for the practice of psychology.

III. Disqualification for Reasons of Health

A. Medical Examination of Applicant for Registration

535. If the registration committee has reasonable grounds for suspecting that the applicant for registration has contracted a dangerous disease, it has the right to demand that the applicant appear before a medical committee for examination. The law defines a dangerous disease as one of the following:

(a) Mental deficiency.
(b) Any disease that may infect people treated by the psychologist.
(c) An illness, or diminished competence that is liable to deprive the psychologist of the ability to practise psychology, completely, partially, or temporarily.

536. The medical committee is appointed by the Ministry of Health's Director General. It consists of three physicians or psychiatrists. Its duty is to deliver its findings and conclusions to the registration committee. An applicant who has refused to be medically examined will be deprived of a listing by the registration committee in the Psychologists' Register.

B. Medical Examination for a Practising Psychologist

537. If it *comes* to the notice of the registration committee that a practising psychologist has contracted a dangerous disease, it has the right to demand that the psychologist be examined by a medical committee. If the psychologist refuses to present for examination, the registration committee has the power to suspend his or her listing in the Register. If the registration committee learns that a psychologist's dangerous disease poses so immediate a threat that a decision on suspension cannot be delayed until the medical committee has reached a decision, which may be followed by an appeal, it may authorize the immediate suspension of the psychologist's activities. Should the registration committee have grounds for supposing that information concerning the physical condition of an applicant for registration or of a practitioner of psychology is lodged with a medical institution, or with a physician who has treated the psychologist or if evidence appertains to another person, it has the right in anticipation of its order that the psychologist present for examination to demand that the possessor of such information or documentary evidence hand it over, and the latter is obliged to do so. Any person who is the recipient of information about an illness is required to treat it as confidential and may not divulge this knowledge unless authorized to do so by the law court, or by virtue of an obligation to answer questions from a person who has been mandated to conduct an enquiry into the commission of crimes.

C. Decision of Registration Committee and Appeal

538. If *the* medical committee has decided that an applicant for registration as a psychologist, or a practising psychologist, is incapable of practising psychology, completely, or for the time being, in view of a dangerous disease; or that he or she can pursue the calling only within limitations, or under specific conditions, the registration committee will not list the applicant's name in the Psychologists' Register, or will delete the name from the Register, or will forbid, or limit, the applicant's activities. The Registration Committee is authorized, upon the applicant's request for reconsideration, if the request is submitted within fifteen days of receiving notification of the request The applicant is entitled to present their arguments before the Registration Committee and may be represented by an attorney or by a person knowledgeable and experienced in the field of psychology.

IV. Specialist Titles

A. Titles

539. Recognized specialists in psychology practise in the spheres of clinical psychology, educational psychology, occupational and social psychology, rehabilitative psychology, and developmental psychology. The law empowers the Minister of Health to determine that there can be specialization in any branch of psychology and to impose conditions for training, examination, and award of title and certificate in each of those branches of the profession. He is also entitled to assign specific activities in psychology to recognized specialists and to order that the latter be listed as recognized specialists in the Psychologist Specialists' Register. The Ministry of Health's Director General is authorized to approve the award of the title of specialist to a psychologist who has completed a specialization course and has passed an examination in accordance with the regulations. The Director General is empowered to award the title of specialist instructor to a person who possesses the following qualifications:

(a) He or she is a psychology specialist in one of the branches of the profession listed in the appendix to the regulations.
(b) He or she has acquired at least three years of professional experience as a specialist in a branch of psychology.
(c) He or she has completed the specialization programme for instructors and has satisfied all the requirements or has been exempted from examination.
(d) The Director General is persuaded that there is no professional or ethical objection to the candidate's appointment as an instructor.

B. *Training for Specialization for Award of Title*

540. Specialization training shall be at a recognized institution under the guidance and control of a specialist instructor. The recognized institution may be any hospital, establishment, ward, professional body, clinic, centre, or service that has been accredited by the Director General.

541. Following the 2024 Amendment to the Psychologists Regulations (Specialization Approval), section 27H was revised to stipulate that the duration of specialization must be a minimum of two years in a recognized institution, with a workload of at least half-time, or a minimum of three years in a recognized institution, with a workload of at least one-third time.

V. Cancellation or Suspension of Title

A. *Disciplinary Sanctions*

542. The law authorizes a disciplinary committee to order the deletion of a psychologist's name from the Register or to ban the *psychologist's* practice for a period of up to five years if it finds him or her guilty of misconduct. The Minister of Health appointed the disciplinary committee, consisting of a lawyer and two psychologists. A complaints committee appointed by the Minister of Health is authorized to investigate grounds for reasonable suspicion that a psychologist has had bad conduct and to decide whether the psychologist must appear before the disciplinary committee. Examples of misbehaviour quoted in the law are as follows:

(a) Conduct unbecoming a practitioner of psychology.
(b) Obtaining a licence or permit with the aid of false evidence.
(c) Demonstration of incapacity, irresponsibility, or gross negligence in the performance of professional duties.
(d) Habitual contravention of the Psychologists' Law and its Regulations.
(e) Conviction of a crime attesting to a lack of the essential responsibility that the practice of psychology requires.

An appeal against the disciplinary committee's decision will be heard by the district court. If the disciplinary committee has reasonable grounds to suspect that a person's mental deficiency makes the person incapable of standing trial or of being held responsible for an act of commission or omission of which he or she is accused, it may request the registration committee to consider removing the name from the Register, as well as exercising its other mandates.

Once the disciplinary committee's decision becomes final, the Director General of the Ministry of Health must present the convicted psychologist's name before the public; this shall be done through the official website of the Ministry of Health. In doing so, the Director General shall make sure that the patient's name and other identification details remain confidential.

B. Director General's Powers

543. The law empowers the Director General of the Ministry of Health to cancel or suspend the approval of a specialist's title if faced with information that the title was obtained by false evidence or that the holder of the title has demonstrated gross negligence or inability to perform the duties in the capacity of a psychology specialist.

VI. Social Workers

544. One of the main objectives of the 1996 Social Workers' Law was to protect the professional standard of social welfare workers and to ensure their fit and proper behaviour. Social welfare is defined by the law as a professional occupation that improves the personal and social functioning of the individual, his or her family and the environment through treatment, rehabilitation, advice, and guidance, all normally controlled by the social welfare worker using the professional methods of treatment that are standard practice in social welfare. The law illegalizes a person's social welfare activity unless he or she is as competent to be a social worker as the law requires and has been duly listed in the Social Workers' Register. However, any action performed out of the kindness of his or her heart by a person, while normal activities or occupation, although not a social worker, shall not be regarded as social welfare work.

§4. THE NURSING PROFESSION

I. General

545. All nurses must obtain licences in order to practise nursing for two reasons: The general public must be safeguarded, and the nursing profession must be safeguarded. The general public must be strengthened by receiving treatment whose quality is of a high standard. The profession must be strengthened by retaining an overall monopoly, a limitation of competition and a prestigious reputation. Nursing without a licence is liable to involve a person in the litigation.

II. Licence for Nursing in Hospital

A. General

546. The 1940 Ordinance for Public Health determines the conditions for the registration of hospitals with the Director of Public Health Services. No hospital may be registered unless the Director has been apprised of the fact that there are enough nurses on the staff and that the senior nurse, or any other person in charge of the nurses, is a qualified nurse and possesses a nursing diploma, or some other certification of nursing studies, both recognized by the Director. The 1940 Ordinance empowered the Health Ministry's Director General to determine regulations with respect to nurses' qualifications in the spheres of education and practical training.

547. The revised version of the Physicians' Ordinance lays down that only a licensed physician may practise medicine. Still, the same Ordinance also decrees that this ruling does not deprive a nurse of authority to tend to patients, nor does it prevent any person, including a nurse, from giving advice, or chance treatment without payment or recompense, or from performing duties under the personal and direct control of a licensed physician. The Ordinance allows a licensed physician to associate nurses under his or her personal control with professional activity. However, any person who is not a licensed physician is debarred from treating, looking after, or operating on a patient when such activity requires the professional judgment and skill of a physician.

548. The 1988 Public Health Regulations, which deal with hospital nursing, lay down that a person shall not be employed in nursing or midwifery at a hospital unless licensed to do so, or in possession of a temporary permit to be employed in nursing or midwifery, being so listed in the relevant section of the Register. This proviso does not apply to a student nurse, who is employed as a nurse in a hospital under the guidance of a person who is licensed to practise nursing in a hospital. The 'practice of nursing' is qualified in the above-mentioned regulations as nursing, being the sole occupation of a person who is a hospital nurse, licensed in accordance with the training in nursing that he or she has completed, as specified in the Public Health Regulations, and including the medical activities and services he or she has rendered, as prescribed in all the laws. The 'holder of a licence for nursing employment' is a person listed in the Register of Licensees 'to practise nursing or midwifery' in a hospital.

B. Skills for Special Activities

549. The revised version of the Physicians' Ordinance lays down that the Director General of the Ministry of Health has the right to exempt nurses from compliance with the Ordinance's Regulations regarding certain activities at such medical centres as having been approved. The Director General is empowered to determine the skills required by the nurses who are assigned to such tasks and issue directives accordingly. After doing so, the directors of the approved medical centres are free to allow nurses who possess the skills to carry out those tasks. In, 1977, the Director General formulated the Physicians Regulations (Skills for the Performance of Special Activities) when defining two kinds of competence, special and general. Nurses who are classified as especially competent are permitted to diagnose and cure patients, even if their work falls within the framework of a 'medical occupation,' if they have completed their training for the performance of the task, as recognized by the Director General. The 'general competence' detailed in the regulations is of two different types which must have been acquired by nurses whose licences are recognized by the Ministry of Health.

550. The first type of general competence that the nurse must have acquired during studies at the nursing school where he or she has graduated enables the nurse to perform the following duties:

(a) The removal of blood from the veins is done for regular analysis.
(b) Taking sterile urine for examination.
(c) The delivery of phlegm for inspection.
(d) The catheterization of the urine bladder is done by way of the urine duct.
(e) The insertion of a pipe into the stomach while the patient is conscious.
(f) Measuring venous blood pressure after a licensed physician has adjusted the instruments.
(g) Supplying oxygen.
(h) Immunization against tetanus.
(i) Changing bandages after an operation.
(j) Removal of stitches.

551. The second type of general competence that a nurse must have acquired by completing a course in emergency treatment recognized by the Director General enables the nurse to perform the following duties, if they are done at a hospital:

(a) withdrawing blood for analysis, including arterial blood samples for gases;
(b) injection of liquids, including blood transfusions, to the veins and medication of the veins in general with preparations for transfusion and extraction of the catheter or needle from the veins;
(c) injection of medication as ordered by a physician in case of serious heartbeat irregularity and in accordance with standard orders;
(d) the administering of medicines at frequencies ordered by a licensed physician;
(e) the attachment of electrodes to determine the rate of heartbeats;
(f) the application of respiratory apparatus, adjustment of oxygen supply, and exchange of appropriate gases;
(g) the clearing of liquids from the nostrils and bronchial tubes;
(h) the insertion of an air passage into the nasal area;
(i) the making of electrocardiograms;
(j) external heart massage, including defibrillation.

Furthermore, after Amendment No. 35 to the Pharmacists Ordinance, the law granted an additional function to nurses. Accordingly, according to the law, a pharmacist may dispense prescription medications only based on a prescription signed by a physician, dentist, veterinarian, or by a certified nurse, under the condition that these nurses have at least five years of experience as certified nurses and have received personal authorization for this purpose from the director, or from the chief medical officer of an HMO as defined in the Health Insurance Law, or from a medical institution authorized by the director for this purpose.

C. Conditions for Registration

1. General Conditions

552. The conditions for listing a person in one of the Register's divisions consist of overall rules with which every applicant for registration must comply as well as other, more precise rules imposed on applicants for listing in a specific division of the Register.

553. The general conditions imposed on an applicant are as follows:

(a) He or she is an Israeli subject and resides in Israel.
(b) He or she has reached the age of 18.
(c) His or her knowledge of Hebrew is at least basic.
(d) He or she has been professionally trained, as prescribed in the above-mentioned regulations.
(e) He or she has not been found guilty of an offence that carries a prison sentence with it, prohibiting the applicant's practice of nursing.

2. Conditions for Registration of Licensed Nurses

554. Listing in the licensed nurses' division of the Register is under the following conditions:

(a) success in a recognized matriculation examination;
(b) successful conclusion of a recognized course of studies for licensed nurses;
(c) success in the examination for licensed nurses of the nursing division of the Ministry of Health.

3. Conditions for Registration of Practising Nurses

555. Listing in the Register's practising nurses' division is subject to the following conditions:

(a) completion of ten years of study at school;
(b) conclusion of a recognized course of studies for practising nurses;
(c) success in the Ministry of Health's nursing division's examination for practising nurses.

4. Conditions for Registration of Nursing Attendants

556. Listing in the nursing attendants' division of the Register requires:

(a) conclusion of a recognized nursing attendants' course of studies;
(b) success in the examination for the registration of a nursing attendant.

5. Conditions for Registration of Midwives

557. Conditions for the listing of midwives in the Register require the following:

(a) previous listing as a licensed nurse;
(b) conclusion of a recognized course of studies for midwives;
(c) success in the examination of the midwives' division of the Ministry.

6. Conditions for Registration of Holders of Certificates in Further Education

558. Listing in the Register's division for holders of recognized certificates of further education will be under the following conditions:

(a) previous listing in the division for licensed or practising nurses;
(b) conclusion of a recognized course in further education;
(c) success in the division's examinations.

559. A *person* who is licensed to practise nursing has completed a course in further education recognized by the Director General and is listed in the Register as the holder of a certificate of further education is exempt from compliance with the regulations of the Physicians' Ordinance and may perform the medical duties and supply the medical services for which he or she has been trained by his recognized further studies.

7. Temporary or Limited Permit

560. The Senior Nursing Officer is empowered to issue a temporary permit for employment as a practising nurse to a person *before* the procedure for his or her registration is completed and a limited permit to a nurse who is not an Israeli subject, or whose home is not in Israel.

8. Medical Examination

561. The Ministry of Health's Director General is empowered to demand an examination of the physical or mental health *and* order the appearance before a medical committee, of a candidate for listing in the Register of Licensed Nurses and of Midwives. The Director General will appoint the committee that will examine the candidate and submit its findings. If the Director General believes that the dangerous illness of a person practising nursing or midwifery is liable to cause such immediate harm to patients or to the person that it is inadvisable to wait for the end of the medical committees' proceedings, the Director is empowered to suspend the nursing worker's listing in the Register. A 'dangerous illness' is defined by the law as including one of the following: mental illness, a disease that may cause harm to the nurse's patients, a disease or diminished competence that is liable to deprive a person of the ability to practise nursing or midwifery, whichever is relevant, completely, temporarily, or partially. If the medical committee has decided that the applicant for listing in the Register, or a nurse who is already licensed to practise nursing or midwifery, is by virtue of a dangerous illness, incapable of doing so, completely, or for the time being; or if the medical committee has decided that a person is able to serve as a nurse or a midwife only to a limited extent, or only under specific conditions; the Director General will instruct the senior nursing officer to refuse to list him or her in the Register, or if he or she is already listed, to delete the name or debar the person from practice for a period of time, or to confine the scope of the person's nursing activities.

9. Appeal

562. A person who feels injured by the decision of the Director General or of the senior nursing officer has the right to appeal to the Minister of Health.

10. Cancellation or Suspension of Registration

563. The Director General of the Ministry of Health is empowered to delete or suspend registration if advised that a person against whom a complaint has been lodged has committed one of the following offences:

(a) He or she is guilty of conduct unbecoming the nursing profession.
(b) He or she has been registered by presenting forged documents.
(c) He or she has demonstrated incapacity, irresponsibility, or gross neglect in the performance of duties.
(d) He or she has been pronounced guilty of an offence that has left a blot on his or her character or shows a lack of the responsibility of a practising nurse.
(e) He or she has not produced credentials for inspection by the chief nursing officer.

III. Licence for Practice of Nursing at Clinics

A. The Legal Monopoly of the Profession

564. The 1981 Regulations for Public Health (Nursing Staff at Clinics) lay down that no person shall practise, or be employed in, nursing at a clinic, unless licensed to practise nursing, or has a temporary permit to do so. The Public Health Ordinance details the penalties imposed on anyone who contravenes the regulations' directives. The ban does not apply to a nursing student working under a person who is licensed to practise nursing. 'A person who is licensed to practise nursing' is one whose name appears in the Register of Nursing Personnel. A licensed nurse at a clinic may not perform any act that may be assigned only to a recognized specialist nurse unless he or she is registered as a specialist in the branch of nursing in whose sphere the Director General has permitted him or her to practise. This ban is not imposed on a specialist student of nursing, who is active in a specialist capacity under the control of a recognized specialist in nursing. A 'clinic' is defined in section 34(c) of the Public Health Ordinance as a place that is not a hospital requiring a licence and whose objective is to supply the public with medical services, dental treatment, and nursing, which may include round-the-clock service for the cure and relief of patients and pregnant women.

B. Conditions for Listing in the Register

565. Any person is eligible for registration, subject to the following conditions:

(a) He or she is an Israeli subject or resides in Israel.
(b) He or she has reached the age of 18.
(c) He or she knows basic Hebrew at least.
(d) He or she has been trained in nursing.

C. Conditions for Registration of Licensed Nurses

566. Listing in the Register of Licensed Nurses is subject to three conditions:

(1) success in recognized matriculation examinations;
(2) successfully completing a recognized course of studies for licensed nurses;
(3) success in the Ministry of Health's Nursing Division's examinations for licensed nurses.

D. Conditions for Registration of Practising Nurses

567. The *listing* of a practising nurse in the appropriate division of the Register is subject to the following three conditions:

(1) completion of the tenth grade of a recognized high school;
(2) completion of a recognized educational course for practising nurses;
(3) success in the Ministry's Nursing Division's examination for practising nurses.

E. Conditions for Registration of Nursing Attendants

568. Listing *as* a nursing attendant in the Register is subject to the following three conditions:

(1) completion of the tenth grade of a recognized high school;
(2) completion of a recognized nursing course for nursing attendants;
(3) success in the Nursing Attendants' Division of the Ministry examinations.

F. Length of Further Training Period

569. The Director General of the Health Ministry is empowered to approve the addition of a further period of nursing apprenticeship in a nursing school's syllabus as a condition for graduation.

G. Recognized Specialization

570. The *Director* General of the Ministry of Health, after consultation with the Female and Male Nurses' Association of Israel, is empowered:

(a) to decide that a specific branch of nursing shall be for recognized specialists only;
(b) to impose conditions regarding the training, examination, degree, and certificate of candidates for specialization;
(c) to reserve certain nursing activities for the possessors of recognized specialization;
(d) to order that the holders of certificates of recognized specialization be listed as such in the Register.

In 2015, the Director General of the Ministry of Health had expanded the list of fields of specialization in nursing, thus including the fields of pain, rehabilitation, and policy and administration. This is besides already-recognized specializations, among others, supportive care, geriatrics, and diabetes.

H. Application for Registration

571. A *request* for listing in the Register must be addressed to the nursing staff's registrar, through the agency of the district health office of the Registration Division of the Ministry of Health, together with a certified copy of documents attesting to the applicant's training in nursing and of a certificate attesting to the applicant's status as a citizen of, or a resident in, Israel.

I. Rejection of Application

572. The Director General has the right to order that a person shall not be registered if found guilty of a crime that is a blot on his *character* or if the offence is of a nature that demonstrates a lack of the essential responsibility characteristic of one who practises nursing.

J. Medical Examination

573. The Director General of the Ministry of Health is empowered to demand an examination of the mental or physical health of an applicant for registration or of a licensed nurse and to order such a person to present before a medical board. The Director General will appoint the medical examination committee, which will deliver its findings. If the Director General believes that the dangerous disease of a licensed nurse is such an immediate threat that it makes it essential to forego the committee's findings, the Director has the right to suspend that person's listing in the Register. A dangerous disease is defined by law as including a mental illness, an affliction that may infect the nurse's patients, or an ailment or *diminished* competence that may deprive the nurse of the capacity to practise nursing completely, temporarily, or partially. Should the committee decide that the applicant for registration or the licensed nurse is incapacitated by a dangerous illness from practising nursing completely, or for the time being, or that the applicant's capacity for nursing is limited, or conditional, the Director General may order the registrar not to list the name, to delete the name, if already listed, to limit, or to prohibit the applicant's nursing activities.

K. Appeal

574. Any person who is affected by the Director General's decision may appeal to the Minister of Health.

L. Cancellation or Suspension of Registration

575. The *Director* General of the Ministry of Health has the authority to delete a listing from the Registry or suspend a listed person if learning that a person, against whom a complaint has been submitted is guilty of one of the following:

(a) His or her conduct is unbecoming a person who practises nursing.
(b) His or her licence has been obtained by forged evidence.

(c) His or her performance of his duties has revealed incapability, irresponsibility, or gross negligence.
(d) He or she has been found guilty of an offence that stains character or demonstrates a lack of responsibility that is essential to the performance of medical duties.
(e) He or she has failed to show credentials to the registrar when required to do so.

§5. Midwives

I. Midwifery, a Legal Monopoly

576. In addition to the regulations formalizing the nursing profession, the Ordinance, which dates to the British Mandate and deals specifically with midwifery, must be regarded as supplementary to the Nurses' Regulations.

577. The Midwives' Ordinance of 1929 makes it illegal for a person to engage in midwifery if he or she is not licensed. The profession of a midwife includes examination for, or diagnosis of, pregnancy, the prescribing of medication for the pregnant, caring for them, and assisting them during childbirth. The ban does not exclude a licensed physician from practising midwifery or a layperson from coming to the rescue of a labouring woman during an emergency, without thought of recompense. The above-mentioned Ordinance decrees that each of the following may be certified to choose midwifery as his or her occupation:

(a) a licence holder;
(b) a person listed in a special division of the Register without holding a licence;
(c) the holder of a temporary licence;
(d) the holder of a temporary permit.

II. Application for a Licence

578. An *application* for a licence for midwifery as an occupation must be addressed to the Director General of the Ministry of Health. The applicant will be eligible for a licence if the minister receives proof of the facts that the applicant has an honest character; is an Israeli subject or has been granted permission to settle in Israel; and if he or she has studied childbirth for at least six months at an institution recognized by the Director General, and has been awarded a midwife's certificate recognized by the Director General.

III. Cancellation of Licence by the Minister of Health

579. If, as a result of a complaint of the Director General or of anyone who feels discriminated against, the minister feels that a person licensed to practise midwifery is guilty of conduct that disgraces his or her calling, or has obtained a licence by false evidence, or has been found incapable, or grossly negligent in the performance of his or her professional duties; or has consistently contravened the directives of the Ordinance; or has been found guilty of a criminal offence; the minister has the right to cancel or suspend that person's licence.

§6. VETERINARIANS

I. General

580. The veterinarian is mandated to prevent and relieve the suffering of animals, to prevent and cure their diseases, to render aid for the maintenance of proper living conditions on animal farms, to protect mankind against risks and injuries caused by animal diseases, and by food or edible products of animal origin and to work for the improved quality of such foodstuffs as contain animal components. Animals are nothing but those listed in the revised version of the 1985 Animals' Ordinance. The Veterinarians' Law defines the work of veterinarians as the medical treatment of animals for the prevention and cure of diseases, examination and diagnosis of disease, or alternatively certifying that their carcases are fit for human consumption.

II. Legal Monopoly of Veterinarian Profession

581. Only persons holding a licence, a permit, or a restricted authorization may choose the practice of a veterinarian for their *livelihood*. This directive does not exclude advice or medical treatment given gratis or work under the vigilant eye of a veterinarian.

III. Conditions for Award of Licence

582. A person who has complied with the following conditions may practise veterinary medicine:

(a) He or she is an Israeli citizen or holder of a certificate of permanent residence in Israel.
(b) He or she has taken a course in veterinary medicine.
(c) He or she has passed examinations as stipulated by the Ministry of Health's Director General or is a graduate veterinarian of a faculty or school for veterinarians at an Israeli institution for higher education and holds a graduation certificate; or is the graduate of an institution of similar status abroad, recognized by the Director General.
(d) He or she has not been found guilty in Israel of an offence that is a blot on his or her character.

583. A fee of ILS 400 must be paid by any applicant who wishes to be admitted to the examination. An examination board appointed by the Director General is authorized to choose the questions for the examination paper, fix dates, conduct the examination, select examiners and supervisors, and estimate the results that will be passed on to the Director General. The examination will be in writing unless the chairperson of the board decides that it will be oral and/or in a foreign language. The subjects in which candidates will be examined will be decided by Israeli legislation with respect to veterinarians, the incidence of diseases in the Animal Diseases Ordinance, diagnosis, prevention, and elimination of disease among domestic animals and control by veterinarians over Israeli products with animal components.

IV. Application for Award of Licence

584. Application for the practice of veterinary medicine addressed to the Director General will have the following attachments:

(a) a copy or photograph of a final certificate as proof of the applicant's veterinary education;
(b) a copy or photograph attesting to the applicant's success in examinations determined by the Director General;
(c) a certificate attesting to the applicant's Israeli citizenship or permanent residence in Israel and permission for information about himself to be forwarded to the Director by Criminal Records.

585. If the applicant complies with all the conditions, the Director General will award him or her a licence. If the latter is not convinced that the applicant has fulfilled all the conditions, the applicant will be referred to an advisory committee appointed by the Director, and the applicant will accept its recommendation unless otherwise persuaded.

The Director General shall issue his decision on the application for a veterinary medical licence within six months from the date of submission of the application. If the director fails to decide by the specified deadline, the applicant shall be considered having been denied. The Director General is authorized to issue a temporary permit allowing a person to practise as a veterinarian.

V. Loss of Licence

586. If a veterinarian mislays his or her licence, he or she must notify the police and the Director General, who is allowed to *replace* the licence with a copy.

VI. Cancellation and Suspension of Licence

587. The Minister of Health is empowered to order the cancellation or suspension of a veterinarian's licence on the strength of a *complaint* from the Director General or from an injured party in the following circumstances or situations:

(a) The veterinarian is guilty of conduct that is unbecoming the profession.
(b) He or she has used false evidence to obtain a licence.
(c) He or she has demonstrated incapability or gross negligence in performing professional duties.
(d) He or she has been found guilty of an offence in circumstances that leave a blot on his or her character.
(e) He or she has contravened directives on self-advertisement.
(f) During a period of service for a local authority, he or she has moonlighted as a private veterinarian in contravention of all legal directives and creating a conflict of interests between two employments.

588. An appeal *against* the cancellation or suspension of a licence may be presented to the district court. A court that finds a person guilty of offences against the Veterinarians' Law, in addition to sentencing, has the authority to cancel or suspend the person's licence to practise as a veterinarian.

§7. Optometrists

I. General

589. The 1991 Law on the Optometrists' Profession defines optometry as the measurement of a person's visual skill or range of sight, *diagnosis* of the human eye's adjustment to, or refraction of, light rays, the preparation of lenses to rectify sight, the issue of prescriptions or directions for the use of optical aids to sight, and prescription for the adjustment and matching of contact lenses for human sight. Orthoptics is described in the law as the measurement of the eye's muscular activity, the amount of cooperation between a pair of eyes, and treatment controlled by an ophthalmic physician for squint, or the lazy eye, using an eye patch or by exercising the eye, or by the application of suitable optical instruments.

II. The Profession's Legal Monopoly

590. No person may practise optometry unless he or she has a legal licence to do so. This prohibition does not apply to an eye specialist or a person who is specializing in ophthalmic diseases, nor does it apply to a person who is specializing in practical optometry under the guidance and control of a licensed physician.

III. Eligibility for a Licence

591. The Director General of the Ministry of Health is legally empowered to issue a licence for the practice of optometry to an applicant who is the possessor of professional training in optometry. A person who is a trained optometrist has all the following qualifications:

(a) He or she has been educated in optometry, which means he or she fulfils one of the following conditions:
   (1) He or she has obtained a degree attesting to the successful completion of studies in optometry at the school for optometrists of a recognized institution in Israel.
   (2) He or she has completed studies in optometry at a foreign university or at a school for optometry of university status, both recognized by the Director General and is in possession of a diploma also recognized by the Director General.

(b) He or she has completed a period of specialization as required by the regulations.

(c) He or she has successfully passed government examinations. The Minister of Health is empowered to issue directives that decree that a particular branch of optometry requires recognized specialization, in which case an optometrist may not provide any service that only a specialist in a specific branch of optometry may render unless he or she is a recognized specialist in that branch of the profession.

IV. Cancellation of a Licence

592. The Director General of the Ministry of Health has the right to cancel a licence or recognition of a specialist, or to suspend a person, either learning that the optometrist has acted ineptly, unprofessionally, or neglectfully; or if the optometrist has obtained a licence or recognition as a specialist by false evidence; or if the optometrist has been convicted of a crime that has left a blot on his or her character. However, the Director General will refrain from taking such action until the optometrist has been given an opportunity to plead his or her cause before a hearings committee appointed by the Director General. Appeal against the latter's decision may be directed to a magistrate's court.

§8. Hypnotists

I. General

593. The 1984 Law on the Use of Hypnotism regularized the use of hypnotism in Israel for the first time. Hypnotism is commonly defined as an action or process that, by the use of one person's suggestion, is intended to, or really does, cause changes in the state of another person's cognition and awareness, leading to deviations in his or her body, consciousness, feelings, memory, and behaviour.

II. Hypnotism as a Monopolistic Profession

594. The law allows no person to hypnotize another unless he or she is a licensed hypnotist. This order does not apply to a physician, dentist, or psychology specialist who has been authorized by the Director General of the Ministry of Health to study hypnotism of the kind practised for the furtherance of studies under the personal supervision of a specialist teacher of hypnotism.

III. Eligibility for Certification

595. A person who complies with the following conditions may become a certified hypnotist:

(a) He or she resides in Israel.
(b) He or she is a physician, dentist, or specialist in psychology.
(c) He or she has completed a recognized course in hypnotism and passed an examination recognized by the Director General. Instruction in hypnotism must be at a recognized institution.

IV. Application and Decision

596. An applicant for a licence to hypnotize will forward his application to the registrar of licensed hypnotists. If the registrar decides that the applicant possesses the attainments conditional to the award of the licence, the registrar will license the applicant and add the name to the list of licensed hypnotists in the Register. The Director General may delay certification if having reason to believe that an applicant's negligence has caused the death or serious injury of a person who had the need of the applicant's services. A certified hypnotist whose licence to practise medicine or dentistry has been suspended by virtue of the Physicians' or Dentists' Ordinance, or who has been struck off, or suspended from the Psychologists' Register, must also have his or her licence to practise hypnotism cancelled or suspended.

V. Cancellation of Licence

597. The Minister of Health has the right to cancel or suspend the licence of a physician or dentist if either of them is guilty of one of the following acts of misconduct; and the disciplinary committee, functioning in accordance with the

Psychologists' Law, may make the same decision with reference to a psychologist who has committed any of the following acts of misconduct:

(a) He or she has behaved in a manner unbecoming a certified hypnotist.
(b) He or she has obtained a licence with the aid of false credentials.
(c) He or she has demonstrated incompetence, irresponsibility, or serious negligence in performing the duties of a certified hypnotist.
(d) He or she has contravened the Law on the Use of Hypnotism or its Regulations.
(e) He or she has been convicted of an offence revealing a lack of such responsibility as must be characteristic of a certified hypnotist.

§9. Physician Assistant

I. The Background for the Establishment of Physician Assistant

598. In 2012, a committee was established to address the need for physician assistants in Israel. The committee determined in its recommendations that 'there is a need justifying the creation of the role of a physician assistant'.

599. Currently, there are approximately 100 physician assistants working in emergency medicine departments (ERs) in the specific medical field of emergency medicine. These are paramedics who underwent training conducted by the Ministry of Health in the past until the decision to promote the law. Following accompanied research that examined the activities of physician assistants in departments, a committee was established to examine the possibility of promoting the development of the physician assistant role to additional medical fields while transforming the role into a primary profession in the existing model in other countries.

600. So far, three training cycles have been held with the participation of about 100 paramedics. The training took place in a specialized course lasting a year and a half, and at its end, the graduates were integrated into emergency medicine departments in Israel. Their authorities were limited and defined in the Physician's Regulations (Qualifications for Performing Exceptional Procedures), 2001, under the supervision of specialist physicians within the emergency medicine department only.

601. The development of healthcare services in Israel poses new daily challenges. The establishment of the physician assistants' profession in Israel assists in dealing with these challenges, as well as in improving the professional response in hospitals and community services in Israel. The theoretical and clinical knowledge accumulated by physician assistants during their academic studies and subsequently during their work will enable department physicians to rely on them to reduce the workload in departments and significantly improve the provision of medical services in the State of Israel.

II. Amendment to the Law

602. On August 2023, Amendment No. 8 to the Health Professions Order Law was published, adding Physician Assistants as a new health profession to the existing eight professions in the law. In July 2023, Amendment No. 8 to the law passed the second and third readings in the Knesset and will come into effect in August 2024.

603. Professional Certification The requirements for obtaining a physician assistant certificate: Academic education – one of the following: second academic degree in Physician Assistant granted by a recognized institution of higher education in Israel. A second academic degree in Physician Assistant granted by a recognized institution of higher education aboard provided it is recognized by the Ministry of Health as equivalent to a second academic degree in Physician Assistant. Academic degree in Medicine granted by a recognized institution of higher education in Israel. An academic degree in Medicine granted by an institution of higher education aboard provided it is recognized by the Ministry of Health as equivalent to a second academic degree in Physician Assistant. Practical training of Physician Assistants included in academic studies. Passing the licensing examinations of the Ministry of Health. After obtaining the licence, Physician Assistant will be able to integrate into all branches of medicine.

III. Work in the Profession and Personal Authorization

604. After receiving a certificate, a Physician Assistant will be able to work concurrently with up to three specialist physicians, under three personal authorizations, and at most in two branches of specialization. Supervision of the Physician Assistant's work will be carried out under personal authorizations granted by the specialist physician or specialist physician performing medical procedures in their field of specialization, provided that the physicians and physician assistant work in the same medical institution.

605. Personal authorization will be granted on a detailed authorization form, renewable every two years. The personal authorization form requires approval from the Ministry of Health in the first two years of the profession's formation. Subsequently, starting from 1 September 2028, the Ministry of Health may delegate its authority to approve the authorization form to the administrators of medical institutions. The law brings with it a true milestone – the creation of a new profession in the world of medicine in Israel, which will lead to a significant improvement in the provision of medical services throughout Israel.

606. In Amendment No. 16 to the Physicians Ordinance, Chapter B2 was added, which addresses personal authorization to a physician assistant. This chapter regulates the granting of authorization to physician assistants by a specialist physician to perform medical procedures within their speciality within the same medical institution. The authorization can only be granted after ensuring medical qualifications professional supervision, and the ability to perform procedures safely and at a high standard. The authorization includes provisions for supervision and protection of the quality and safety of the medical procedure. Additionally, conditions for granting personal authorization will be determined by the medical director and published on the Ministry of Health's website. Furthermore, there is a requirement to inform the medical institution's director of any decisions regarding personal authorization.

607. The validity period of personal authorization is two years, with the option for early cancellation upon prior notice. The director will determine authorization approval and any amendments according to conditions set by the Minister. All sections in this chapter aim to ensure the safe and highly professional standard execution of medical procedures and the adequacy of treatment provided under the authorization.

IV. Revocation, Suspension, Restriction, or Amendment of Personal Authorization

608. The law stipulates that if the Director General deems that any of the following circumstances exist regarding a personal authorization, he may revoke it, order changes to it, or restrict it:

(1) It has ceased to comply with the conditions under this statute or under the Health Professions Regulation Law.
(2) It was granted based on incorrect or misleading information.
(3) Under the circumstances, it is not effective or justified to maintain it.

609. Further stipulated by the law that the Director General shall not decide under subsection (a) unless he has provided the colleague physician and the specialist physician, and if the authorization was approved under section 17(h)(c), also the medical institution Director General, an opportunity to present their claims. However, if the Director General is convinced that there is a serious threat to public health, he may immediately suspend the validity of the personal authorization in a reasoned decision, if he gives the aforementioned parties an opportunity to present their claims as soon as possible after the suspension, and no later than fourteen days from the date of the decision.

610. It should be noted that the Director General's Decision shall take effect upon notification to the colleague physician.

V. Study Programmes

611. In April 2024, the Council for Higher Education (CHE) approved guidelines for second-degree programmes in the field of Physician Assistant (PA). To enable Physician Assistants to assist physicians by performing some of the routine medical and administrative tasks currently carried out by physicians, they must receive appropriate para-medical training and work closely and under the supervision of departmental physicians, both professionally and administratively.

612. The new study programmes will include theoretical and clinical components in accordance with CHE requirements, allowing highly skilled graduates to provide quality and professional care within the Israeli healthcare system. The decision emphasizes stringent conditions and requirements for the implementation of these programmes to ensure the quality and professionalism of graduates.

613. Initially, the study programme will be conducted exclusively within faculties or medical schools, focusing on preparing students for various medical specialities using advanced teaching methods such as Problem-Based Learning (PBL), Case-Based Learning (CBL), and Simulation-Based Learning (SBL). The CHE will reconsider in two years whether to extend these programmes to institutions with faculties of health sciences and will reassess admission criteria accordingly.

Chapter 2. Relations with Healthcare Providers

§1. Hospitals

614. Paragraph 24A of the Public Health Ordinance instructs that the erection of a hospital, or any change of structure or policy by a hospital, requires the approval of the Health Ministry's Director of Health Services. In addition to the medical implications, the Director's decisions will be guided by his answers to the following questions:

(a) Will the erection and day-to-day operation of a medical centre impose a burden on public health expenditure?
(b) Will the addition of beds cause an unwarranted change in the quota of beds allocated to the requirements of the area's population?
(c) The Director will authorize the setting up of a unique professional unit only if its addition does not cause a change in the quota of beds in the specific medical area for which the approval has been requested.
(d) The Director is authorized to order the closure of a medical unit in his hospital to lessen public expenditure on health, to preserve public health, or to prevent injury to public health.

On the strength of the authority invested in him by the Ordinance, the State of Israel's Minister of Health formulated the 1966 Public Health Ordinances. Among other directives, these Ordinances require a hospital with more than 300 beds to house and operate a computed tomography machine. The Ordinances prescribe the number of beds that must be made available in the hospital in proportion to the area's population, as follows. There must be 2.4 beds ready for the occupation of persons afflicted by general diseases per thousand of the population, and 1.3 beds for psychiatric patients. The revised paragraph 26 states that a hospital directed by a person who is not a licensed physician must appoint a medical director who is a licensed physician and will advise the director on the medical affairs of the hospital. The above-mentioned Ordinances empowered the Minister of Health to act as a controlling authority. In this capacity, the minister has the right to appoint a government physician with powers to demand and receive complete information on what is happening in the hospitals. On the strength of the authority vested in him by the Ordinance, the minister formulated the Public Health Regulations of 1970, published in 'Reshumoth,' detailing the nature of the documents that hospital directors must forward to the Director General of the Ministry of Health and that must be kept in the registry and readily available for reference. The 1976 Regulations on Public Health (Preservation of Records) specify methods for keeping hospital records on hold. The 1974 Ordinance (Presentation of Extraordinary Information) orders the hospital Director to supply a government physician with information about the hospital's activities in general and about patients' complaints in particular. The 1998 Public Health Ordinances (Preservation of Reports) require the hospital Director to report every case of hospitalization at the hospital to the government physician, and the 1980 Ordinance demands that every case of death and every extraordinary event be reported. This Ordinance authorized the Minister of Health to formulate regulations ordering the hospital Director to notify the police of every wounded or dead person admitted to the hospital if there is suspicion of violence. In addition, the Ordinance authorizes the manager of a particular medical institute to forbid a person from entering the institute, entirely or partially, if recidivism is proven against a violent person who acts against the hospital and/or its staff.

By virtue of his authority, the Minister of Health promulgated the 1975 Public Health Regulations (Notification of Suspected Violence). More and more extensive use of these regulations is now being made in matters concerning the disclosure and report of child abuse cases. Smoking in hospitals, except in rooms singled out for this purpose, is prohibited by the 1982 Public Health Regulations (Prohibition of Smoking in Hospitals).

§2. Clinics

615. The Public Health Ordinance authorized the Minister of Health to formulate directives to ensure the proper establishment, registry, and operation of clinics. By virtue of the authority vested in him, the minister instituted the 1987 Public *Health* Regulations (Registration of Clinics) detailing the conditions for the registration and operation of clinics. The 1987 Public Health Regulations (Conditions to be Complied with in Clinics) require the attendance of a physician in clinics as specified in the regulations.

§3. Laboratories

616. The 1977 Public Health Regulations (Medical Laboratories) detail conditions for obtaining a permit to establish and operate *medical* laboratories in Israel.

617. However, a 2020 amendment states that notwithstanding the provisions of these regulations, a medical laboratory may not be administered to perform laboratory tests for the new coronavirus 2019 NCoV-2019 Coronavirus Novel infection and deal with it, provided that a registration certificate has been issued to the laboratory in accordance with Regulation 2(a(1)) and under conditions as specified by the Director in the registration certificate. However, it should be noted that Regulation 2A was a temporary regulation defined as an emergency measure during the COVID-19 period, and it expired on 1 September 2022.

The National Authority's Law to License Laboratories is entitled to the authority to determine areas and types of examinations which will decide the licensing of laboratories. The authority is also entitled to fix standards for the education and technical training of laboratory workers and for the performance of inspection and inspection kits.

Selected Bibliography

Azar, A. *Medical Negligence and Issues in Torts* (Perlstein-Genosar 1994).
Azar, B. *A Person's Wishes Should Be Respected: The Informed Consent Doctrine in Clinical Experiments on Human Beings.* Dissertation submitted for the LLM Degree, Faculty of Law, Tel Aviv University, 1994.
Ben-Basat, Y. *Physician-Patient Relationship: Professional Literature Review* (Sold Institute 1997).
Beran, R. *Epilepsy and Law* (Yozmot 1998).
Bniel, S. *Fathers against Their Will* (Yediot Aharonot 1992).
Carmi, A. *Dentistry and Law* (Tamar 1984).
Carmi, A. *Euthanasia* (Springer-Verlag 1984).
Carmi, A. *Health Law* (Nevo 2003).
Carmi, A. *Law and Medicine* (Tamar 1987).
Carmi, A. *Medical Experimentation* (Turtledove 1973).
Carmi, A. *Medicine and Law* (Maariv 1971).
Carmi, A. *Nursing and Law* (Maariv 1973).
Carmi, A. *Nursing Law* (Tamar 1984).
Carmi, A. *The Doctor, the Patient and the Law* (Maariv 1977).
Carmi, A. & A. Sagiv. *Medical Negligence in Judaism and in Israel* (Tamar 1986).
Carmi, A. & S. Schneider. *Drugs and Alcohol* (Springer-Verlag 1986).
Carmi, A. & S. Schneider. *Experiencing Graphology* (Freund 1988).
Carmi, A. & S. Schneider. *Hospital Law* (Springer-Verlag 1988).
Carmi, A. & S. Schneider. *Nursing Law and Ethics* (Springer-Verlag 1985).
Carmi, A. & S. Schneider. *Psychiatry Law and Ethics* (Springer-Verlag 1986).
Carmi, A. & H. Zimrin. *Child Abuse* (Springer-Verlag 1984).
Carmi, A., E. Chigier & S. Schneider. *Disability* (Springer-Verlag 1984).
Davis, J. *Medicolegal Case Law in Obstetrics and Gynaecology* (Avi Law Books Ltd 1999).
De Vries, A. & A. Carmi. *The Dying Human* (Turtledove 1979).
Ishay, R. *Between Doctor and Patient* (Shocken 1998).
Kaspi, J. *Dangerous Drugs: Policy, Control, Enforcement and Law* (Tamar 1996).
Levy, A., D. Nachshon & A. Carmi. *Forensic Psychiatry* (Yozmot 1999).
Mohammed S. Wattad (ed.). *Amnon Carmi, Health Law* (Nevo 2013).
Shapira, A. *Informed Consent to Medical Treatment: Legal Aspects* (University of Tel Aviv 1970).
Steinberg, A. *Encyclopedia of Jewish Medical Ethics* (Shlezinger 1988).
Yelinek, S. *Wrongful Birth* (Eshly 1997).

Index

The numbers here refer to paragraph numbers.

Index

Index